T0206934

Communications in Computer and Information Science 1743

Editorial Board Members

Joaquim Filipe
Polytechnic Institute of Setúbal, Setúbal, Portugal

Ashish Ghosh
Indian Statistical Institute, Kolkata, India

Raquel Oliveira Prates
Federal University of Minas Gerais (UFMG), Belo Horizonte, Brazil

Lizhu Zhou
Tsinghua University, Beijing, China

More information about this series at https://link.springer.com/bookseries/7899

V. Arunachalam · K. Sivasankaran (Eds.)

Microelectronic Devices, Circuits and Systems

Third International Conference, ICMDCS 2022
Vellore, India, August 11–13, 2022
Revised Selected Papers

 Springer

Editors
V. Arunachalam (iD)
Vellore Institute of Technology
Vellore, India

K. Sivasankaran (iD)
Vellore Institute of Technology
Vellore, India

ISSN 1865-0929   ISSN 1865-0937 (electronic)
Communications in Computer and Information Science
ISBN 978-3-031-23972-4   ISBN 978-3-031-23973-1 (eBook)
https://doi.org/10.1007/978-3-031-23973-1

© The Editor(s) (if applicable) and The Author(s), under exclusive license
to Springer Nature Switzerland AG 2022
This work is subject to copyright. All rights are reserved by the Publisher, whether the whole or part of the material is concerned, specifically the rights of translation, reprinting, reuse of illustrations, recitation, broadcasting, reproduction on microfilms or in any other physical way, and transmission or information storage and retrieval, electronic adaptation, computer software, or by similar or dissimilar methodology now known or hereafter developed.
The use of general descriptive names, registered names, trademarks, service marks, etc. in this publication does not imply, even in the absence of a specific statement, that such names are exempt from the relevant protective laws and regulations and therefore free for general use.
The publisher, the authors, and the editors are safe to assume that the advice and information in this book are believed to be true and accurate at the date of publication. Neither the publisher nor the authors or the editors give a warranty, expressed or implied, with respect to the material contained herein or for any errors or omissions that may have been made. The publisher remains neutral with regard to jurisdictional claims in published maps and institutional affiliations.

This Springer imprint is published by the registered company Springer Nature Switzerland AG
The registered company address is: Gewerbestrasse 11, 6330 Cham, Switzerland

Preface

It is our great pleasure to collect the research papers for the 3rd International Conference on Microelectronic Devices, Circuits and Systems (ICMDCS 2022) and publish them in Springer's prestigious Communications in Computer and Information Science (CCIS) series.

ICMDCS 2022 was organized by the Department of Micro and Nano Electronics, School of Electronics Engineering (SENSE), at the Vellore Institute of Technology (VIT), Vellore, India, during August 11–13, 2022. The conference was technically supported by the industry partner GlobalFoundries, India. Due to the global COVID-19 pandemic scenario, the conference was conducted in virtual mode.

The conference received 84 research papers in subject areas including system level design, digital design, analog/RF/mixed signal design, and emerging technologies. After the plagiarism check and rigorous review process, with each paper receiving at least XX reviews in an XX blind process, 28 articles were accepted for presentation in the five technical sessions.

The conference had nine keynote speeches given by eminent academicians and industry leaders including Subramanian S. Iyer from University of California, Los Angeles, USA; Prabha Sundaravadivel from the University of Texas at Tyler, USA; and experts from General Motors, USA; GlobalFoundries, India; Intel, India; and Marvell Semiconductors, India.

In addition to the keynote and technical paper presentations, pre-conference industry-sponsored tutorial sessions on recent advancements in the abovesaid areas were offered by experts from GlobalFoundries, Intel PSG, Marvell Semiconductors, and Cadence, India, on August 11, 2022.

ICMDCS 2022 provided a platform to hear, demonstrate, and witness the growth of microelectronic, embedded, and smart systems with more than 32 presenting authors and 60 delegates.

We express our sincere thanks to the Vellore Institute of Technology for providing the encouragement and facilities to organize this conference. Futhermore, Vipin Madangarli, Director of Design Enablement at GlobalFoundries, Bangalore, India provided constant support in organizing the event. Also, we are thankful to the faculty and staff of SENSE for their wholehearted contributions from the inception of the conference to the final submission of the papers for publication in this CCIS volume.

V. Arunachalam
K. Sivasankaran

Organization

Chief Patron

G. Viswanathan   Vellore Institute of Technology, India

Patrons

Sankar Viswanathan   Vellore Institute of Technology, India
(Vice-president)
Sekar Viswanathan   Vellore Institute of Technology, India
(Vice-president)
G. V. Selvam (Vice-president)   Vellore Institute of Technology, India
Rambabu Kodali (Vice   Vellore Institute of Technology, India
Chancellor)
S. Narayanan (Pro-vice   Vellore Institute of Technology, India
Chancellor)

General Chair

Sivanantham S.   Vellore Institute of Technology, India

Organizing Chairs

Arunachalam V.   Vellore Institute of Technology, India
Sivasankaran K.   Vellore Institute of Technology, India

Publication Chair

Kumaravel S.   Vellore Institute of Technology, India

Registration Chair

Sri Abibhatla Sridevi   Vellore Institute of Technology, India

Technical Session Chairs

R. Sakthivel   Vellore Institute of Technology, India
Kittur Harish Mallikarjun   Vellore Institute of Technology, India
Ravi S.   Vellore Institute of Technology, India

Sasikumar P.	Vellore Institute of Technology, India
Jagannadha Naidu K.	Vellore Institute of Technology, India
Arun Dev Dhar Dwivedi	Vellore Institute of Technology, India
Govardhan K.	Vellore Institute of Technology, India
Kannadassan D.	Vellore Institute of Technology, India
Penchalaiah Palla	Vellore Institute of Technology, India

Tutorial Chairs

P. Jayakrishnan
Dhanabal R.
B. Karthikeyan
Antony Xavier Glittas X.
Rajeev Pankaj Nelapati

Technical Program Committee

Aditya Deulkar	Samsung Semiconductor India, Bangalore, India
Abhishek Ramanujam	Analog Devices, Ireland
Xiao-Zhi Gao	Helsinki University of Technology, Finland
Roy Paily	Indian Institute of Technology, Guwahati, India
Parameswaran Ramanathan	Wisconsin-Madison University, USA
Vignesh Rajamani	Oakland University, USA
Navin Bishnoi	Marvell Semiconductors, Bengaluru, India
Sreehari Veeramachaneni	BITS Hyderabad, India
Debesh K. Das	Jadavpur University, India
Maryam Shojaei Baghini	Indian Institute of Technology, Bombay, India
P. Krishnamoorthi	Philips India Pvt. Ltd, Bengaluru, India
P. Sakthivel	Anna University, India
P. Ramesh	Amritha University, Kolkata, India
G. Lakshminarayanan	National Institute of Technology, Tiruchirappalli, India
Sang Hyeon Kim	Korea Advanced Institute of Science and Technology, South Korea
Sudarshan Srinivasan	Intel, Bengaluru, India
Tapan K. Nayak	CERN, Switzerland
Vanathi P. T.	PSG College of Technology, India
Venkata Vanukuru	Global Foundries, Bengaluru, India
Venkateswaran	SSN College of Engineering, India
Virendra Singh	Indian Institute of Technology, Bombay, India
Vita Pi-Ho Hu	National Chiao Tung University, Taiwan
Xingsheng Wang	University of Glasgow, UK

Anis Suhaila Mohd Zain	Technical University of Malaysia, Malacca, Malaysia
Ashok Govindarajan	Zilogic Systems, Chennai, India
Balamurugan G.	Honeywell, Bangalore, India
Chandrasekar	Colorado State University, USA
Changhwan Shin	Sungkyunkwan University, South Korea
Hyungcheol Shin	Seoul National University, South Korea
Jawahar Senthil Kumar V	Anna University, India
Gaurav Goel	Intel, Bangalore, India
Jayaraman K.	Maxim Integrated, Bangalore, India
Ling Guo	University of Florida, USA
Jongwook Jeon	Konkuk University, South Korea
Yang Hao	Queen Mary University of London, UK
Lavakumar A.	Synopsys, Bangalore, India
Meganathan D.	Anna University, India
Moorthi S.	National Institute of Technology Tiruchirappalli, India
Nirmal Kumar P.	Anna University, India
Pradeep Nair	Texas Instruments, Bangalore, India
N. Balamurugan	Thiagarajar College of Engineering, India
C. P. Ravikumar	Texas Instruments, Bengaluru, India
Vipin Madangarli	Global Foundries, Bengaluru, India
M. Raja	BITS Dubai, UAE
Kewal K. Saluja	University of Winsconsin-Madison, USA
Krishnendu Chakrabarty	Duke University, USA
Xiao-Zhi Ga	Helsinki University of Technology, Finland
Subramaniam Ganesan	Oakland University, USA
Anand Paul	Kyungpook National University, South Korea
K. Bharanitharan	Taiwan
Vijaya Samara Rao Pasupureddi	Carinthia University of Applied Sciences, Austria
Vishwani D.Agrawal	Auburn University, Alabama
Balamurugan G.	Honeywell, Bangalore, India
V. Kamakoti	Indian Institute of Technology, Madras, India
Susmita Sur-Kolay	Indian Statistical Institute, India
M. Sabarimalai Manikandan	Indian Institute of Technology, Bhuvaneshwar, India

Sponsors

Contents

System Level Design

Tapered Fed Modified Patch Antenna for SWB Communications Using DGS

Ch. Murali Krishna[1]([⊠]) [iD], Er. Jeetamitra Satapathy[2], N. Suguna[3] [iD],
R. Saravanakumar[4] [iD], Manohar Golait[5] [iD], and Puneet Narayan[6] [iD]

[1] Birla Institute of Technology and Science, Pilani - Hyderabad Campus, Hyderabad,
Telangana, India
krishnasri780@gmail.com

[2] Government Industrial Training Institute, Bhubaneswar, Odisha, India

[3] School of Electronics Engineering, Vellore Institute of Technology, Vellore, India

[4] Saveetha School of Engineering, Saveetha Institute of Medical and Technical Sciences,
Chennai, India

[5] School of Engineering and Technology, G H Raisoni University, Saikheda, Madhya Pradesh,
India

[6] Government Engineering College, Bharatpur, Shyorana, Rajasthan, India

Abstract. In this paper, a new approach to obtain extended wide bandwidth characteristics named as super wide band (SWB) operation from modified monopole antenna with defected ground structure (DGS) is presented. The designed antenna is made on dielectric material Flame retardant glassy epoxy (FR-4) having electrical properties of dielectric constant 4.4, loss tangent of 0.02 and its thickness 1.6 mm. Overall compact size of the printed antenna is 31 mm × 18 mm (electrical dimensions are $0.14\lambda_0 \times 0.08\lambda_0$ at lowest resonant frequency of 1.31 GHz). Bandwidth and gain parameters of the designed antenna are improved by introducing the defective ground structure with semi-circular structure & slots. The proposed antenna resonates at 3.20 GHz, 7.85 GHz and 12.80 GHz frequencies with wide impedance bandwidth (IBW) of 16.7 GHz (1.31–18.01 GHz) bandwidth concerning the − 10 dB reference line of the reflection coefficient. Fractional bandwidth (FBW) and bandwidth ratio (BR) are 172.88% and 13.75:1. Furthermore, the bandwidth dimension ratio (BDR) of 15,435.72 signifies the miniaturization in the structure w.r.t to super wide band characteristics. The radiation patterns are semi-omnidirectional, omnidirectional. The current design can have L – band (1–2 GHz), S – band (2–4 GHz), C – band (4–8 GHz), X – band (8–12 GHz) and Ku – band (12–18 GHz) applications.

Keywords: Modified rectangular patch · Defected ground structure (DGS) · Tapered feedline · Monopole · SWB applications · FBW · BR

1 Introduction

Federal communication commission (FCC) allocated the frequency spectrum from 3.1–10.6 GHz for commercial, industrial-scientific-medical (ISM) applications [1]. Still the

© The Author(s), under exclusive license to Springer Nature Switzerland AG 2022
V. Arunachalam and K. Sivasankaran (Eds.): ICMDCS 2022, CCIS 1743, pp. 3–14, 2022.
https://doi.org/10.1007/978-3-031-23973-1_1

ultra-wide band spectrum (3.1–10.6 GHz) can't be used for high speed long-range communications, high data rate and limited transmission power. In order to overcome the limitations of the UWB spectrum, bandwidth can be extended by proposing the extended ultra-wide band (EUWB) or also named it as super wide band (SWB) characteristics which is designed on the single device. The EUWB antenna supports the short range as well long range applications with efficient power transmission characteristics helps in useful for wireless personal area networks (WPAN) [2–4]. Authors proposed a new fractal circular patch antenna by employing various iterations of the self-similar circles on the radiating patch in order to achieve the wide bandwidth characteristics ranging from 3.1–10 GHz [5]. The designed integrated with split – ring resonator (SRR) and reconfigurable switching to provide the notch bands. Irregular U – shaped patch antenna implemented with T – modelled resonator for low power applications designed on FR – 4 substrate, which encloses frequency range from 2.27–7.53 GHz [6]. Planar UWB antenna designed on FR – 4 substrate with the pentagonal slot fractals are inscribed in the circular metallic structure with tapered U – slit defected ground structure (DGS), which covers frequency from 2.9–15 GHz. Radiation efficiency (η) has limited in this structure. [7]. Co-planar waveguide (CPW) fed tapered slot ground is proposed for UWB applications along with the controllable notch band characteristics [8]. This antenna has been designed within the size of 35 mm × 30 mm and achieved 126% of fractional bandwidth (FBW). In [9], the researchers reported that transmission line (TL) loaded wideband square slot antenna is modeled for wide band communications. The obtained gain and efficiency values are 3.84 dB and 88%. Wideband rectangular patch antenna is printed for Ku – band interests which covers impedance bandwidth from 9.8 to 17.55 GHz with FBW of 56.67% [10]. U – Shaped transmission line fed antenna with sub ground is projected to fit the UWB applications designed on 52 mm × 46 mm size [11]. Octal shape fractal integrated on the rhombus monopole antenna is fed with coplanar wave guide geometry is simulated. This designed antenna achieves wide bandwidth characteristics ranging from 2.86 to 14.38 GHz with an FBW of 132.48% [12]. Modified semi sierpinski fractal is loaded on the rectangular patch to get the UWB characteristics. Due to self – similar structure property and slot introduced in the ground results the UWB performance [13].

In this paper, open ended semicircles are loaded at the corners of the rectangular geometry to achieve the super wide band (SWB) characteristics at S11 $\leq$ −10 dB along with the defected ground structure (DGS). This antenna is projected on flame retardant (FR) – 4 epoxy dielectric material with thickness of 0.8 mm and its dielectric constant is 4.4 with tapered line fed technique. The use of semi-circular arcs in the patch and ground plane are enhances the fractional bandwidth (FBW), bandwidth ratio (BR) and bandwidth dimension ratio (BDR) of the designed antenna. The proposed antenna can be used for microwave devices, long distance radio telecommunications (Bluetooth, WLAN), and satellite and radar communications.

2 Design Methodology and Its Geometrical Configuration

The radiating element layout of suggested monopole antenna has been printed on dielectric material having dielectric constant of 4.4, loss tangent 0.02 and its thickness of 1.6 mm. It is a three layered structure, which is composed of two radiating conductors are printed on both sides of the dielectric material. Three dimensional view and top view of proposed antenna with DGS is shown in Fig. 1. Compact size (Ls × Ws × h) of the proposed modified rectangular patch antenna with defected ground structure is 31 mm × 18 mm × 1.6 mm. Optimized dimensions of the proposed design are tabulated in Table 1. All the parameters are measured in millimeter (mm).

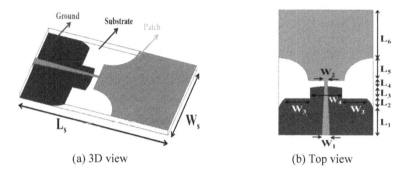

(a) 3D view   (b) Top view

Fig. 1. Proposed monopole antenna with DGS in three dimensional view

Table 1. Geometrical dimensions of proposed monopole antenna with DGS (Units: mm)

L_S	W_S	L_1	L_2	L_3	L_4
31	18	6	3	2.65	1.85
L_5	L_6	W_1	W_2	W_3	W_4
5.5	11.9	1.5	0.5	4.8	6

The conventional microstrip patch antenna with partial ground are designed by using standard mathematical expressions [14] and is designed at operating frequency of 3 GHz is illustrated in Fig. 2(a). The designed antenna has been simulated using Finite Element Method (FEM) electromagnetic High Frequency Structure Simulator (HFSS) tool. Figure 2(b) presents the area of the partial ground can be increased by merging semi-circle with the partial ground. It will enhances the performance of Ant – 1. Open ended semi-circular arcs are etched on the metallic patch as presented in Fig. 2(c). Another novel technique to enhance the bandwidth of the suggested geometry, 50 Ω feed line is modified into tapered fed structure and it has 50 Ω characteristics at the input feed point as shown in Fig. 2(d). From the analysis of simulation characteristics, ultra – wide band characteristics has non-uniform reflection coefficient throughout the bandwidth. To maintain the unique impedance matching characteristics and improving the gain and radiation efficiency performance ground has been modified with open ended rectangular slots loaded on it as shown in Fig. 2(e).

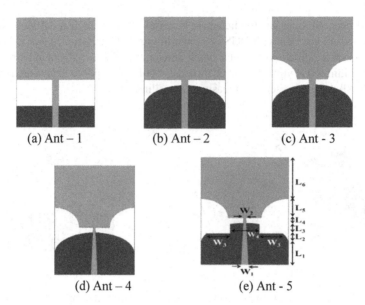

(a) Ant – 1   (b) Ant – 2   (c) Ant - 3

(d) Ant – 4   (e) Ant - 5

Fig. 2. Implementations of the proposed structure from the conventional geometry

3 Performance Analysis of Proposed Antenna

Figures 3, 4, 5, 6, 7, 8, 9 and 10 represents the impedance bandwidth (IBW) performance and impedance matching of designed iterations interms of reflection coefficient & VSWR characteristics. Figure 11 illustrates the evaluation of reflection coefficient (S_{11}) characteristics of the proposed antenna in different iterations. To achieve the super wide band characteristics, single rectangular monopole antenna is converted into modified defected metallic structure (DMS) and defected ground structure (DGS). These open ended circular and rectangular arcs are optimized to get the better response. In Ant – 1, simple rectangular was introduced with partial ground showed the resonance at 2.90 GHz from 2.51 to 3.43 GHz with peak S11 value of −30.42 dB. This was further modified with the loaded semi slots at the open ends of the radiating element and partial ground structure. Design characteristics of all the evaluations are reported in Table 2 from the characteristics shown in Fig. 2. Proposed antenna (Ant - 5) achieves the super wide band characteristics operating from 1.31 to 18.01 GHz at S11 $\leq$ −10 dB. The proposed antenna attains impedance bandwidth (IBW) of 16.7 GHz. The bandwidth ratio ($BR = f_h/f_l$, where f_h – higher operating frequency and f_l – lower operating frequency) and fractional bandwidth ($FBW = \frac{2*(f_h - f_l)}{(f_h + f_l)} \times 100$) are 13.75:1 and 172.88% respectively.

Figure 12 represents the VSWR and group delay characteristics of the suggested antenna. It is noticed that the resistive portion is oscillating around 50 Ω while the reactive portion fluctuates around 0 Ω from Fig. 13. This states that the Zin is close to 50 Ω. This input impedance and group delay characteristics within the wideband has three resonances at 3.20 GHz, 7.85 GHz and 12.80 GHz. Table 3 represents the input impedance, VSWR and group delay parameters at the resonances.

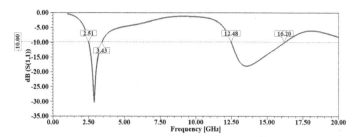

Fig. 3. S11 performance of the Ant – 1

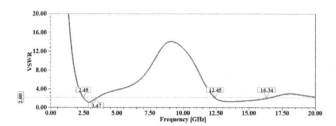

Fig. 4. VSWR performance of the Ant – 1

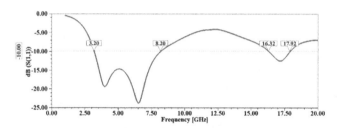

Fig. 5. S11 performance of the Ant – 2

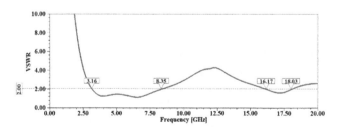

Fig. 6. VSWR performance of the Ant – 2

The two dimensional radiation characteristics interms of E – plane and H - plane of the proposed design can be presented using the simulated 3D plots as exposed in Fig. 14. The E – plane radiation patterns at low frequencies shows the Omni directional and bidirectional at high frequency. H – Plane has bidirectional characteristics at the

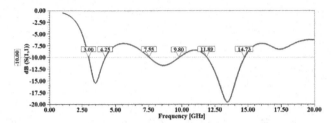

Fig. 7. S11 performance of the Ant – 3

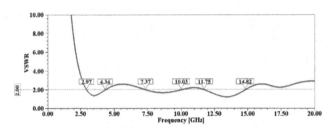

Fig. 8. VSWR performance of the Ant – 3

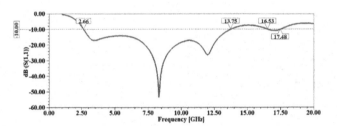

Fig. 9. S11 performance of the Ant – 4

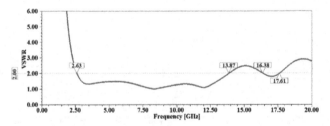

Fig. 10. VSWR performance of the Ant – 4

low frequencies 3.20 GHz, 7.85 GHz and multidirectional at high frequency. Computed antenna parameters of the proposed antenna at selected resonances 3.20 GHz, 7.85 GHz and 12.80 GHz are presented in Table 4.

The current variation on the radiating elements at resonant frequencies of 3.20 GHz, 7.85 GHz and 12.80 GHz is given in Fig. 15(a–c). The current flow on the antenna

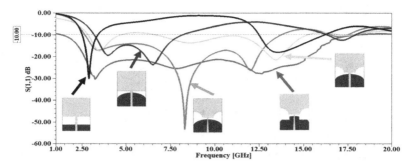

Fig. 11. S11 performance of the proposed structure from the conventional geometry

Table 2. Reflection coefficients characteristics summary of the designed antennas

Design	Band	f_L, GHz	f_U, GHz	IBW, GHz	BR	FBW, %
Ant – 1	Narrow	2.51	3.43	0.92	1.37:1	30.98
	Narrow	12.48	16.2	3.72	1.30:1	25.94
Ant – 2	Wide	3.2	8.2	5	2.56:1	87.72
Ant – 3	Narrow	2.84	4.75	1.91	1.67:1	50.33
	Wide	6.66	15.24	8.58	2.29:1	78.36
Ant – 4	UWB	2.66	13.75	11.09	5.17:1	135.16
Ant – 5	SWB	1.31	18.01	16.7	13.75:1	172.88

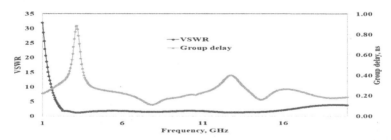

Fig. 12. VSWR and group delay characteristics of the proposed monopole antenna

represents that larger part of the current is scattered along the feedline and edge of the ground plane. On the patch, one half-cycle of current variation is observed, which indicates the fundamental mode of the radiating element at 3.20 GHz. The current flow at 7.85 GHz has two half cycle of current variations on the patch. At 12.80 GHz, strong currents are observed on the ground plane. Existence of strong currents on the ground plane indicates that ground plane dimensions have effect on bandwidth of the antenna. Figures 16 and 17 shows the gain and radiation efficiency characteristics of the proposed design in the frequency spectrum from 0 to 20 GHz. The simulated peak gain of the proposed modified patch antenna with partial DGS is given in Fig. 16. It is observed that

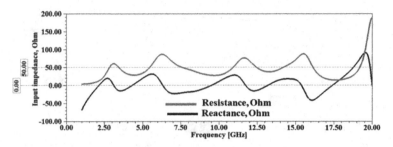

Fig. 13. Input impedance characteristics of proposed monopole antenna

Table 3. VSWR, Group delay and input impedance parameters at the resonances

Resonance	f_r, GHz	Resistive part (R_{in})	Reactive part (X_{in})	Group delay (t_d)	VSWR
1	3.20	57.96 Ω	−8.44 Ω	0.84 ns	1.28
2	7.85	46.90 Ω	−18.37 Ω	0.12 ns	1.46
3	12.85	45.12 Ω	−11.27 Ω	0.40 ns	1.28

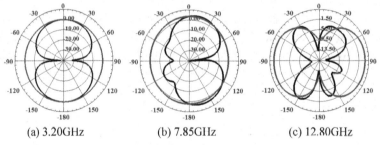

(a) 3.20GHz   (b) 7.85GHz   (c) 12.80GHz

Fig. 14. Two dimensional radiation patterns of proposed monopole antenna (Red – Elevation plane & Black – Azimuthal plane)

the gain increases with the increase in frequency. This effect occurs because at higher frequencies the electrical dimensions of radiation element are larger than the wavelength. The radiation efficiency of the proposed antenna is shown in Fig. 17. The peak radiation efficiency is observed as 96.56% for the 3.20 GHz frequency, 91.69% for the 7.85 GHz resonant frequency and 86.41% for the 12.80 GHz resonant frequency. The efficiencies are in-between 85 and 97% in the entire bandwidth.

Table 4. Computed antenna parameters at three resonances

S. No	Quantity	3.8 GHz	7.8 GHz	12.8 GHz
1	Max U	1.0437 mW/Sr	2.0994 mW/Sr	1.6815 mW/Sr
2	Peak directivity	1.4309 dB	2.9856 dB	2.4845 dB
3	Peak gain	1.3653 dB	2.7375 dB	2.1468 dB
4	Peak realized gain	1.3116 dB	2.6383 dB	2.1131 dB
5	Radiated power	9.1665 mW	8.8367 mW	8.5054 mW
6	Accepted power	9.6069 mW	9.6375 mW	9.8433 mW
7	Incident power	10 mW	10 mW	10 mW
8	Radiation efficiency	95.41%	91.69%	86.40%

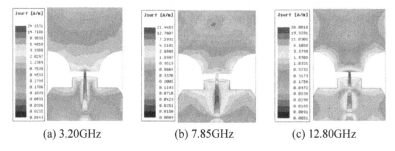

(a) 3.20GHz   (b) 7.85GHz   (c) 12.80GHz

Fig. 15. Surface current distributions of proposed monopole antenna at resonances

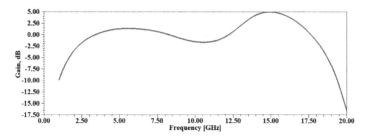

Fig. 16. Gain plot of the proposed antenna

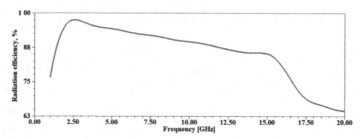

Fig. 17. Radiation efficiency of the proposed antenna

4 Performance Comparison of the Proposed Antenna with the Existed Models

The designed and simulated antenna results have several advantages interms of compact size, coverage frequency spectrum, operating impedance bandwidth, fractional bandwidth and radiation efficiency are compared with the some recently available works are tabulated in Table 5.

Table 5. Advantages of the proposed design compared with the existed works

Ref	Size, mm^2	Electrical size, $\lambda_0{}^2$	Operating spectrum, GHz	IBW, GHz	FBW, %	BDR	Gain, dB	η, %
[5]	25 × 21	0.26 × 0.22	3.1–10	6.9	105	1841.79	4.4	90
[6]	34 × 20	0.26 × 0.16	2.27–7.53	5.26	107.35	2580.53	4.91	>70
[7]	32 × 32	0.31 × 0.31	2.9–15	12.1	135.2	1406.87	4.85	79.21
[8]	35 × 30	0.33 × 0.28	2.78–12.3	9.52	126	1366.46	4.3	85
[9]	50 × 50	0.35 × 0.35	2.1–11.5	9.4	138	1128.49	3.84	88
[10]	36 × 36	1.18 × 1.18	9.8–17.55	7.75	56.67	40.71	2.08	NR*
[11]	52 × 46	0.49 × 0.43	2.8–15	12.2	137.07	650.6	1.51	88.23
[12]	83 × 41.5	0.8 × 0.4	2.86–14.38	11.42	132.48	417.66	4.18	NR
[13]	34 × 34	0.36 × 0.36	3.1–10.6	7.5	109.48	844.84	4.75	>75
Proposed	18 × 31	0.08 × 0.14	1.31–18.01	16.7	172.88	15435.72	4.38	85–97

* NR – Not reported.

5 Conclusion

The main goal of this research work is to extend the wide bandwidth for future generation wireless applications. In this paper, open ended single element antenna with partial DGS ($31 \times 18 \times 1.6$ mm^3) has been designed on the FR-4 dielectric and is simulated using HFSS tool for SWB applications. IBW, FBW, BDR, gain and radiation efficiency are improved by implementing a defective ground structure on the bottom layer of the substrate. The proposed antenna provides an impedance bandwidth of 16.7 GHz over the operating range from 1.31–18.01 GHz frequencies and its fractional bandwidth is 172.88%. According to the results obtained, this proposed design is sustainable for wireless systems. Therefore, this proposed antenna is worthful for WPAN, short and long range indoor applications.

References

1. Federal Communications Commission: Federal Communications Commission Revision of Part 15 of the Commission's Rules Regarding Ultra-wideband Transmission System from 3.1 to 10.6 GHz, pp. 98–153. ET-Docket, Washington, DC, USA (2002)
2. Schantz, H.G.: A brief history of UWB antennas. IEEE Aero. Electron. Syst. Mag. **19**, 22–26 (2004)
3. Balani, W., Sarvagya, M., Ali, T., Anguera, J., Andujar, A., Das, S.: Design techniques of super-wideband antenna–existing and future prospective. IEEE Access **7**, 141241–141257 (2019)
4. Chen, K.R., Row, J.S.: A compact monopole antenna for super wideband applications. IEEE Antennas Wirel. Propag. Lett. **10**, 488–491 (2011)
5. Nazeri, A.H., Falahati, A., Edwards, R.M.: A novel compact fractal UWB antenna with triple reconfigurable notch reject bands applications. AEU—Int. J. Electron. Commun. **101**, 1–8 (2019)
6. Tiwari, R.N., Singh, P., Kanaujia, B.K.: Asymmetric U-shaped printed monopole antenna embedded with T-shaped strip for bluetooth, WLAN/WiMAX applications. Wireless Netw. **26**(1), 51–61 (2018). https://doi.org/10.1007/s11276-018-1781-5
7. Mohandoss, S., Thipparaju, R.R., Balarami Reddy, B.N., Palaniswamy, S.K., Marudappa, P.: Fractal based ultra-wideband antenna development for wireless personal area communication applications. AEU—Int. J. Electron. Commun. 93, 95–102 (2018)
8. Tu, Z., Li, W., Chu, Q.: Single-layer differential CPW-fed notch-band tapered-slot UWB antenna. IEEE Antennas Wirel. Propag. Lett. **13**, 1296–1299 (2014). https://doi.org/10.1109/LAWP.2014.2332355
9. Paul, P.M., Kandasamy, K., Sharawi, M.S., Majumder, B.: Dispersion-engineered transmission line loaded slot antenna for UWB applications. IEEE Antennas Wirel. Propag. Lett. **18**(2), 323–327 (2019). https://doi.org/10.1109/LAWP.2018.2889931
10. Khandelwal, M.K., Kanaujia, B.K., Dwari, S., Kumar, S., Gautam, A.K.: Analysis and design of wide band Microstrip-line-fed antenna with defected ground structure for Ku band applications. AEU – Int. J. Electron. Commun. **68**(10), 951–957 (2014). https://doi.org/10.1016/j.aeue.2014.04.017
11. Kumar, S.S., Rao, G.S., Pillalamarri, R.: Rectangular slotted microstrip line fed compact printed antenna with etched ground plane for UWB communications. Microsyst. Technol. **21**(10), 2077–2081 (2014)
12. Kumar, R., Shinde, J.P., Shinde, P.N., Uplane, M.D.: On the design of CPW-fed square octal shaped fractal UWB antenna. In: 2009 Applied Electromagnetics Conference (AEMC) (2009)

13. Choukiker, Y.K., Behera, S.K.: Modified Sierpinski square fractal antenna covering ultra-wide band application with band notch characteristics. IET Microwaves Antennas Propag. **8**(7), 506–512 (2014)
14. Balanis, C.A.: Antenna Theory: Analysis and Design, 3rd ed. Wiley (2005)

Design of Hardware Accelerator for Facial Recognition System Using Convolutional Neural Networks Based on FPGA

Anshul Dalal, Manoj Choudhary, V. Aakash, and S. Balamurugan$^{(\boxtimes)}$

School of Electrical and Electronics Engineering,
Vellore Institute of Technology, Vellore 632 014, Tamil Nadu, India
sbalamurugan@vit.ac.in

Abstract. Convolutional Neural Networks (CNN) are being widely used for a variety of real-world image processing and facial recognition applications. CNN is computationally intensive which makes it difficult to deploy them in latency-critical applications. Several studies have proposed the use of Field Programmable Gate Arrays (FPGA) for accelerating CNN implementation. Its structure inherently is such that parallelizing its hardware implementation can lead to considerable performance improvement. In this paper, we present an FPGA-based implementation of a CNN accelerator for a facial recognition system. We propose a design approach with a focus on exploring the parallel operation of convolution kernels within each layer and on exploring parallelism between individual convolutional layers in the CNN, along with a Data quantization strategy that helps in reducing the bit-width down to 16-bit with negligible accuracy loss. A custom 4-8-16 CNN model with three convolution layers, two max-pooling layers, and one full-connected layer was trained on an augmented ORL face dataset using TensorFlow in Google Colaboratory. Hardware architectures were designed using Verilog Hardware Descriptive Language (HDL). The proposed neural accelerator implemented on Artix-7 100t FPGA provides a speed-up of nearly 1097 and 66 times over the Central Processing Unit (CPU) and Graphics Processing Unit (GPU) implementation (on Google Colaboratory) of the same CNN network.

Keywords: CNN · Convolutional neural networks · Hardware accelerator · Facial recognition system · FPGA · ORL dataset · Block-RAM · BRAM · Parallelism · Row-buffering

1 Introduction

Facial Recognition remains the new face of innovation. This technology is bound to influence all of our lives, as new tools powered by this innovative technology are launched. CNN is being widely used in facial recognition technology, a rather time-critical application. Implementing CNN-based technology in time-critical applications is challenging. They are computationally intensive and require repeated multiplication and accumulation operations. The software implementations of CNN using conventional general purpose

© The Author(s), under exclusive license to Springer Nature Switzerland AG 2022
V. Arunachalam and K. Sivasankaran (Eds.): ICMDCS 2022, CCIS 1743, pp. 15–26, 2022.
https://doi.org/10.1007/978-3-031-23973-1_2

CPUs are not optimal and yield high latencies. Their high memory-footprint often bottlenecks the model due to repeated memory accesses. Their structure is inherently such that parallelizing their implementation can lead to performance improvements. Large performance gains can be obtained by implementing them on specialized hardware like Application Specific Integrated Circuits (ASIC), and GPU [1]. Hardware accelerators for neural networks (or neural accelerators) are being extensively researched to move the computational load from software to specialized hardware.

GPUs, FPGAs, and custom ASICs are promising platforms for hardware acceleration due to their capacity for parallel processing. ASICs superior in performance but they offer little flexibility, have high cost and time-to-market. It is challenging to attain a desirable cost/performance ratio [2, 3]. Studies have shown that GPU can be suitable for implementing CNNs [4]. However, its power consumption makes it undesirable for real-time applications. FPGAs provide a sweet-spot between the programmability of GPUs, and the speed and power-efficiency of ASICs [5]. They are fast, flexible, reconfigurable, energy-efficient, have fast design cycles and allow implementing exactly the necessary design. There has been an increasing interest in developing architectures with improved parallelism and energy-efficiency [6]. Thus, FPGAs are becoming the primary choice for designing hardware accelerators for CNN [2]. Attempts have been made to optimize the convolution hardware in some of the FPGA based CNN implementation [7, 8]. AlexNet, VGG, ResNet, GoogleNet, etc. are some of the CNNs architectures that have been implemented on FPGA for applications like character recognition and object detection [9]. FPGA implementation of a facial recognition system based on CNN [10] and Eigen-face algorithm [11], along with the facial expression recognition system [12], have also been proposed in previous works. The present trend is to exploit the parallel computational nature of CNN by designing architectures with varying levels of parallelism [13]. Thus, as suggested in 2018, Bailey, parallelism between all the convolution kernels within each layer was implemented in this work. The design proposed in [10] for facial recognition using CNN fails to exploit the potential performance improvements that can be attained by operating all the individual convolutional layers in parallel. We propose improvements by eliminating result storing stages between successive convolution layers and by replacing the raster-scan based convolution unit in their design with a row-buffering based convolution unit.

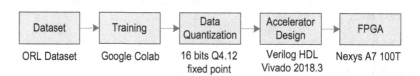

Fig. 1. Design flow

The CNN Hardware Accelerator is designed in Verilog HDL using Xilinx Vivado 2018.3 tool. Our CNN architecture was trained on Google Colab using the TensorFlow framework. Figure 1 gives a brief overview of the design flow which is explained in detailed in the following sections. We have evaluated the speed-up achieved on FPGA over GPU (Tesla K80 on Google Colab), and native CPU (Intel i5 7th generation CPU running Google Colab).

2 Methodology

This paper is split into two sections, software and hardware implementation. In the software part, the focus is on the design and training of CNN using python on Google Colaboratory. Along with this, Matlab scripts were used to generate all the necessary COE files (Xilinx Coefficient File). The hardware part deals with the design and implementation of the network on the Artix 7 FPGA board.

2.1 Dataset Preparation

We have used the standardized Oracle Research Lab (ORL) dataset images to train our network. It is a standard dataset commonly used for facial recognition in deep learning applications [10]. It has ten greyscale images of dimensions 56×46 of all the 40 individuals. This dataset was then expanded to 43 individuals including the authors. Further, the training dataset was artificially expanded using various standard dataset augmentation techniques like image manipulation, rotation by small angles, shift, flip, zoom so that CNN gives correct inference for input/testing images which are not in their usual orientation. These measures are increasingly necessary to make the CNN robust and reduce errors in real-time applications.

2.2 CNN Architecture Design on Software

Since implementation of complex networks, that require millions of parameters, on FPGA is difficult owing to limited on-chip memory, we decided to design a custom CNN architecture. Several networks were tested until the design had an acceptable balance between accuracy and number of parameters. Figure 2 presents our 4–8–16 CNN model with 3 convolution layers, 2 max-pooling layers and 1 full-connected or dense layer.

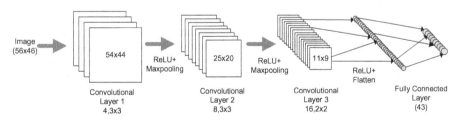

Fig. 2. The architecture of the proposed Convolutional Neural Network model

The first layer has 4 convolution kernels of dimension 3×3 and outputs 4 feature maps. Layer-2 has 8 kernels (dimension 3×3) for each output feature map produced by layer-1 (32 kernels) and outputs 8 feature maps. Similarly, layer-3 has 16 kernels of dimension 2×2 for each feature map produced by layer-2 (128 kernels) and outputs 16

Layer (type)	Output Shape	Param #
conv2d (Conv2D)	(None, 54, 44, 4)	36
max_pooling2d (MaxPooling2D)	(None, 27, 22, 4)	0
conv2d_1 (Conv2D)	(None, 25, 20, 8)	288
max_pooling2d_1 (MaxPooling2	(None, 12, 10, 8)	0
conv2d_2 (Conv2D)	(None, 11, 9, 16)	512
flatten (Flatten)	(None, 1584)	0
dense (Dense)	(None, 43)	68112
activation (Activation)	(None, 43)	0

Total params: 68,948
Trainable params: 68,948
Non-trainable params: 0

Fig. 3. Feature map dimensions and parameter distribution in each layer

feature maps. Figure 2 also shows the dimensions of kernels and feature maps in each layer of the CNN.

Figure 3 shows the number of parameters in each layer along with the feature map dimensions. The trained parameters obtained were of 32-bit floating-point format. From hardware point-of-view, fixed-point arithmetic is faster than floating-point arithmetic because it requires less complex hardware and utilizes fewer resources. Since facial recognition systems are expected to work in real-time, using fixed-point arithmetic over floating-point will reduce inference time with negligible performance degradation. Since 16-bit Q4.12 fixed-point format has an acceptable accuracy, all the trained parameters were quantized to 16 bit Q4.12 fixed-point format.

3   Hardware Design on FPGA

The direction of flow of data between the layers is indicated by arrows. The trained parameters after quantization were written to COE files using Matlab scripts. Block-RAMs (BRAM) of the FPGA configured as ROMs were initialized using these files. Layer-1,2 and 3 have 4, 32 and 128 convolution kernels, respectively. The block diagram in Fig. 4 gives an abstracted view of all the layers in the system. Every layer is assigned a separate BRAM for holding its kernel parameters. For every kernel, its parameters are concatenated and stored at a unique address in the BRAM corresponding to the layer the kernel belongs to. Since layer-1 has 4 kernels, a total of 36 parameters (4×9) are stored at 4 unique address locations. BRAMs corresponding to layer-2 and 3 has also been configured similarly.

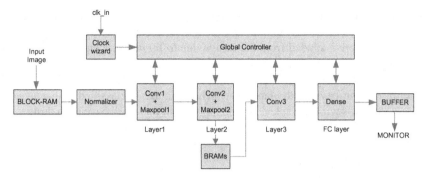

Fig. 4. Layer-wise schematic of CNN Implementation on FPGA

Parameters stored in these BRAMs are fetched in parallel and cached into registers after the system starts. This approach prevents the design from slowing down the system compared to the method employed in [14]. Instead of waiting for the current layer to process its input and then fetching the parameters of the following layer in the next few clock cycles [14], pre-fetching the parameters saves few clock cycles and is conducive to parallel operation of all the convolution layers. The global controller generates all the control signals and derived clocks for the design. As suggested in [14], parallelism between all the convolution kernels within each layer was implemented in this work. Thus, the design achieves high throughput and requires lesser clock cycles to process a frame and produce an output. The initial layers of CNN require high processing time as their inputs are of larger dimensions relative to the subsequent layers. To minimize the processing time of the initial layers, layer-1 and layer-2 are completely parallelized, because of this, the feature maps produced by layer-1 are referenced by layer-2 only once. Hence by passing them directly to layer-2, the need for buffering outputs of layer-1 in BRAMs [10] can be eliminated. For images of large dimensions, this approach will bypass the stage of buffering large feature maps. This way, architecture proposed in [10] can be improved, where the output feature maps produced by each layer is stored in BRAMs before passing these results to the subsequent layer which adds to the overhead delays. It also inherently prohibits the scope of operating layers in parallel.

Input feature maps of the successive layers have relatively smaller dimensions and require lower processing time. As a trade-off between scalability and resource utilization on hardware, layer-3 has only 8 convolution kernels operating in parallel instead of 128 kernels. The summation of outputs produced by these 8 convolution kernels produce a feature map. Thus, in layer-3 one feature map is produced at a time in contrast to the previous layers that produce all feature maps simultaneously. This process is iterated 16 times to produce all 16 output feature maps. Due to this approach the 8 output feature maps produced by layer-2 are referenced multiple times in layer-3 and thus they are stored in BRAMs. Fully connected (FC)/Dense layer takes input from layer-3 pixel-by-pixel. FC layer contain 43 neuron instances and has a comparison tree to find the neuron that was activated the most. The result of this comparison tree is passed through an activation layer. The control unit enables layer-2 after layer-1 produces its first valid output, and thereafter, both the layers operate in parallel. Layer-3 is enabled after layer-2 produces all of its output. Layer-3 and the dense layer are synchronized with the master clock. High-level functionalities like softmax, global average pooling, bias terms, and zero paddings were excluded from the design due to limited on-chip resources and to reduce the hardware complexity [14].

The input image is displayed on a monitor screen via a Video Graphics Array (VGA) connector. Post processing, the label to which the image is classified is displayed on the board's seven-segment display. All the modules in this work have been designed in Verilog using Xilinx Vivado 2018.3 with Nexys Artix-7 100T as the target. The hardware is designed for 16-bit Q4.12 fixed-point representations.

3.1 Convolution Module

Convolution is the most computationally intensive operation in CNN. The input image is convolved with a kernel/filter to extract spatial features from it. After finding the convolution results, the output is passed through a Rectified Linear Unit (ReLU) activation function. Architecture for the convolution module is shown above in Fig. 5.

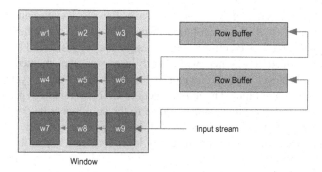

Fig. 5. Architecture for the convolution module and concept of line/row buffering used in convolution

The convolution module's speed largely determines the design's latency. The raster scan method of image caching used in [10] is an inherently slower method due to the overheads involved [15]. We have used row-buffering method for caching or buffering of pixels, to attain nearly true single-pixel per clock cycle processing, with minimal overheads at the end of each row. Theoretically, raster-scan method processes an input image of n × n dimensions, in $\{(n-2) * (3 * (n-3) + 9)\}$ clock cycles while row-buffering method requires $\{(n-2) * n + (2 * n) + 3\}$ clock cycles to process an image with same dimensions. Figure 6 shows a plot of the number of clock cycles required for inference by the raster-scan and row-buffering method. For inputs of large dimensions, the difference in their performance is pronounced.

3.2 Maxpooling Module

Max-pooling involves the pooling of the pixels in a window of the feature map and finding the maximum pixel value. Convolution produces a feature map that identifies

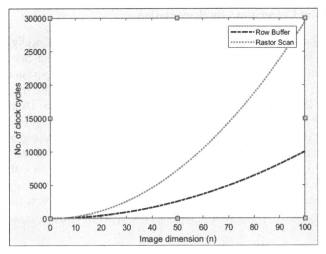

Fig. 6. Clock cycles required by raster-scan and row buffering for processing an image of dimensions nxn.

certain features in the input image. Max-pooling with a stride of 2 on this feature map compresses the image evenly in both dimensions by a factor of 2. The row buffering technique used in the convolution module for caching of pixels has also been used in max-pooling. The global controller unit generates clock signals for max-pooling units. We have used a subsampling window of 2×2 dimension and a stride of 2 pixels in our Max-pooling module. Increasing the window dimension or the stride is useful only if the input images have high dimensions and might lead to loss of features or data in images of smaller dimensions. Architecture for the Max-pooling module is shown below in Fig. 7.

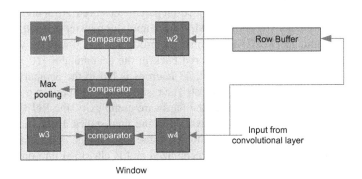

Fig. 7. Architecture for the Max-pooling module

3.3 Fixed Point Calculations Implementation

Data quantization helps in reducing the bit-width down to 16-bit with negligible accuracy loss. Software implementation employs floating-point arithmetic for calculations. The trained parameters obtained on Google Colab were of 32-bit floating-point format. From hardware point-of-view, fixed-point arithmetic is faster than floating-point arithmetic, because it has less complex hardware and utilizes fewer resources. Using fixed-point arithmetic over floating-point arithmetic will reduce inference time with negligible performance degradation. Since 16-bit Q4.12 fixed-point format has an acceptable accuracy, all the trained parameters were quantized to Q4.12 fixed-point format and the hardware was designed to perform calculations in fixed-point representation. Modules for signed addition and multiplication in fixed-point format were designed. Input image and parameters were normalized to limit the output values produced in each layer to the range {0,1} [14].

3.4 Global Controller Unit

Global Controller Unit generates all the control signals. The input to the controller is the master clock and system reset. It handles generation of derived clock signals for every layer along with control signals that synchronize and control all the data flow between the layers. It is also responsible for generating control signals and addresses for prefetching of parameters from BRAM.

3.5 Fully-Connected (Dense) Layer

The final stage of CNN is the fully-connected/dense layer and operates at the main clock's frequency. The output of layer-3 is serially fed pixel-by-pixel (essentially flattening) as input to the FC. All the 43 neurons in this layer are connected to this input. Each neuron in this layer has a separate BRAM configured as ROM that stores parameters corresponding to that neuron. Each address location has a 16-bit parameter stored. An address generator is used to fetch parameters from the ROM. An accumulator register stores the results of multiply and accumulate (MAC) operations. The product is added with the value stored in the accumulator register and then stored back in the accumulator [10]. The result stored in the accumulator registers of all 43 neurons is fed to the comparison tree to find the neuron that was activated the most. The result of this comparison tree is passed through an activation layer. To reduce the hardware complexity, the ReLU activation function is used instead of Softmax activation in the final stages. If the output of this comparison is less than a threshold (set to zero), the input image is not classified into any of the 43 labels, else the image is recognized and is classified into one of the 43 labels.

4 Results

Experimental results show that our network achieves nearly 95.61% testing accuracy and 99.7% training accuracy. The latency/execution time per image of the CPU and GPU

Table 1. Performance with varying frequencies

Frequency (MHz)	Latency/Execution Time (us) per image	Speedup ratio	
		CPU	GPU
50	91.16	5485	329
30	151.94	3291	197
20	227.9	2194	131
10	455.8	1097	66

implementations is nearly 500–1000 ms and 30–50 ms respectively. The implementation of the same CNN network on FPGA, takes nearly 4558 clock cycles for inference.

Table 1 illustrates the performance of our design on FPGA against CPU and GPU platforms. Since CPU and GPU operate at variable frequencies, their best-case execution time is considered for performance evaluation. Since the FPGA implementation operates at a fixed frequency, clock cycles required for inference is used for performance evaluation.

Table 2. Resource utilization report

Resources	Available	Resource utilization
LUT	63400	48362
LUTRAM	19000	540
FF	126800	5970
BRAM	135	56
DSP	240	240
IO	210	25
MMCM	6	1

The resource utilization of our design on Nexys Artix-7 100t FPGA board is shown in Table 2. Due to the complete utilization of Digital Signal Processing (DSP) slices on FPGA board, Look Up Tables (LUT) are utilized to implement multipliers. Table 3 shows the layer-wise resource utilization of our design on FPGA.

Figure 8 shows result of our hardware implementation. Simulation waveform result are presented in Fig. 9. All the necessary signals along with derived clocks have also been captured. A combination of selector switches chosen by the user selects the input test image which is fed to the CNN network for inference. Label indicates the label to which the input image is classified into.

Table 3. Layer-wise resource utilization

Module name	LUTs (63400)	Block RAM (135)	DSPs (240)	LUT as Logic (63400)	LUT as memory (19000)
Layer 1	8471	6	24	8299	172
Layer 2	20142	2	184	19902	240
Layer 3	7216	5	32	7088	128
Dense layer	4984	43	0	4984	0
Clock generator	0	0	0	0	0
Global Controller	78	0	0	78	0
Seven segment display	2	0	0	2	0

Fig. 8. Hardware implementation

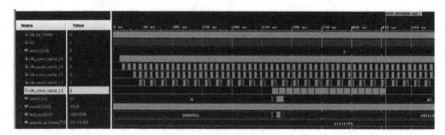

Fig. 9. Behavioral simulation waveforms

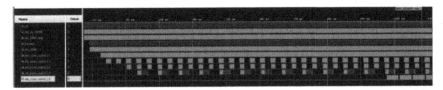

Fig. 10. Behavioral simulation for the global controller unit

Count keeps track of the number of clock cycles required for inference. Signals led_out and anode_activate are used to interface seven-segment display. Figure 10 shows the behavioral simulation of the global controller unit. All the synchronization clock signals for convolution and maxpooling units in all the layers is also shown. The label to which the image is classified is displayed on a seven-segment display. The input image is also displayed on a monitor via VGA connector. Figure 11 shows the on-chip power utilization report.

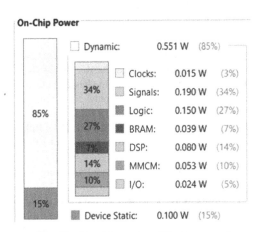

Fig. 11. On-chip power utilization report

In this paper, Xilinx's Nexys A7 100T FPGA development board was the platform used to implement our design. High-end FPGAs with abundant resources like Zync 7000, Zync UltraScale + MPSoC can make possible a better and efficient implementation.

5 Conclusion

In this work, we have proposed an FPGA implementation of a CNN accelerator for a facial recognition system. In this paper, our main focus was on exploring parallel operation of convolution kernels within each layer and also on exploring parallel operation of individual convolution layers in CNN to attain high throughput and low latency. Our design approach is scalable and can be easily implemented on medium-to-low end FPGAs. Hardware design of all the essential components of CNN has been explained in detail. The network designed has approximately 95.61% testing accuracy and 99.7%

training accuracy. FPGA implementation of the design provides a speed-up of nearly 1097 and 66 times over the CPU and GPU implementation of the same network on Google Colab.

References

1. Bailey, D.G.: Image processing using FPGAs. J. Imaging **5**(5), 53 (2019)
2. Chen, T., et al.: Diannao: a small-footprint high-throughput accelerator for ubiquitous machine-learning. ACM SIGARCH Comput. Archit. News **42**(1), 269–284 (2014)
3. Glorot, X., Bengio, Y.: Understanding the difficulty of training deep feedforward neural networks. In Proceedings of the Thirteenth International Conference on Artificial Intelligence and Statistics, pp. 249–256. JMLR Workshop and Conference Proceedings (Mar 2010)
4. LeCun, Y., Bengio, Y., Hinton, G.: Deep Learning. Nature **521**(7553), 436–444 (2015)
5. Ovtcharov, K., Ruwase, O., Kim, J.Y., Fowers, J., Strauss, K., Chung, E.S.: Accelerating deep convolutional neural networks using specialized hardware. Microsoft Research Whitepaper **2**(11), 1–4 (2015)
6. Phan-Xuan, H., Le-Tien, T., Nguyen-Tan, S.: FPGA platform applied for facial expression recognition system using convolutional neural networks. Procedia Comput. Sci. **151**, 651–658 (2019)
7. Qiao, S., Ma, J.: Fpga implementation of face recognition system based on convolution neural network. In: 2018 Chinese Automation Congress (CAC), pp. 2430–2434. IEEE (2018)
8. Sharma, H., et al.: From high-level deep neural models to FPGAs. In: 2016 49th Annual IEEE/ACM International Symposium on Microarchitecture (MICRO), pp. 1–12. IEEE (Oct 2016)
9. Solovyev, R.A., Kalinin, A.A., Kustov, A.G., Telpukhov, D.V., Ruhlov, V.S.: FPGA implementation of convolutional neural networks with fixed-point calculations. arXiv e-prints, arXiv-1808 (2018)
10. Sreejith, M.: Development of an FPGA based Image Processing Intellectual Property Core. NIT, Roukela (2014)
11. Sriram, V.B., Sawant, P., Kamath, K., Wadhwa, K., Gore, G., Revankar, S.: Implementation of 2d convolution algorithm on FPGA for image processing application, International Journal of Electrical, Electronics and Data Communication, ISSN: 2320–2084, 3.12, 22–25 (2015)
12. Šušteršič, T., Vulović, A., Filipović, N., Peulić, A.: FPGA implementation of face recognition algorithm. In: Oliver, N., Serino, S., Matic, A., Cipresso, P., Filipovic, N., Gavrilovska, L. (eds.) MindCare/FABULOUS/IIOT 2015-2016. LNICSSITE, vol. 207, pp. 93–99. Springer, Cham (2018). https://doi.org/10.1007/978-3-319-74935-8_13
13. Szegedy, C., et al.: Going deeper with convolutions. In: Proceedings of the IEEE Conference on Computer Vision and Pattern Recognition, pp. 1–9 (2015)
14. Zhang, C., Li, P., Sun, G., Guan, Y., Xiao, B., Cong, J.: Optimizing fpga-based accelerator design for deep convolutional neural networks. In: Proceedings of the 2015 ACM/SIGDA International Symposium on Field-Programmable Gate Arrays, pp. 161–170 (Feb 2015)
15. Zhuge, C., Liu, X., Zhang, X., Gummadi, S., Xiong, J., Chen, D.: Face recognition with hybrid efficient convolution algorithms on FPGAs. In: Proceedings of the 2018 on Great Lakes Symposium on VLSI, pp. 123–128 (May 2018)

Digital Design

Advanced TSV-BIST Repair Technique to Target the Yield and Test Challenges in 3-D Stacked IC'S

Vethamuthu Renold Sam[1] , S. Sivanantham[1] , Akkapolu Sankararao[2(✉)] ,
and G. Vaishnavi[2]

[1] VIT University, Vellore, India
Ssivanantham@vit.ac.in
[2] AMD India Pvt. Ltd, Bangalore, India
{Sankararao.Akkapolu,VAISHNAVI.G}@amd.com

Abstract. The efficient technique to increase the yield and target the test challenges of 3D Stacked ICs by using a Novel TSV-BIST Repair mechanism is introduced in this paper. This technique provides an optimistic solution for identifying the advanced manufacturing faults, power, and interconnect delays during TSV bonding and stacking of 3D Integrated Circuits. The proposed TSV-BIST Repair mechanism is capable to identify all the potential defects of TSVs like short, open, void formation, pin-hole, etc. and the Redundancy feature provides a mechanism to replace the faulty TSVs with spare TSVs to increase yield and productivity of the chip. Detailed analysis was performed on different layers of 3D stacked ICs with help of the proposed methodology. The industrial results of the conventional approach are compared with the proposed TSV-BIST repair mechanism. This methodology is proven with a significant improvement in yield of 11.5% and test time of 18.5% by potentially recovering all eminent defective chips.

Keywords: TSV (Through-Silicon-Vias) · 3D ICs · BIST · Repair · Yield

1 Introduction

As per Moore's law, semiconductor industry has been a center to integrate multiple functionality and specifications into tiny chips or System-On-Chip (SoC). As the technology node cone decreasing, there is a huge demand for high performance and less tester cost device due to decrease in technology nodes [1]. Currently, 2D (Two-dimensional) devices had conventional CMOS scaling, various cores on one die (SoC), different dies on one package (Multi-Chip Package, MCP), Printed Circuit Board (PCB) containing multiple dies. Many chips encountered challenges in high performance, yield improvement, lower tester cost due to dense functional logic [2]. In this scenario, Three-dimensional (3D) technology is a promising solution in current industry due to its high scope of stacking multiple dies with Through-Silicon-Vias (TSV) [3]. Traditionally, 3D Stacked-ICs had

© The Author(s), under exclusive license to Springer Nature Switzerland AG 2022
V. Arunachalam and K. Sivasankaran (Eds.): ICMDCS 2022, CCIS 1743, pp. 29–42, 2022.
https://doi.org/10.1007/978-3-031-23973-1_3

achieved great interest with respect to less power consumption, performance improvement and stacked connectivity between the dies with small interconnect lengths. TSV based design provides larger package density, reduced package body by removing the need for wired bond [4, 5].

3D Stacked-ICs with TSV based approach also comes with few defects such as: short, Open, void formation, inappropriate Cu-metal filling, metal pillar breakage due to impurities, thermal stress, misalignment, different heights of pillar, etc. However, Yield challenges observed during the 3D-ICs was a huge obstacle across all semiconductor industries [6]. As a key-role in 3D technology, TSV based 3D Stacked-ICs were incorporated as there was high variation in range of 0.004% to 8% of yield rate in 3D ICs [7–9]. This variation hits 3D-ICs yield exponentially as stacked die number increases. As per general study, yield loss occurs mainly due to two reasons – yield loss due to defect in stacking one or more dies; yield loss observed due to defects during IC assembly process [10–12, 16].

In this paper, we are briefly walk-through the 3D-Stacked ICs design requirements and its obstacles. Consequently, the existing test solutions for stacked device testing has been discussed to overcome the challenges addressed. However, due to clustering effect if a TSV is defective during bond process, this influences neighboring TSVs to be defect prone. Hence, we propose a novel TSV Repair technique to identify the defective TSV and repair them using BIST operations is explained in Sect. 3. The detailed yield analysis, test time results from proposed methodology are reported in Sect. 4. The challenges and future scope were discussed in Sect. 5 and finally the paper is concluded in Sect. 6.

2 Motivation

The 3D IC functionality includes superset of TSV bonding. According to study, the conventional IC manufacturing process has reported relatively lower yield compared to standard 2D IC process. Designs with TSV-based technology is not error-prone as there is high chance of defective TSV due to shorts creating high resistance and opens created due to variable TSV heights. Hence, the eminent test methodologies and design-for-testability (DFT) solutions have been a promising topic in semiconductor industry [13, 14].

Pre-bond (Known-good-die) test plays an important role in 3D-IC yield improvement by diagnosing the TSV defects even before stacking multiple dies. However, the failures will not be detected only because of defective TSV formation but also due to the inappropriate distribution of small TSVs across a thin wafer at minimal tester cost. Whereas Post-bond (Known-good stack) test plays vital role while testing TSV interconnects between two or more dies [7, 15]. This test easily reports all the defective failure caused due to TSV stacking when multiple dies are vertically stacked. If dies are identified faulty, it results in discarding of chip permanently which then abruptly affects wafer cost. Currently, we have various methodology to identify the TSV faults by applying different test techniques. TSV BIST is one such hot topic in industry [16–19]. Also, it is important to have quality test structure that creates digital response from the short or open defects causing high resistance between the substrate and the TSV [20]. The digital responses need to be stored on-chip and read-out later for testing, characterization, and target to recover defective TSV. Figure 1 briefs about pre and post bond test in 3D stacked IC's.

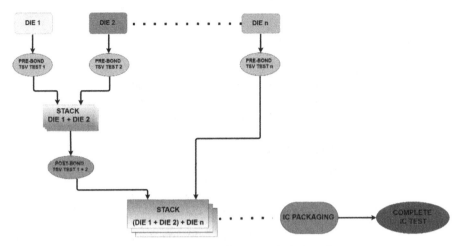

Fig. 1. Flow diagram for 3D stacked IC testing

In this paper, we present an advanced 3D Stacking-IC TSV Repair methodology. The proposed architecture explains the integrated design and test methodology to identify the defective signals and repair using the read and write operation through the fuse controller logic.

3 Proposed TSV-BIST Repair Mechanism

In this section, we describe the newly proposed TSVBIST architecture and Repair mechanism. The proposed architecture of the TSVBIST repair mechanism, as shown in Fig. 2. Here, in a 3D stacked IC, we considered that the bottom chip functions as a master chip and the chip on top of the bottom chip functions as a slave chip or a stacked chip. Therefore, the TSV's are placed between the master die and the stacked die to provide the interaction between dies without much interconnect congestion issues.

TSV is a macro, and it is consisting of a separate transmitter (Tx) and receiver (Rx) parts. These Transmitter and Receivers are acts as interface between the stacked dies. The testing of TSVs is very challenging and complex in nature during stacking process of the die, requires an advanced TSV testing approaches. It places an important role w.r.t yield and test cost. In order to reduce the complexity and cost of the 3D IC testing and increase the productivity of TSVs, we need to group the TSVs and tested together. The TSV grouping mechanism provides a simple testing approach and test time reduction by testing all the TSVs in a group at once. The size of the TSV group can vary based on the physical location of the TSVs and the number of TSVs present in block. Generally, the TSVs which are sitting in the same block can be grouped and tested together. Whereas in this proposed architecture, the TSV grouping can be done based on the read and write operations of the TSVs. Usually, in this approach the read or write group includes 70 to 80 TSVs in each group. Along with this we are using 2 Redundant TSVs in each group, in order to repair the faulty TSVs which are identified by the TSV BIST Repair mechanism during TSV test.

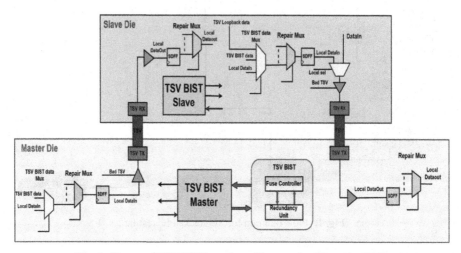

Fig. 2. Proposed TSV-BIST repair architecture for 3D stacked IC's

The proposed TSV BIST Repair architecture has a Built-In-Self-Test mechanism to test the TSVs and performing repair and redundancy analysis for failing TSVs. TSV-BIST logic present in all the dies of the packaged die. The BIST logic which is present in the master die or bottom die is called TSV-BIST master and the logic which is present in stacked dies called as TSV-BIST slave. The TSV BIST Master Controls the execution of the TSV BIST for all modes of operation and even it controls the other TSV-BIST slaves in stacked dies. It receives information and execution information via JTAG TDRs. It also Interfacing to the fuse controller to pass repair information and to force fuse distribution. The TSV-BIST master consisting of the BIST data generator, address generator and comparator units. Whereas in case of TSV-BIST slave has only the data generations, there is no data comparator units on it. So, the TSV-BIST data comparison always happens in master die. TSVBIST_CONTROL signal is used to make the synchronization always between the TSV-BIST master and salve logics in master and salve dies. It minimizes the number of control signals between the Master and Slave and always try to use a single signal to interface between Master and Slave. Generally, TSVs must be tested at High-speed functional frequencies, if any design consisting multiple clock domains an individual TSV-BIST master needed for each clock domain.

As shown in TSV-BIST architecture diagram in Fig. 2, each TSV macro consisting of 2 mux's at transmitter side, one is TSV BIST data mux and other one is TSV repair mux, whereas in receiver side only the TSV Repair Mux is present, these mux's are used to shift-out the one TSV data to another TSV if there is any failing TSV is identified. A pair of flops and buffers are added to each side of the TSVs, in order to shift the data and capture the response and overcome the critical timing effects. These TSV flops are acts as wrapper flops during EXTEST mode and connected as chain in SCAN mode in order to generate ATPG patterns. When there is no failing TSV is identified, then all the signals are passing through original TSVs. if any TSV is identified as failing TSV, then it is replaced with spare or redundant TSV by shifting all the signals between failing TSV and redundant TSV.

In this proposed methodology, we introduced 2 types of TSV groups, TSV write groups and TSV read groups. In Read groups the data is always driven from slave (stacked) dies to master (base) die, whereas in case of Write groups the data is always drive from base die to stacked dies. The TSV groups can be determine if the group is read or write based upon group number provided by the TSV-BIST controller. It also provides the feature to tracking which TSV Group is being executed and what type of the TSV group and the Pass/Fail status of the TSV BIST. The testing and repair of TSV groups can be done one after one before moving to the next TSV group until all the TSV groups have been tested and repaired. Within each group different data patterns are used in order to identify all the potential faults existing in TSVs. The testing process for TSV read and write groups are different, and the detailed testing information w.r.t each group provided in the below sub-sections.

Similar to Memory BIST, TSV-BIST also has the Repair feature provided by the Redundancy unit and fuse controller interfaces as shown in Fig. 2. The redundant unit provides capability to identify the failing TSVs based on status register values and calculates the repair signature for the particular failing TSVs. The fuse controller consisting of memory device usually a read only memory (ROM), it stores the repair signature values for all the repairable TSVs in the design. The TSV-BIST enables the fuse distribution mechanism to provide the repair information to faulty TSVs in the design. Along with these features the TSV-BIST also provides facilitates to the test data generation, response data comparisons, tacking of the failing TSVs based on the error status and calculates the repair signatures and loaded into the repair registers.

The proposed TSV-BIST also provides some of the important unique diagnostic features during TSV testing, we will also call it as TSV BIST operating modes such as.

Normal mode: In this mode that we allow all the TSVs to be tested for all groups. During this process, the TSVs are repaired, and the repair information placed at an interface for the fuse controller to process. This mode is set up for looping where the repair only happens on the final pass through the loop, with the addition of another pass to verify that the repairs worked. This mode may also allow a diagnostic capability if enabled.

Programmable: The programmable feature of TSV BIST allow the user to configure TSV test to.

- The number of times to execute TSV BIST
- Allows the TSV BIST to execute on a single layer or sequence of layers
- Allows the TSV BIST to execute on a single slice or sequence of slices
- Allows the TSV BIST to execute on a particular group or sequence of groups
- Enable Diagnostic Mode to read out comparison data

If multiple layers, slices, or groups is used, this will operate on a sequential sequence.

GO/NO-GO: This mode is designed to verify the fuses that are programmed fixes all the issues in the TSV and we get a clean TSV BIST run. In this mode the fuses are applied to the TSVs for repair and then TSV BIST will execute between the master and slave dies and verify that the TSVs run clean.

3.1 TSV Read Group Test

TSV Read groups are the once which drives data from stacked or slave dies to base die or master die. The TSV master and slave shares the same data generator. Since the TSV master consisting of data comparator logic, it must need to know when to compare the valid data which is driven from the TSV slave data generator. The TSVBIST_CONTROL signal keeps the master and slave in sync and there are a known number of flops in the path from the slave to the master so that the comparator knows when to sample valid data. The Fig. 3 shows the read operation of the TSV BIST data path between the master and the slave.

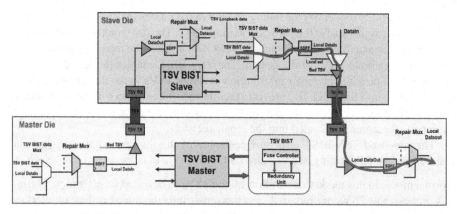

Fig. 3. Read group data path in TSV-BIST repair flow for 3D ICs

The slave Die has the TSV BIST data mux, and it will take TSV BIST data as input and sends the data through one flop on the slave die and another flop on the base die before comparing it to the expected data. In this scenario the read path consisting of 2 flops in the data path and there are 4 different combinations of test patterns can be applied and compared. These 4 basic data patterns are applied multiple times up to the width of the read group for identifying all the potential defects in the TSVs during read operation. There can be inverses applied to the base data pattern depending on the contents of the shift register, whose width is equal to the width of the read group. For this TSV data select register are used to select the data between actual data and inversion data. The complete read data path which is traversing from stacked die to base die as shown in Fig. 3.

Once all the data patterns are applied to the read group, if these is any failing TSVs, which are identified through the BIST status registers. In such failing scenarios the algorithm pauses the execution and calculates the Repair signature by using Redundancy analysis unit and stores that into fuse controller of the TSV BIST master. Generally, the fuse controller collects all the failing information and stores within it, and it will distribute to the repair signatures through TSV BIST master to repair the failing TSVs by replacing with Redundant TSVs. the TSV master is notified once the repair has completed so that it can complete the testing. Based on the status register values The TSV BIST master is notified if a repair is needed or not. Generally, the repair status registers are two bits per each group, and the 2-bit register decides, whether repair is needed or not and how many repairs required so on.

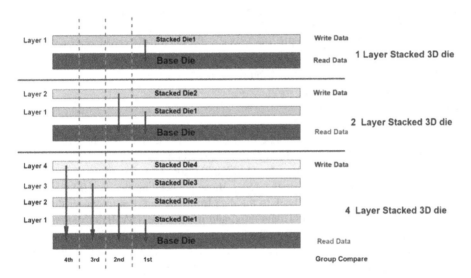

Fig. 4. Read group data paths in TSV w.r.t multi-layer 3D SIC's

The Fig. 4 shows the basic read operation performed for different layers of stacked dies. Here we will consider the 3 different configurations of multiple layers of stacked dies, like 1-layer, 2-layer, and 4-layers of stacked dies. In each case the read operations are performed form slave die or stacked die to base die, which is represented with arrow paths in the Fig. 4 (Table 1).

Table 1. Repair status register values of TSV BIST.

BIST status register value	Description
2'b00	No repair required
2'b01	One repair required
2'b10	Two repairs required
2'b11	Non-Repairable: more than two repairs needed (Fatal error reported)

We are using 2 redundant TSVs per each group in order to repair the failing TSVs with redundant one. So, the maximum repairs we can perform up to 2 here, if any TSV group have more than 2 failing TSVs then it will generate a fatal error and those TSVs are non-repairable TSVs. generally, the lower order bits of the repair register belong read group and upper order bits are belongs to the write TSV groups. The below table-1 gives the detailed information about 2-bit repair status register.

3.2   TSV Write Group Test

To test a read or write group, the read groups must be tested first since the write groups are tested by feeding them back through a read group only. Once the testing of all the TSVs read groups completed, then the TSV BIST starts the write group test since the TSV write group created on the TSVs, those are sending the data from base die to stack dies and again reading back to the data from stacked dies to master die. Here the master die has the TSV BIST data mux, and it takes the TSV BIST data as input which is generated by TSV-BIST master present in bottom die and sends the data to the stacked dies through the flops, and the slave dies loopback this written data down through read groups to the base die again for data comparison. In this write scenario the data path consisting of total 4 flops. This is important because the data generator cycles

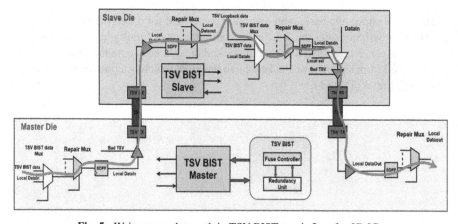

Fig. 5. Write group data path in TSV-BIST repair flow for 3D ICs

over four different data patterns so that the TSV master comparator will be lined up with the correct expected data once it has traversed through the loopback path back to the base die.

The write group testing also includes the read group, so the same set of patterns will be reused for read group testing. In case the number of write groups are more than read groups, some of the read groups used more than once while testing the write groups. Generally, the write groups are paired with the read groups to provide the feedback to write group data to the bottom die. The complete write data path which is traversing from base die to stacked and again feedthrough from stacked die to base die as shown in Fig. 5.

Similar to Read group testing, once all the data patterns are applied to the write group, if these is any failing TSVs, which are identified through the BIST status registers. In such failing scenarios the algorithm pauses the execution and calculates the Repair signature by using Redundancy analysis unit and stores that into fuse controller of the TSV BIST master. The fuse controller collects all the failing information and stores within it, and it will distribute to the repair signatures through TSV BIST master to repair the failing TSVs by replacing with Redundant TSVs.

The Fig. 6. Shows the basic write operation performed for different layers of stacked dies. Here also we will consider the 3 different configurations of multiple layers of stacked dies, like 1-layer, 2-layer, and 4-layers of stacked dies. In each case the write operations are performed form base die or stacked die and read back to base die, which is represented with arrow paths in the fig.

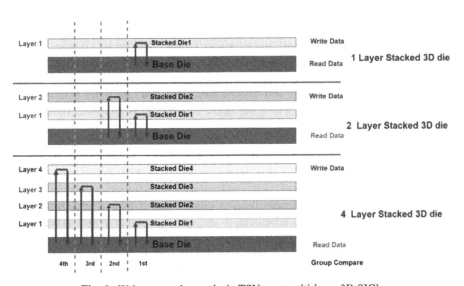

Fig. 6. Write group data paths in TSV w.r.t multi-layer 3D SIC's

The Fig. 6 shows the complete write data paths how it is traversing from base die to stacked and again reading back to base die.

The fuse controller which is present in TSV BIST master has 32-bit fuse value for each fuse register. The generalized 32-bit fuse register shown in Fig. 7, usually this fuse controller stores all the repair information and when the system is powered on all the fused will be burned. Inside each fuse register consisting different fields to identifies the correct repair signature for a failing TSV. It is consisting of the staked die id and TSV group id and finally the repair signature values as shown in the figure Fig. 7.

31	30	29	28	27	26	25	24	23	22	21	20	19	18	17	16	15	14	13	12	11	10	9	8	7	6	5	4	3	2	1	0
Repair Signature [20:31]												TSV Group ID [11:19]										TSV Group Column [0:9]									

Fig. 7. Fuse register for TSV-BIST repair

4   Results and Yield Analysis

In this paper, the performance of the proposed TSV-BIST Repair mechanism is analyzed. The industrial results are verified w.r.t different layers of 3D stack packaged ICs. The Yield and test time Analysis was performed on various chaplet-based designs w.r.t different numbers of stacked layers. Those results are closely compared with standard TSV testing approaches. Generally, the yield loss in 3D stacked ICs is mainly due to failing TSVs during the assembling process. The main manufacturing challenges for 3D ICs occurs at wafer thinning and TSV bonding process which cause TSV faults, using a redundant TSVs to repair the failing TSVs is one of the important yield improvement techniques. Many of the TSV testing techniques fallows the standard uniformly distributed TSV fault mechanisms, keeping these factors in mind and we developed a new TSV BIST Repair mechanism by grouping and testing TSVs based on the data communications paths between base die and stacked dies. It gives a significant improvement in yield and test time reduction with a negligible area overhead. Here we consider the dies which are going for staking are fault free and it was tested and proven during the pre-bond testing.

The proposed technique was implemented in our recent industry design production phase w.r.t various layers of staked dies. Here in this case, we have provided the results w.r.t 3 layers and 6 layers of 3D staking ICs and compared with the previous conventional TSV BIST approach results. Currently the dies which are used in our recent stacked 3D designs are heterogenous and are belongs to different technology nodes, whereas in case of previous conventional TSV-BIST approach was implemented on homogenous 3D stacked dies and all the stacked layer dies are belongs to same technology node. Compared to homogenous 3D stacked dies, heterogenous stacked Dies from different technology node design is very complex and required high test time. In this current TSV BIST approach the read and write groups consisting of an optimal number of TSVs (80–90) per group.

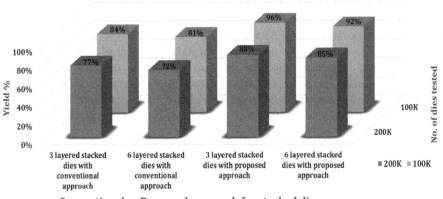

Fig. 8. Yield analysis graph between conventional and proposed TSV BIST approach

The industrial design data were analyzed on two sets of 3D ICs w.r.t 3-layes and 6 layers stacking devices, the first set is testing of 100K 3D stacked devices and the second set consisting of 200K device testing. All these devices are testing at post-bond during production time on ATE interface.

The proposed TSV-BIST repair solution gives yield of 96% and 92% for the first set of 100K 3D stacked devices testing w.r.t 3 layers and 6 layers of stacked dies. For the same set of stacked 3D IC testing, the conventional TSV-BIST approach provides yield of 84% and 81% w.r.t 3 layers and 6 layers of stacked 3D ICs. Similarly, we have verified the proposed approach for 2nd set of 200k 3D stacked devices, with that the proposed TSV_BIST repair approach provides yield of 88% and 85% w.r.t 3 layer and 6 layer

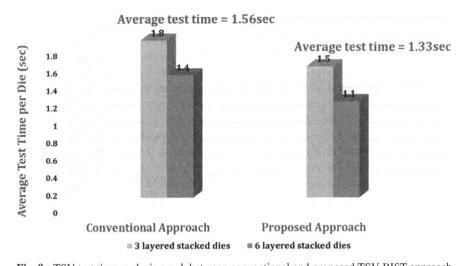

Fig. 9. TSV test time analysis graph between conventional and proposed TSV BIST approach

stacked ICs, whereas the conventional approach gives 77% and 72% w.r.t 3layer and 6 layer stacked 3D dies for same set of 200K devices as shown in Fig. 8 the complete yield analysis results are summarized and provided in the Table 2. Form these experimental results proven that the proposed TSV-BIST approach gives a significant improvement in design yield, and the average yield improvement is approximately 11.5%.

Similarly, the average test time was analyzed while testing the same set of devices during production w.r.t proposed TSV-BIST approach and conventional approach. While using the proposed architecture the average time taken to test one stacked 3D IC is 1.33 s, where the conventional approach takes an average time of 1.56 s to test the one 3D stacked IC as shown in Fig. 9. So, the average test time reduction is ~18.5%.

5 Challenges and Future Scope

The main challenges for implementing the proposed TSV BIST Repair architecture are, to generate test vectors for TSV self-test need an extra BIST logic and for providing the TSV Repair mechanism need a dedicated extra memory to store the TSV repair signatures in fuse controller. It gives the area overhead problems. The verification of TSV's during pre-silicon is little complex to create the test bench including all the stacked dies in overall design compared to conventional BIST approach. while testing the 3D staked dies form the bottom die, always we need to verify first the TSV-BIST sequence. So, for that always an extra bootup sequence requited to test the TSVs. we need to provide some extra cycles to perform the TSV-BIST repair mechanism during boot operation. currently the research trend is moving towards to achieve the above-mentioned challenges.

6 Conclusion

In this paper, we have presented a novel TSV-BIST Repair mechanism for testing 3D stacked IC's. This architecture provides a promising solution to identify all the potential defects like, opens, shorts, void and all the structural damages happened during the TSV bonding process of stacked die. This approach also provides diagnosis and repairing feature for failing TSVs in 3D stacked ICs in order to achieve the targeting goals w.r.t Yield and test time. a novel TSV grouping mechanism is introduced based on TSV read and write operations of the TSVs. the test results are conducted and performed on various sets of 3D stacked devices w.r.t 3 layer and 6layer design of stacked ICs by using proposed architecture. Also, the numbers compared with conventional approach, as a result a significant improvement in manufacturing yield in terms of 3D stacked devices with a minimal area overhead. While compared to the conventional approach, the proposed TSV BIST Repair mechanism provides an average of 11.5% improvement in Yield. This approach not only targeting towards the yield improvement, but it also provides a great impact in test time reduction of around 18.5% compared to standard approach.

References

1. Xu, K., Yu, Y., Peng, X.: TSV fault modeling and a BIST solution for TSV pre-bond test. In: 2021 IEEE 39th VLSI Test Symposium (VTS), pp. 1–6 (2021). https://doi.org/10.1109/VTS 50974.2021.9441058.

2. Cheng, S.-F., Huang, P.-T., Wang, L.-C., Chang, M.-C.F.: Built-in self-test/repair methodology for multiband RF-interconnected TSV 3D integration. IEEE Des. Test **36**(6), 63–71 (2019). https://doi.org/10.1109/MDAT.2019.2932935

3. Jani, I., Lattard, D., Vivet, P., Durupt, J., Thuries, S., Beigné, E.: Test solutions for high density 3D-IC interconnects – focus on SRAM-on-logic partitioning. In: 2019 IEEE European Test Symposium (ETS), pp. 1–2 (2019). https://doi.org/10.1109/ETS.2019.8791531

4. Wang, R., Deutsch, S., Agrawal, M., Chakrabarty, K.:The hype, myths, and realities of testing 3D integrated circuits. In: 2016 IEEE/ACM International Conference on Computer-Aided Design (ICCAD), pp. 1–8 (2016). https://doi.org/10.1145/2966986.2980097

5. Jani, I., Lattard, D., Vivet, P., Beigné, E.: Innovative structures to test bonding alignment and characterize high density interconnects in 3D-IC. In: 2017 15th IEEE International New Circuits and Systems Conference (NEWCAS), pp. 153–156 (2017). https://doi.org/10.1109/ NEWCAS.2017.8010128.

6. Kumar, A., Reddy, S.M., Becker, B., Pomeranz, I.: Performance aware partitioning for 3D-SOCs. In: 2012 International SoC Design Conference (ISOCC), pp. 163–166 (2012). https:// doi.org/10.1109/ISOCC.2012.6407065

7. Chi, C.-C., Lin, B.-Y., Wu, C.-W., Wang, M.-J., Lin, H.-C., Peng, C.-N.: On improving interconnect defect diagnosis resolution and yield for interposer-based 3-D ICs. IEEE Des. Test **31**(4), 16–26 (2014)

8. Salah, K.: DfT techniques and architectures for TSV-based 3D-ICs: a comparative study. In: 2016 18th Mediterranean Electrotechnical Conference (MELECON), pp. 1–4 (2016). https:// doi.org/10.1109/MELCON.2016.7495444.

9. Fkih, Y., Vivet, P., Flottes, M.-L., Rouzeyre, B., Di Natale, G., Schloeffel, J.: 3D DFT challenges and solutions. IEEE Comput. Soc. Annu. Symp. on VLSI **2015**, 603–608 (2015). https://doi.org/10.1109/ISVLSI.2015.11

10. Lee, H.S., Chakrabarty, K.: Test challenges for 3D integrated circuits. IEEE Des. Test Comput. **26**(5), 26–35 (2009)

11. Loi, I., Mitra, S., Lee, T.H., Fujita, S., Benini, L.:A low-overhead fault tolerance scheme for TSV-based 3D network on chip links. In: 2008 IEEE/ACM International Conference on Computer-Aided Design, pp. 598-602 (2008)

12. Noia, B., Chakrabarty, K.:Pre-bond testing of die logic and TSVs in high performance 3D-SICs. In: 2011 IEEE International 3D Systems Integration Conference (3DIC), 2011 IEEE International, pp. 1–5 (2012)

13. Benabdeladhim, M., Fradi, A., Hamdi, B.:Interconnect BIST based new self-repairing of TSV defect in 3D-IC. In: 2017 International Conference on Engineering & MIS (ICEMIS), pp. 1-4 (2017)

14. Hu, S., Wang, Q., Guo, Z., Xie, J., Mao, Z.: Fault detection and redundancy design for TSVs in 3D ICs. In: 2015 IEEE 11th International Conference on ASIC (ASICON), pp. 1–4 (2015)

15. Wang, C., et al.: BIST methodology, architecture and circuits for pre-bond TSV testing in 3D stacking IC systems. IEEE Trans. Circuits Syst. I: Regular Papers **62**(1), 139–148 (2015)

16. Dai, L., Yu, N., Yang, Y., Wang, C., Xi, X.:A scan-based pre-bond test of through-silicon vias with open and short defects. In: 2017 International Conference on Electromagnetics in Advanced Applications (ICEAA), pp. 1037–1040 (2017)

17. Hsieh, A., Hwang, T.: TSV redundancy: architecture and design issues in 3-D IC. IEEE Trans. Very Large Scale Integr. (VLSI) Syst. **20**(4), 711–722 (2012)

18. Huang, H., Huang, Y., Hsu, C.:Built-in self-test/repair scheme for TSV-based three-dimensional integrated circuits. In: 2010 IEEE Asia Pacific Conference on Circuits and Systems, pp. 56–59 (2010)
19. Goel,S.K.: Test challenges in designing complex 3D chips: what in on the horizon for EDA industry?: designer track. In: 2012 IEEE/ACM International Conference on Computer-Aided Design (ICCAD), pp. 273–273 (2012)
20. Arumí, D., Rodríguez-Montañés, R., Figueras, J.: Prebond testing of weak defects in TSVs. IEEE Trans. Very Large Scale Integr. (VLSI) Syst. **24**(4), 1503–1514 (2016). https://doi.org/10.1109/TVLSI.2015.2448594.

Redundancy Allocation Problem Evaluation Using Interval-Based GA and PSO for Multi-core System Consisting of One Instruction Cores

Shashikiran Venkatesha[1]([✉]) [iD] and Ranjani Parthasarathi[2]

[1] Smart Computing, Vellore Institute of Technology, Vellore, India
shashikiran.annauniv@gmail.com
[2] College of Engineering Guindy, Anna University, Chennai, India

Abstract. Selection of redundant resources and optimizing the system reliability to maximization would form a redundancy allocation problem (RAP). The article proposes a formulation for RAP for multi-core system consisting of one instruction cores. The one-shot system model is the reliability model used to derive system reliability expression for the multi-core system considered here. The system reliability expression would be the objective function with non-linear cost constraints is formulated as a non-linear programming problem, or RAP formulation. The one instruction cores (OIC) support conventional larger cores like MIPS core when they fail to execute an instruction. The OICs support to larger cores like MIPS core is highly imprecise in a multi-core scenario. To address impreciseness, interval numbers is introduced, thereby RAP becomes interval- RAP. Interval-RAP is a NP-Hard problem. Two-phase interval-based GA and interval-based PSO is proposed to solve the interval-RAP. Simulation studies illustrate that two-phase interval-based GA and interval-based PSO are fair efficacious in determining superior solutions.

Keywords: Redundancy allocation problem · Genetic Algorithm · Particle swarm optimization · Reliability optimization

1 Introduction

The performance and sustenance of engineering applications deployed on a hardware platform (such as multi-core computing system) depends on the reliability of the host system. In recent times, reliability has become a noteworthy parameter in the design of multi-core systems. Reliability can be defined as the probability of a function efficaciously meeting the requirements within the aegis of constraints in a stipulated time period. In order to improve the reliability of the system, in a multi-core context, two approaches are adopted. Firstly, when the reliability of the single core improves, the reliability of the multi-core system also improves. Enhancing the reliability of a core is very expensive approach that requires hardening of the devices at the physical layer.

© The Author(s), under exclusive license to Springer Nature Switzerland AG 2022
V. Arunachalam and K. Sivasankaran (Eds.): ICMDCS 2022, CCIS 1743, pp. 43–71, 2022.
https://doi.org/10.1007/978-3-031-23973-1_4

Secondly, augmenting or adding redundant core to the multi-core system would enhance the system reliability. The problem of choosing redundant cores and concurrently optimizing the system reliability to maximization within the stated constraints can be called as redundancy allocation problem (RAP). The paper proposes a formulation for RAP in a multi-core scenario.

The RAP is formulated using the system reliability expression. The system reliability expression is derived using a reliability model configured for a multi-core system. Traditionally, k-out-of-n systems: G(F)[1] system is used as reliability model to estimate the system reliability for a multi-core system. In such machines, at least k cores are operational among n cores in the system. For generalized k-out-of-n systems: G(F) systems, Coit et al. & Smith et al. [2], Coit et al. & Liu et al. [3], and Aghaei et al. [4] proposed RAP formulations. For a multi-core scenario, Huang et al., & Xu et al. [5] used k-out-of-n systems: G system-based reliability model to estimate system reliability using Weibull distribution. The k-out-of-n systems: G system cannot be used as a reliability model for **multi-core system consisting of one instruction cores** (or shortly named as MSOIC). Hence a RAP formulation used for k-out-of-n systems: G cannot be used for multi-core system consisting of one instruction cores. Because, the one instructions core (OIC) is not used as a spare core. In MSOIC, the OICs are small support cores for conventional cores or million instruction per second (MIPS) core (or cores larger in die size) in MSOIC. The MIPS cores when they fail to execute an instruction, faulty instruction is migrated to small support cores or OICs in MSOIC. The OICs execute the faulty instruction and the results are uploaded in the appropriate pipeline registers in MIPS core for the stalled instruction to continue its execution. To model this scenario, reliability model for MSOIC which uses One-Shot System (OSS) model is proposed in this article. The OSS model is one such reliability model that abstracts the interdependency between larger cores and supports cores in MSOIC. The RAP for One-Shot System based reliability modelled MSOIC, is formulated as single objective function non-linear programming problem (or optimization problem) is presented in this paper.

In the single objective function non-linear programming problem for MSOIC, the system reliability is maximized when the number of functions start-up policed (X) in OICs and function level/component level redundancy (A) increases. X (start-up policed matrix) and A (availability matrix) are the decision variables in non-linear programming problem for MSOIC. However, there is a cost associated in terms of performance overheads in executing the functions on the OIC. Hence, the system reliability has to be optimized by determining values for X and A with the overhead cost C as the constraint. Further, another factor to be considered is that the reliability of migrating instructions from conventional core to OICs and executing the function on OICs, $r(t)$, is imprecise. This impreciseness could be due to manufacturing complexity, or complexity in design and the environment where it is deployed. In order to address impreciseness, conventionally three approaches are available, namely, interval analysis, fuzzy and stochastic fuzzy. Among these, Interval analysis is used to address impreciseness. Hence Interval valued reliabilities are assigned to $r(t)$. Thus, the RAP is referred to as Interval RAP. RAP is a NP-Hard problem [6]. In NP-hard problem, problem space is large and one solution cannot be claimed as inferior to the other alternatives [7]. Contemporary heuristic algorithms are used where an effort to determine exact solutions are computationally high and expensive. The heuristic algorithms like the Genetic Algorithm provide near optimal solutions for complex problems. In this paper, Interval RAP is formulated and solved using a modified interval-based Genetic Algorithm (GA) and interval-based Particle Swarm Optimization (PSO) algorithms. As a prelude to that, the background related to interval analysis presented in the following Sect. 3. A brief background on microarchitecture and OSS based reliability model for multi-core system consisting of one instruction cores is presented in Sect. 2, will lay the foundation for RAP formulation and its evaluation using Interval – GA and Interval – PSO.

Contributions of this paper:

In order to improve the system reliability, redundant components are included to support the system during failure. The allocation of functional redundant components (OICs) in the multi-core system needs to be addressed. The contribution related to RAP and reliability optimization are listed below:

1) Interval RAP with objective function for maximization of system reliability is formulated.
2) Monotonicity, reliability of function and maximum system reliability that are integral to Interval RAP are evaluated.
3) Interval RAP is solved by using modified interval-based GA. The optimal solution for an evaluation example-one and evaluation example-two having smaller problem size and larger problem size respectively are evaluated. The system reliability of regular GA and proposed GA are compared.
4) By performing sensitivity analysis, impact of GA parameters on system reliability are analyzed.
5) Interval RAP is solved using modified interval-based PSO. Two variants of PSO, local best PSO and global best PSO are used to evaluate the interval RAP. The optimal solutions are compared for the same set of constraints for an evaluation example-one and evaluation example-two.
6) The solutions of interval-based GA and interval based PSO are compared and analyzed.

2 Background on Multi-core System Consisting of One Instruction Cores

In our earlier research article, which presents the evaluation of hardware parameters such as dynamic power, leakage power, area, and critical path for a novel, low cost ("low cost" means low power and lower die area) fault tolerant OIC [8]. The reliability model and analysis for OICs were also presented in the article. The OICs execute only one instruction named "subleq" instruction. The faulty instruction opcode sent by conventional core is decoded by the OIC and the subleq instruction is executed by three subtractors repeatedly to emulate the faulty instruction. The voter logic decides the correct result after evaluating results from three subtractors. Triple modular redundancy (or three subtractors) is adopted in OIC to enhance the reliability of the instruction execution. Thereby, it enhances the reliability of OIC. The OIC consumes dynamic power of 1.41 mW and area of $8,122 \ \mu m^2$ which is better than its contenders.

Further, an integrated solution such as MSOIC (multi-core system consisting of small support OICs supporting conventional cores like MIPS core) is presented in the research article [9]. The reliability analysis, performance and yield estimation for MSOIC are our significant contribution. The power and area estimation are analyzed for MSOIC consisting of one MIPS core connected to one OIC. The fault detection logic unit in MSOIC detects the fault in the result produced by arithmetic logic unit after instruction execution. The opcode of the faulty instruction sent to OIC from MIPS core. The OIC executes faulty instruction by decoding its opcode and invokes a sequence of subleq instruction or called subleq micro-routine. This subleq micro-routine undergoes execution in three subtractors + one self-correcting subtractor. Finally, the result produced by the OIC is updated in the pipeline registers of MIPS core. The migration of fault instruction from MIPS core to low-cost fault tolerant OIC can be abstracted by a reliability model named One-Shot System (OSS) model. The different levels of abstraction that exist in the functional support by provided by OIC to conventional cores (or MIPS cores) is appropriately captured by OSS based reliability model.

The OSS based reliability model provides three model parameters and they are (a) wakeup probability (b) start-up policy, and (c) readiness probability. The wakeup probability denotes the probability of invoking a function on OIC when the faulty instruction is decoded. It denotes functional-level successful activation. The start-up policy denotes well tested functions and are enabled in OIC prior to operationalizing the multi-core eco-system. The function that undergoes start-up policy will have "one" as the wakeup probability. The readiness probability is the probability of OIC to successfully get activated and functionally ready to acknowledge the request from MIPS core (or conventional core). It denotes component-level readiness. Appropriate choice of (a) functions with start-up policed or high wakeup probability, and (b) OICs with high readiness probability determines the system reliability for multi-core system consisting of OICs. Assuming that, all selected OICs are functional and working in the system consisting of (a) L number of conventional cores or MIPS cores, (b) M number of candidate OICs, and (c) N number of functions executing correctly in the system, the system reliability for MSOIC is stated in the Eq. (1).

$$
\textit{System Reliability}_{MSOIC} = \left[\prod_{u \in \Psi_0} read_u\right] \cdot \prod_{j \in N}\left[1 - \prod_{i \in \Psi_0}\left(1 - \right.\right.
$$
$$
\left.\left.\sum_{d_i=0}^{|\Psi_0|} e^{-\sum_{i=1}^{L} \lambda_i t} \cdot \prod_{i=1}^{L} \frac{(\lambda_i t)^{d_i}}{d_i!} e_{ij}\right)^{avail_{ij}}\right], \ i = 1, \ldots, L \text{ when } k = 0. \tag{1}
$$

In the Eq. (1), readiness level of the OICs is denoted by $read_u$; selected OICs set is denoted by Ψ_0; function j is available in the ith OIC is denoted by $avail_{ij}$ or A matrix is known Availability Matrix consisting decision variables; number of logical elements in the micro-architecture is denoted by λ_i; $e_{ij} = (1 - wakep_{ij})x_{ij} + wakep_{ij}$; e_{ij} denotes wakeup probability($wakep_{ij}$) when the function is not start-up policed (x_{ij}); $e_{ij} = 1$ when function is start-up policed (x_{ij}); k denotes the number of failed OICs among the selected

OICs. Equation (1) reduces to Eq. (3) when the value of $r(t)$ as stated in the Eq. (2) is submitted in the Eq. (1).

$$r(t) = \sum_{d_i=0}^{|\Psi_0|} e^{-\sum_{i=1}^{L} \lambda_i t} \cdot \prod_{i=1}^{L} \frac{(\lambda_i t)^{d_i}}{d_i!} \tag{2}$$

In the Eq. (2), $r(t)$ denotes the successful completion of a migrated faulty instruction to OIC. The reliability of function j on i^{th} OIC is denoted by r_{ij}. It is an integral part of $r(t)$. Substitution of r(t) in Eq. (1), it results in Eq. (3).

$$System\ Reliability_{MSOIC} = \left[\prod_{u\in\Psi_0} read_u\right] \cdot \prod_{j\in N}\left[1 - \prod_{i\in\Psi_0}(1 - r(t).e_{ij})^{avail_{ij}}\right],\ when \tag{3}$$

$k = 0$.

3 Formulations for Interval RAP

Equation (3) restated below in Eq. (4), is the objective function to maximize the system reliability with decision variables X and A, with no failure in the selected OICs.
   Maximize:

$$System\ Reliability(X, A) = \left[\prod_{i\in\Psi_0} read_i\right] \cdot \prod_{j\in N}\left[1 - \prod_{i\in\Psi_0}(1-\right.$$
$$\left. r(t)e_{i,j})^{avail_{i,j}}\right] read_i,\ r(t) \in [0, 1], 0 < t_l < t < t_r\ when\ L \le M\ and\ k = 0. \tag{4}$$

subject to the constraints:

$$e_{ij} = (1 - wakep_{ij})x_{ij} + wakep_{ij}, wakep_{ij} \in [0, 1] \tag{5}$$

$$\sum_{i=1}^{m} \sum_{j=1}^{n} C_{ij}x_{ij} \le C \tag{6}$$

$$x_{ij} \in [0, 1] \tag{7}$$

The decision variable X denotes the start-up strategy x_{ij} and A denotes the availability a_{ij}. In the nonlinear constraint (Eq. (6)), the cost C_{ij} is the execution time in clock cycles for the function j on component i. C denotes the maximum waiting time for a conventional core seeking computation from the given set of OICs. $t \in [t_l, t_r]$ is the interval time. The event defining conventional core seeking functional support from OIC may vary within interval time and is called interval mission time. Within the interval, with mission time reaching the lower bound, the OIC reliability may reach the upper bound. With the mission time reaching the upper bound, reliability of the OIC may reach lower bound. It implies that for $t = t_L$, $r(t_L) = r_R$ and for $t = t_R$, $r(t_R) = r_L$. Now, the objective function can be restated as per Definition 1.2 as given in the Sect. 3 and is given in Eq. (8). The formulation in Eq. (8) is an interval RAP in the form of non-linear programming problem with interval coefficients.

Maximize

$$System\ Reliability_{MSOIC}(X,A) = \begin{bmatrix} \prod_{i \in \psi_0} read_i . \prod_{j \in N} \left[1 - \prod_{i \in \psi_0}(1 - r_R e_{i,j})^{avail_{i,j}}\right], \\ \prod_{i \in \psi_0} read_i . \prod_{j \in N} \left[1 - \prod_{i \in \psi_0}(1 - r_L e_{i,j})^{avail_{i,j}}\right] \end{bmatrix} \tag{8}$$

The constraints remain the same for Eq. (8). Hence the system reliability estimation involves interval arithmetic and order relations. The background on interval arithmetic and order relation is presented in the next section thereby article becomes self-contained.

3.1 Interval Analysis

Interval analysis was first introduced by [10] to address impreciseness. Interval arithmetic and Order relations are important for crossover/mutation and selection process for finding the better solution in the Genetic algorithm. In PSO, Order relations is used in updating *GLbest*, *LCbest, i* and *PSbest, i* parameters and Interval arithmetic in updating velocities. Interval arithmetic and Order relations are discussed below. Interval analysis is used to address impreciseness in electric power system [11], microelectronics circuits [12], structure safety analysis [13], and damage identification [14]. Wang et al. [15] proposed interval analysis for standby redundancy-based system optimization problems. Bhunia and Samanta [16] proposed interval analysis for theoretical multi-objective optimization problem in the interval domain. Gupta and Bhunia [17], used interval-valued reliability for components in the series systems.

Arithmetic for Interval Numbers

Consider W to be an interval valued number. It is defined as set of real numbers '*a*', such that, $w_L \le a \le w_R$, *i.e.*, $a \in [w_L, w_R]$, $w_L, w_R \in R$. R is set of real numbers. w_L and w_R are left and right boundaries of the interval respectively. W is expressed in Eq. (9).

$$W = [w_L, w_R] = \{a : w_L \le a \le w_R, a \in R\} \tag{9}$$

An interval valued number W can also be expressed in terms of radius and centre and is expressed in Eq. (10).

$$W = <w_c, w_r> = \{a : w_c - w_r \le a \le w_c + w_r, a \in R\} \tag{10}$$

where $w_c = (w_L + w_R)/2$ and $w_r = (w_R - w_L)/2$ are the centre and the radius of the interval, respectively, and R is the set of real numbers.

Definition 1.1: Arithmetic operations: Consider $X = [X_L, X_R]$ and $Y = [Y_L, Y_R]$ are closed intervals. Then addition, subtraction multiplication and division are defined as given below.

Addition of two intervals X and Y is given in Eq. (11).

$$X + Y = [X_L + Y_L, X_R + Y_R] \tag{11}$$

Subtraction of two intervals and Y is given in Eq. (12).

$$X - Y = [X_L - Y_L, X_R - Y_R] \tag{12}$$

Multiplication of an interval by a real number λ is given in Eqs. (13) and Eq. (14).

$$\lambda.X = \lambda.[X_L, X_R] = [\lambda X_L, \lambda X_R] \; if \; \lambda \geq 0 \tag{13}$$

$$\lambda.X = \lambda.[X_L, X_R] = [\lambda X_R, \lambda X_L] if \; \lambda < 0 \tag{14}$$

Multiplication of two intervals is given in the Eq. (15).

$$X \times Y = [\min(X_L Y_L, X_L Y_R, X_R Y_L, X_R Y_R), \max(X_L Y_L, X_L Y_R, X_R Y_L, X_R Y_R)] \tag{15}$$

Division of interval Y by interval X is given in the Eq. (16).

$$\frac{Y}{X} = Yx\frac{1}{X} = [Y_L, Y_R]x\left[\frac{1}{X_L}, \frac{1}{X_R}\right] provided \; X_L \neq 0, X_R \neq 0. \tag{16}$$

Definition 1.2: Power of interval: Consider $X = [X_L, X_R]$. For a non-negative integer N, the Nth power of the interval X is given in Eq. (17).

$$
\begin{aligned}
X^N &= [1, 1], \; if N = 0. \\
X^N &= \left[X_L^N, X_R^N\right], \; if X_L \geq 0, \; or \; if \; N \; is \; odd \\
X^N &= \left[X_R^N, X_L^N\right], \; if \; X_R \leq 0, \; or \; if \; N \; is \; even \\
X^N &= \left[0, \max\left(X_L^N, X_R^N\right)\right], if \; X_L \leq 0 \leq X_R, N > 0 \; is \; even.
\end{aligned}
\tag{17}
$$

Order Relations for Interval Numbers
The order relations between pairs of intervals valued numbers rest on the perception the decision taker has in the optimization problem. The selection of the best alternative between pair of intervals valued numbers for maximization problems is discussed in this section.

Two interval numbers $X = [X_L, X_R]$ and $Y = [Y_L, Y_R]$ can be categorized into the following three types.

(i)   Both the intervals are disjoint.
(ii) Partially overlapping intervals.
(iii) One interval contained in the other.

Mahato and Bhunia [18] developed definitions for these cases in the perspective of optimistic and pessimistic decision maker's standpoint on order relations for maximization problems.

Optimistic Decision Making
Definition 1.3: The order relation $\geq_{omax}$ between X and Y for maximization problems is given in Inequality – (18) and Inequality – (19).

$$X \geq_{omax} Y \; iff \; X_R \geq Y_R \tag{18}$$

$$X >_{omax} Y \text{ iff } X \geq_{omax} Y \text{ and } X \neq Y \tag{19}$$

The optimistic decision taker accepts the interval X which is superior to Y. Order relation $\geq_{omax}$ is symmetric but not transitive.

Pessimistic Decision-Making

Definition 1.4: The order relation $\geq_{omax}$ between the intervals $X = [X_L, X_R] = \langle X_c, X_r \rangle$ and $Y = [Y_L, Y_R] = \langle Y_c, Y_r \rangle$ from pessimistic decision taker's standpoint for maximization problems is given in Inequality – (20) and Inequality – (21).

$$X >_{pmax} Y \text{ iff } X_c > Y_c \text{ for disjoint and partially ovelapped intervals.} \tag{20}$$

$$X >_{pmax} Y \text{ iff } X_c \geq Y_c \text{ and } X_r < Y_r \text{ when one interval is contained in the other.} \tag{21}$$

Optimistic decision making may have to be considered for $X_c > Y_c$ and $X_r > Y_r$.

3.2 Characteristics of Proposed RAP

Important characteristics integral to the RAP are discussed below.

(a) *System Reliability$_{MSOIC}$ (x_{ij}, avail$_{ij}$) is monotonically increasing with* avail$_{ij}$ *(i = 1... m; j = 1...n).*

We know that $r_{ij} \in [0, 1]$, $e_{ij} \in [0, 1]$, and $r(t) \in [0,1]$. r_{ij} is an integral part of $r(t)$ and $avail_{ij} \geq 0$. It is known that $(1 - r(t)e_{ij})_{ij}^a \in [0, 1]$. i^* and j^* which are arbitrary values of i and j, are fixed and not varied. For two instances $avail_{i*j*}^{(2)}$, $avail_{i*j*}^{(1)}$, if $avail_{i*j*}^{(2)} > avail_{i*j*}^{(1)}$ then two conditions S1 and S2 arise which are examined below.

S1: Consider $avail_{i*j*}^{(1)} \geq 1$ and that $\Psi_0^{(2)} = \Psi_0^{(1)}$, subsets of selected components of both $\Psi_0^{(2)}$ and $\Psi_0^{(1)}$ are same. Consider $F \subset \Psi_0^{(1)} = \Psi_0^{(2)}$. For the F which does not contain i^*, the system reliability determined using Eq. (22) for $avail_{ij} = avail_{i*j*}^{(2)}$ and $avail_{ij} = avail_{i*j*}^{(1)}$ are identical. But, for the F that contains i^* and $avail_{i*j*}^{(2)} > avail_{i*j*}^{(1)}$, the inequality in the Eq. (23) holds. Hence, the sum of all subsets F containing $avail_{i*j*}^{(2)}$ is greater than or equal to F containing $avail_{i*j*}^{(1)}$.

$$S^R = \left[\prod_{u \in F} read_u\right] \cdot \left[\prod_{v \in \Psi_0 \backslash F}(1 - read_v)\right] \cdot \prod_{j=1}^{n}\left[1 - \prod_{i \in F}(1 - r(t)e_{ij})^{avail_{ij}}\right] \tag{22}$$

$$\left(1 - r(t)^* e_{i*j*}\right)^{avail_{i*j*}^{(2)}} \leq \left(1 - r(t)^* e_{i*j*}\right)^{avail_{i*j*}^{(1)}}, \text{ where } r_{i*j*} \text{ is an integral part of } r(t)* \tag{23}$$

S2: Consider $avail_{i*j*}^{(1)} = 0$, then $avail_{i*j*}^{(2)}$ is greater than zero, and $i^* \in \Psi_0^{(2)}$. But i^* does not belong $\Psi_0^{(1)}$. For $F^{(2)} \subset \Psi_0^{(2)}$ and $F^{(1)} \subset \Psi_0^{(1)}$, two conditions S3 and S4 are analysed and are discussed below.

S3: i^* does not belong to $F^{(2)}$ *and* $F^{(1)}$. The system reliability determined using $F^{(2)}$ and $F^{(1)}$ are same and is given in Eq. (24).

$$\left[\prod_{u\in F^{(2)}} read_u\right]\cdot\left[\prod_{v\in\Psi_0\backslash F^{(2)}} (1-read_v)\right]\cdot\prod_{j=1}^{n}\left[1-\prod_{i\in F^{(2)}} (1-r(t)e_{ij})^{avail_{ij}}\right] =$$

$$\left[\prod_{u\in F^{(1)}} read_u\right]\cdot\left[\prod_{v\in\Psi_0\backslash F^{(1)}} (1-read_v)\right]\cdot\prod_{j=1}^{n}\left[1-\prod_{i\in F^{(1)}} (1-r(t)e_{ij})^{avail_{ij}}\right] \tag{24}$$

S4: i^* belongs to $F^{(2)}$ such that $F^{(2)} = F^{(1)} \cup \{i^*\} \subset \Psi_0^{(2)}$ and $F^{(1)} \subset \Psi_0^{(1)}$. System reliability determined using $F^{(2)}$ is greater than or equal to system reliability using $F^{(1)}$. Then following inequality in the Eq. (25) holds.

$$\left[\prod_{u\in F^{(2)}} read_u\right]\cdot\left[\prod_{v\in\Psi_0\backslash F^{(2)}} (1-read_v)\right]\cdot\prod_{j=1}^{n}\left[1-\prod_{i\in F^{(2)}} (1-r(t)e_{ij})^{avail_{ij}}\right] \geq$$

$$\left[\prod_{u\in F^{(1)}} read_u\right]\left[\prod_{v\in\Psi_0\backslash F^{(1)}} (1-read_v)\right]\cdot\prod_{j=1}^{n}\left[1-\prod_{i\in F^{(1)}} (1-r(t)e_{ij})^{avail_{ij}}\right] \tag{25}$$

It is obvious from Eq. (25), that system reliability determined using $F^{(2)}$ is greater than or equal to system reliability resulting by $F^{(1)}$. Additional component i^* is included in $F^{(2)}$. Enhancement in the system reliability is observed. Monotonicity of system reliability with increasing $avail_{ij}$ is proved.

(b) Reliability of Function j:

The reliability of the function j can be evaluated for the selected components and is given in Eq. (26).

$$r_{fj} = 1 - \prod_{i\in I_j}\left[1 - rd_i(1 - (1 - r_{ij}.e_{ij})^{avail_{ij}}\right] \tag{26}$$

r_{ij} is an integral part of $r(t)$. I_j represents the index set of the components that can perform function j in Eq. (26).

(c) Maximum System Reliability:

Assuming Availability($avail_{ij}$) is known for a system, in order to maximize the system reliability, best start-up strategy is initialized to one, i.e. $x_{i,jj} = 1$ for function j where $\tilde{i}_j$ is stated in the Eq. (27).

$$\tilde{i}_j = \arg \max_{i\in\Psi_0}\left\{1 - \prod_{l\in I_j}\left[1 - read_l(1 - (1 - r_{lj}.e_{lj}^{(i)})^{avail_{ij}})\right]\right\}e_{lj}^{(i)} = 1, \; if \; l =$$

i; otherwise $wakep_{lj}$

$$\tag{27}$$

4 Genetic Algorithm for Interval RAP

Genetic algorithm is proposed for the nonlinear integer programming with the objective function given in the Eq. (8) as the fitness function. The stochastic based selection procedure, crossover, mutation and elitism are the computational techniques adopted in the proposed GA. The proposed GA has two phases: primary phase and the secondary phase. In the primary phase, d independent runs are performed to initialize the solutions in the initial population. The solutions from the runs with subsequent consecutive solutions effectively improving the system reliability are included in the initial population.

This approach of choosing the initial population will set solution evolution in the right direction and improve the efficiency of the GA. Notably, the regular GA without elitism uses the randomly initialized population to evolve solutions. Two problems, evaluation example-one with smaller problem space and evaluation example-two with larger problem space are evaluated using GA. For evaluation example-two or large problem, additional changes are made to the primary phase of the proposed GA to highlight the effectiveness of the proposed GA as compared to regular GA. They are discussed below.

Firstly, for maximizing the system reliability, Availability ($avail_{ij}$) is estimated without considering into x_{ij}. Then the start-up policed x_{ij} is set according to Eq. (27). The reliability of the function j without considering a start-up policed can be determined by replacing e_{ij} by $wakep_{ij}$ in Eq. (26) and is given in Eq. (27).

$$r_{fj} = 1 - \prod_{i \in I_j} \left[1 - read_i(1 - (1 - r_{ij}.wakep_{ij})^{avail_{ij}} \right] \tag{28}$$

Secondly, estimating $avail_{ij}$ or Availability matrix involves two steps and they are as follows.

1. Choosing components that increase functional reliability (r_{fj}) is performed by enabling functions such that maximum latency is within C. 2. Choosing between two OICs (say a, b), enabling one function in 'a' and disabling the same in 'b' such that r_{fj} improvement is maximal is selected. Availability ($avail_{ij}$) is determined and set to X according to $\tilde{t}_j$ as in Eq. (27).

Finally, the solution obtained in the primary phase is included in the initial population for the secondary phase of the proposed GA. The secondary phase of the proposed GA is described below.

1. The GA parameters, P_SIZE: population size, P_MUTAT: the probability of mutation, P_CROSS: the probability of crossover and M_GEN: number of generations arc initialized. The encoding of the chromosome for the problem is given in Fig. 1. The chromosome comprises of decision variables X (which denotes the start-up policy) and U (which denotes the number of functions of each type used or sum of every column in Availability matrix). Number of ones in the binary encoded string represent the functions that are start-up strategized (X) as shown in Fig. 1.

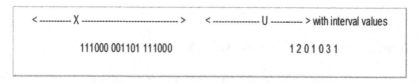

Fig. 1. Example for chromosome encoding

2. Each chromosome is evaluated for fitness. The fitness function is used to select the best chromosome in the population. The value of the interval valued objective

function of the chromosome is taken as the fitness function for RAP systems. Only chromosomes with fitness value greater than a threshold value are considered for selection.

3. Selection: The primary objective is to evolve better solutions and eliminate below average solutions from the current population for the next generation. In the proposed GA, individuals are stochastically selected from the current population according to their fitness value. Definitions 1.3 and 1.4 (mentioned in the Sect. 3) are appropriately used to determine the reliability intervals for the selection of quality chromosomes.

4. Crossover for chromosomes/individuals with probability (P_CROSS) is allowed to participate to produce offspring. The 2-point crossover operator is used.

5. New species are not suddenly created. Hence, the mutation probability P_MUTAT is chosen to create new population. The mutation creates new diversity in the population.

6. Elitism: the best optimal solution is retained in all iterations to improve the performance of GA.

7. The iterations are repeated until the maximum optimal solution with respect to reliability and cost are attained. The objective function is evaluated to determine the system reliability. The best results of the system reliability at jth and $(j + 1)$th generation are compared and superior among them are accepted. The steps 1 to 7 are repeated until changes in the system reliability are insignificant.

4.1 Evaluation for Genetic Algorithm

The initialization and evaluation of model parameters of OSS used in the estimation of system reliability are examined here. The following is also applicable for evaluation of PSO.

(a) Readiness probability $read_i$: In a multi-core system involving OICs, component level readiness is high in the initial stages of operation. Hence, $read_i$ is set to 0.99. In the subsequent requests, previous readiness is considered for evaluating system reliability.

(b) Wakeup probability $wakep_{ij}$: In the OICs, wakeup probability of functions that have undergone start-up strategy are set to one. The functions that have not undergone start-up strategy will have a wakeup probability between 0.1 and 0.9. Functions on OICs turned on with in a time period will have higher wakeup probability compared to the other functions which fail to meet the dead line. Thus, same function on different OICs may have different wakeup probability.

(c) Parameter $r(t)$ (which includes r_{ij}): The interval values are assigned due to impreciseness in operation that includes migration and execution of instruction on OICs. The sample set of interval values given in the Table 1 are taken from the work by Roy et al. [19]. This interval value set has been used (a) to study system entropy [19], and (b) to study maximum load point variations and voltage stability in electric power systems [11]. The significance of this set of intervals valued numbers is that it contains all types of intervals: disjoint, partially overlapping and one interval contained in the other. Disjoint interval numbers are present in the set 1 given in Table 1. A mixture of disjoint and partial overlapping interval numbers is present in sets 2–4 given in Table 1. One interval number contained in the other are present in interval numbers set 5 in Table 1. These sets of interval numbers will oscillate the decision making between optimistic and pessimistic for maximization of system reliability. The stability of the system is put to test in a realistic sense and is examined in the sensitivity section.

Two problems are considered for evaluation – "evaluation example-one" and "evaluation example-two large" as mentioned earlier. In evaluation example one, six functions and three OICs is considered. In the evaluation example two, 10 functions and six OICs is considered.

4.2 Simulation Platform

The Borland C/C++ integrated edition platform is used to evaluate proposed interval-based GA on multi-core system with quad-core i5 processor with clock frequency 2.5 Ghz. The system has 64-bit operating system namely WINDOWS PRO 10 with 8 GB DRAM. Both the problems, evaluation example-one and evaluation example-two large are evaluated in the system with configuration mentioned above.

Evaluation Example-One

In the primary phase, ten independent runs are used to initialize the solutions in the initial population. The evaluation example-one with six functions and three OICs is evaluated by performing 20 independent runs in the secondary phase of the proposed GA for each interval number set stated in Table 1. The six functions supported by OICS are ADD, MOV, INC, DEC, SUB, and DIV. The population size is initialized to 100 and the number of generations to 200. The two-point crossover operator is used to generate new offspring. Over 80% of the population undergo two-point crossover operation. 6% of individuals are mutated. The wakeup probability and readiness parameters are tabulated in Table 2. The cost C_{ij}, the execution time in clock cycles for the function j on component i is shown in Table 2. In Eq. (6), C is set to 50 clock cycles for the evaluation example one.

The GA parameters like selection function, crossover and mutation are set similarly for both proposed GA and Regular GA. The best results for system reliability in the form of System Reliability (Lower) and System Reliability (Upper) are tabulated in Table 3. The optimal solution given by the proposed GA and regular GA are shown in the Table 4. The proposed GA provides better system reliability (lower/upper) solution compared to regular GA for all data samples in Table 4. From Table 4, in the first column, X: 101000 000010 101101, first six bits denote that ADD and INC functions in the first OIC are start-up policed functions; second six bits denote that SUB function in second OIC is a start-up policed function; third six bits denote that ADD, INC, DEC, and DIV functions in third OIC are start-up policed functions. From Table 4, in first column, U: 2 2 2 3 3 3 denotes number of copies of functions ADD, MOV, INC, DEC, SUB and DIV available in the system. For a given X and U in the Table 4, the optimal system reliability (lower/upper bound) attained by proposed GA is 0.969002/0.970178 for C = 44 clock cycles. Similarly other entries in the Table 4 can be interpreted.

From Table 3, the gap between system reliability (upper/lower bound) values given by regular GA and proposed GA respectively is more visible for all the samples given in Table 1. From Table 4, difference in the near optimal solutions given by both GAs concludes that primary phase has improved the efficiency of proposed GA.

Table 1. Interval numbers (r_R, r_L)

Interval number Set no	Type of Interval numbers	Interval numbers formatted as [lower bound, upper bound]
SET 1	Disjoint intervals	[0.68,0.72], [0.73,0.75], [0.78,0.81], [0.80,0.88], [0.89,0.95]
SET 2	Disjoint and partially overlapped intervals	[0.65,0.70], [0.71,0.73], [0.80,0.88], [0.82,0.87], [0.90,0.92]
SET 3	Disjoint and partially overlapped intervals	[0.60,0.67], [0.72,0.78], [0.78,0.83], [0.80,0.90], [0.87,0.956]
SET 4	Disjoint and partially overlapped intervals	[0.64,0.65], [0.72,0.74], [0.80,0.88], [0.83,0.85], [0.90,0.95]
SET 5	One interval contained in the other, Disjoint and Partially overlapped intervals	[0.63, 0.66], [0.64, 0.68], [0.65, 0.70], [0.65, 0.70], [0.73, 0.74], [0.75, 0.79], [0.76, 0.86], [0.75, 0.80], [0.77, 0.80], [0.75, 0.81], [0.78, 0.84], [0.80, 0.87], [0.88, 0.92], [0.89, 0.90], [0.91, 0.96]

Table 2. Cost, wakeup probability and readiness parameters for evaluation example-one

Cost (C_{ij})	Wakeup probability ($wakeup_{ij}$)	Readiness $read_i$
4 5 4 1 1 35	0.98 0.9 0.9 0.96 0.87 0.87	$rd = rd_1 = rd_2 = rd_3 = 0.99$
4 5 4 1 1 35	0.82 0.82 0.82 0.9 0.9 0.9	
4 5 4 1 1 35	0 0.9 0.9 0.9 0.9 0.9	

Table 3. Best System reliability (Lower/Upper) for the evaluation example-one with 3OICs and 6 functions using GA

Proposed GA	Table 1 (Set 1)	Table 1 (Set 2)	Table 1 (Set 3)	Table 1 (Set 4)	Table 1 (Set 5)
System reliability (Lower) (Best)	0.969006	0.969328	0.968163	0.969328	0.969591
System reliability (Upper) (Best)	0.970178	0.969802	0.970178	0.970178	0.970237
Regular GA	Table 1 (Set 1)	Table 1 (Set 2)	Table 1 (Set 3)	Table 1 (Set 4)	Table 1 (Set 5)
System reliability (lower) (best)	0.968975	0.968452	0.967877	0.968454	0.962434
System reliability (upper) (best)	0.970132	0.969230	0.970132	0.969947	0.968746

Table 4. Optimal solution for evaluation example-one with 3OICs and 6 functions using GA

Proposed GA		Table 1 (Set 1)	Table 1 (Set 2)	Table 1 (Set 3)	Table 1 (Set 4)	Table 1 (Set 5)
X		101000 000010 101101	110100 000111 011000	010000 000011 110111	111011 000110 001000	111110 001111 011110
A	U: OICs	2 2 2 3 3 3 3	2 2 2 3 3 3 3	2 2 2 3 3 3 3	2 2 2 3 3 3 3	1 2 3 3 3 1 3
System reliability lower/upper		0.969002/ 0.970178	0.968437/ 0.969224	0.958130/ 0.966943	0.951516/ 0.963214	0.962376/ 0.968744
Cost (in cycles)		44	40	46	49	41
Regular GA		Table 1 (Set 1)	Table 1 (Set 2)	Table 1 (Set 3)	Table 1 (Set 4)	Table 1 (Set 5)
X		010111 000001 111111	111101 000111 101111	111101 000110 011111	011011 000111 101001	110110 000010 111101
A	U: OICs	2 2 2 3 3 3 3	2 2 2 3 3 3 3	2 2 2 3 3 3 3	2 2 2 3 3 3 3	2 2 3 3 3 1 3
System reliability lower/upper		0.968780/ 0.970131	0.960412/ 0.964004	0.953624/0.967867	0.968101/0.968977	0.958415/0.967867
Cost (in cycles)		41	49	49	45	49

Evaluation Example-Two

The evaluation example-two with 10 functions and six OICs is evaluated by 10 independent trials of 60 runs each with 20000 generations for data samples in Table 1. The 10 functions are designated as F1, F2, F3,..., F10. The wakeup probability, cost Cij (and C = 3000 cycles) and readiness parameters are tabulated in the Table 5. The best system reliability (lower/upper) results for the evaluation example two problem are tabulated in Table 6. The optimal solution by the proposed GA for the evaluation example two are shown in the Table 7. From the Table 7, X: 1 0 0 0 0 0 1 1 1 0, 0 0 0 0 0 0 1 1 0 0, 0 0 0 0 0 0 0 0 0 1, 0 1 0 0 0 0 0 0 0 0, 0 1 0 0 1 1 0 1 1 0, 0 0 0 0 1 0 0 0 0 1, first ten bits denote F1, F7, F8, and F9 are start-up strategized in the first OIC. Similarly remaining bit strings can be interpreted. From Table 7, U: 3 3 3 1 3 3 3 3 4 4 denotes number of copies of functions F1, F2, F3,..., F10 available in the system. For a given X and U in the Table 7, the optimal system reliability (lower/upper) attained by proposed GA is 0.989966/0.989997 for C = 2500 clock cycles. Similarly other entries in the Table 7 and 8 can be interpreted. The solutions for system reliability by proposed GA are compared with the regular GA. From the Table 6 and Fig. 2, the solution of the proposed GA converges faster as compared to the regular GA. The proposed GA stabilizes at 0.989998/0.990000 against 0.989966/0.989997 given by the regular GA. The faster convergence of the solution in large problem space is due to changes made in the primary phase of the proposed GA and is evident from Fig. 2. From Table 7 and 8, the system reliability (lower/upper) given by proposed GA is 0.989966/0.989997, which is better than 0.989876/0.989991 given by regular GA.

Table 5. Cost, Wakeup probability and Readiness parameters for evaluation example-two

Cost C_{ij}	100 100 250 250 500 500 600 600 800 800
	100 100 0 250 500 500 600 600 800 800
	100 100 250 0 500 500 600 600 800 800
	100 100 250 250 500 500 600 600 800 800
	100 100 250 250 500 500 0 600 800 800
	100 100 250 250 500 500 0 600 800 800
Wakeup probability (*wakep$_{ij}$*)	0.9 0.7 0.7 0.9 0.9 0.7 0.8 0.8 0.8 0.7
	0.9 0.7 0 0.7 0.9 0.9 0.8 0.8 0.8 0.7
	0.9 0.7 0.9 0 0.7 07 0.8 0.8 0.8 0.7
	0.9 0.7 0.9 0.7 0.9 0.7 0.8 0.8 0.8 0.7
	0.9 0.8 0.8 0.9 0.9 0.9 0 0.8 0.8 0.8
	0.9 0.8 0.8 0.9 0.9 0.8 0 0.8 0.8 0.8
Readiness *read$_i$*	$rd_1 = rd_2 = rd_3 = rd_4 = rd_5 = rd_6 = 0.99$

Table 6. Best System reliability (Lower/Upper) for the evaluation example-two with 6 OICs and 10 functions using GA

Proposed GA	System Reliability (Best) (Lower)	System Reliability (Best) (Upper)	Regular GA	System Reliability (Best) (Lower)	System Reliability (Best)(Upper)
Table 1 (set 1)	0.989998	0.990000	Table 1 (set 1)	0.989966	0.989997
Table 1 (set 2)	0.999983	0.999993	Table 1 (set 2)	0.999833	0.999906
Table 1 (set 3)	0.999923	0.999996	Table 1 (set 3)	0.999887	0.999976
Table 1 (set 4)	0.999968	0.999995	Table 1 (set 4)	0.999857	0.999989
Table 1 (set 5)	0.999989	0.999999	Table 1 (set 5)	0.999936	0.999953

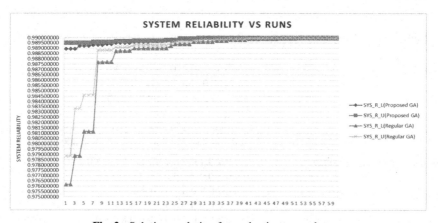

Fig. 2. Solution evolution for evaluation example-two

Table 7. Optimal solution for the evaluation example-two with 6OICs and 10 functions using GA

Proposed GA	Table 1(set 1)	Table 1(set 2)
X	1 0 0 0 0 0 1 1 1 0	0 1 0 0 0 1 0 0 1 0
	0 0 0 0 0 0 1 1 0 0	0 1 0 0 0 0 1 1 0 0
	0 0 0 0 0 0 0 0 0 1	0 0 1 0 1 0 1 0 0 0
	0 1 0 0 0 0 0 0 0 0	0 0 0 0 0 0 0 0 0 1
	0 1 0 0 1 1 0 1 1 0	1 0 0 0 1 1 0 0 1 0
	0 0 0 0 1 0 0 0 0 1	0 0 0 1 0 0 0 0 0 0
A U:/OICs	3 3 3 1 3 3 3 3 4 4	5 2 4 2 3 2 4 3 3 2
	/6	/6
System reliability lower/upper	0.989966/0.989997	0.999968/0.999984
Cost (in cycles)	2500	1900
Regular GA		
X	1 0 0 0 0 1 1 1 0 0	0 0 0 1 0 1 1 0 0 0
	0 1 1 0 1 0 1 0 0 0	0 0 0 1 0 0 0 0 0 1
	0 0 0 0 0 1 0 0 1 0	1 0 0 0 1 1 0 0 1 0
	1 0 0 1 0 0 0 0 0 0	0 0 0 1 0 1 0 0 0 0
	1 1 0 0 0 0 0 0 0 0	1 0 1 0 0 0 0 0 0 0
	1 0 0 0 1 1 0 1 1 0	0 0 0 0 0 0 0 0 0 0
A U:/OICs	4 3 3 3 3 3 3 3 4 4/6	4 4 5 3 6 5 3 5 3 3/6
System reliability lower/upper	0.989876/0.989991	0.999006/0.999646
Cost(in cycles),	2500	1900

4.3 Sensitivity Analysis

The sensitivity analysis is performed to study the impact of GA parameters on the objective function. The analysis also helps to study the stability of the system when impreciseness is addressed with interval valued numbers in the objective function. GA parameter values are also selected using this analysis. Here the stability of the proposed GA for all interval numbers (Table 1) are illustrated using graphs in the Fig. 3, 4, 5 6 and 7 with respect to GA parameters (P_SIZE, P_MUTAT, P_CROSS, and M_GENER). It is observed from the Fig. 3, 4, 5 6 and 7 proposed GA is steady and unchanging, thereby providing quality solutions for the proposed RAP formulation. A few important observations are enumerated below with respect to GA parameter selection and their consistency.

Table 8. (Continued from Table 7) Optimal solution for the evaluation example-two with 6OICs and 10 functions using GA

Proposed GA	Table 1(set 3)	Table 1(set 4)	Table 1(set 5)
X	0 0 0 0 0 0 1 1 0 0 0 1 0 0 0 0 0 0 0 0 0 0 0 0 0 0 1 1 0 0 0 0 0 0 0 0 1 0 0 0 0 0 0 1 0 0 0 0 1 0 0 0 0 0 0 1 0 1 1 0	0 0 0 1 0 1 0 1 0 0 0 1 0 0 0 0 0 0 0 0 1 0 0 1 0 0 0 0 1 0 1 0 0 0 1 0 0 0 0 0 0 0 0 0 0 0 0 1 0 0 0 0 0 1 1 0 0 1 0 1	0 0 0 0 0 0 1 1 0 1 0 0 0 0 0 1 1 0 0 0 0 1 0 0 0 0 0 0 0 0 0 0 1 0 0 1 0 0 0 1 0 0 0 0 0 1 0 0 0 1 0 0 0 0 1 0 0 0 0 0
A U:/OICs	3 3 2 2 3 3 3 2 3 3 /6	4 3 3 3 3 2 3 3 3 4/6	2 3 3 3 3 3 4 3 3 3 /6
System reliability lower/upper	0.999602/0.999968	0.999903/0.999945	0.999977/0.999997
Cost (in cycles)	1900	2150	2000
Regular GA			
X	0 0 0 0 0 0 0 1 0 0 0 0 0 0 0 0 0 0 0 0 0 1 0 0 1 0 0 1 1 1 0 1 0 0 0 1 0 0 0 0 0 0 0 0 0 0 0 0 1 0 0 0 0 0 1 1 0 0 1 0 1	0 0 0 0 0 0 0 0 0 0 0 1 1 0 0 0 0 0 0 0 0 0 0 0 0 0 0 0 0 0 0 0 1 0 0 0 0 1 0 0 0 0 0 0 0 0 0 0 0 0 0 0 0 1 1 1	1 1 1 0 0 0 0 1 0 1 0 0 0 0 1 0 0 0 0 1 0 0 0 1 0 0 0 0 0 0 1 0 1 1 0 0 0 0 0 0 1 1 1 1 0 1 0 0 1 0 0 0 0 1 1 1 1 1 0 0
A U:/OICs	3 3 2 2 4 3 3 4 3 3 /6	4 3 3 3 3 2 3 3 3 3 /6	3 3 3 4 3 3 4 3 3 3 /6
System reliability lower/upper	0.999791/0.999991	0.999860/0.999917	0.999851/0.999952
Cost (in cycles),	2350	2200	2350

(a) System Reliability (Lower/Upper) in Fig. 3a, 4a, 5a, 6a and 6a is monotonically increasing with generations. The parameter M_GENER = 200 is a suitable value that reflects the stability of system reliability (lower/upper) for all interval numbers stated in Table 1.

(b) P_SIZE (population size) is varied with respect to the system reliability (lower/upper) in Fig. 3b, 4b, 5b, 6b, and 7b. Notably, the stochastic selection is adopted in the proposed GA. Even then, system reliability (lower/upper) is increasing proportionally with respect to a population size and stabilizes at P_SIZE = 100. P_SIZE does not impact the optimal solution of our proposed GA with population size of 100 or above.

(c) P_CROSS: the impact of crossover on the system reliability is shown in Fig. 3c, 4c, 5c, 6c, and 7c. It is factual from these figures, that an increase in crossover rate does not have any impact on the system reliability (lower/upper). An increase in crossover rate does not result in an abnormal change in the system reliability values.

(d) P_MUTAT: A higher mutation level generates greater genetic assortment and some-times does have an impact on the system. Figure 3d, 4d, 5d, 6d, and 7d reflect stability in the system reliability. Higher mutation rate with elitism in the proposed GA sets the population for better solution evolution in the due course with recovery of lost solutions in the earlier generations. Both P_CROSS and P_MUTAT rate chosen for the RAP are suitable to sustain stability over a large range.

(e) Choice of the class of interval numbers for component reliabilities is not relevant because, there can be only one optimal system with M and N. Selection of interval valued numbers does not influence the optimal solution of the system as discerned from sensitive analysis. The system reliability monotonically increases with the number of components and functions deployed. Thus, the optimal solution by the proposed GA is not affected. The stability of the system is ascertained.

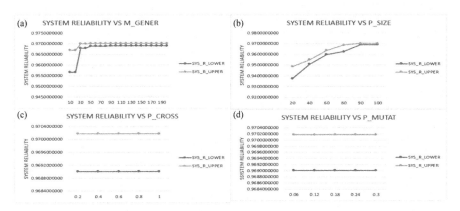

Fig. 3. (a) System Reliability Vs Generations (b) System Reliability Vs Population Size (c) System Reliability Vs Probability of Crossover (d) System Reliability Vs Probability of Mutation for set 1 interval numbers in Table 1.

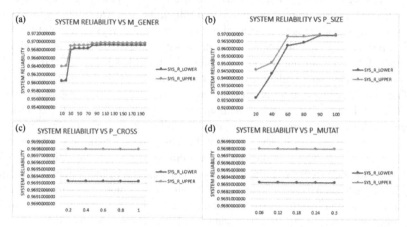

Fig. 4. (a) System Reliability Vs Generations (b) System Reliability Vs Population Size (c) System Reliability Vs Probability of Crossover (d) System Reliability Vs Probability of Mutation for set 2 interval numbers in Table 1.

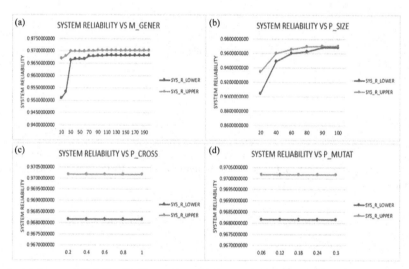

Fig. 5. (a) System Reliability Vs Generations (b) System Reliability Vs Population Size (c) System Reliability Vs Probability of Crossover (d) System Reliability Vs Probability of Mutation for set 3 interval numbers in Table 1.

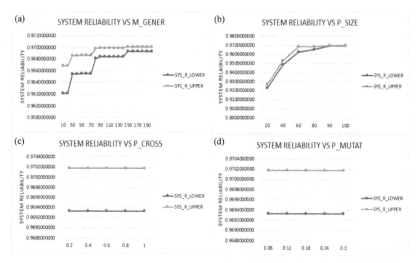

Fig. 6. (a) System Reliability Vs Generations (b) System Reliability Vs Population Size (c) System Reliability Vs Probability of Crossover (d) System Reliability Vs Probability of Mutation for set 4 interval numbers in Table 1.

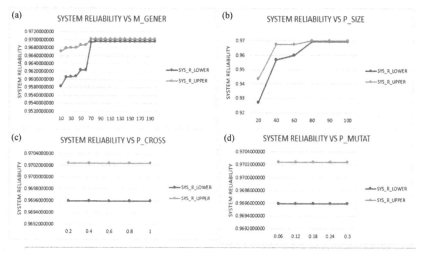

Fig. 7. (a) System Reliability Vs Generations (b) System Reliability Vs Population Size (c) System Reliability Vs Probability of Crossover (d) System Reliability Vs Probability of Mutation for set 5 interval numbers in Table 1.

5   Particle Swarm Optimization for Interval RAP

The Particle Swarm Optimization (PSO) is an effective alternative to solve large non-linear optimization problems. PSO is proposed for Interval RAP with the objective function given in the Eq. (8) as the fitness function. The flocking of birds is used for conceptualising the search framework in PSO. This conceptual framework assists in finding local and global solution for the optimization problem unlike GA where only global search is performed. In PSO, a swarm of particles, each represents a candidate solution for a given optimization problem is maintained. All the particles traverse the search space adjusting their positions with information from neighbouring particles and its own past positions. Let us consider pos_i^t as the position of the particle i at time step t in the search space, the movement of particles is governed by the following Eq. (29).

$$pos_i^{t+1} = pos_i^t + vel_i^{t+1} \tag{29}$$

In our proposed PSO, Particle position is mapped to $r(t)$ which is an interval number, the Eq. (29) can be restated as given in Eqs. (30) and (31).

$$pos_{i(R)}^{t+1} = pos_{i(R)}^t + vel_{i(R)}^{t+1} \tag{30}$$

$$pos_{i(L)}^{t+1} = pos_{i(L)}^t + vel_{i(L)}^{t+1} \tag{31}$$

$pos_{i(R)}^t, pos_{i(L)}^t, [pos_{min}, pos_{max}]$ are mapped to $[\mathbf{r_R}, \mathbf{r_L}]$ Interval values tabulated in the Table 1. Since $r(t)$ is the event defining conventional core seeking functional support from OIC may vary within interval time and is called interval mission time. Within the interval, the OIC reliability may reach the upper bound or lower bound. Hence $r(t)$ is confined to the interval. $vel_{i(R)}^t, vel_{i(L)}^t$ are the velocities of the ith particle pair in the swarm at time t. The cognitive influence and social influence from all the particles to move towards known better solutions is governed by velocity parameter. $pos_{i(R)}^t, pos_{i(L)}^t$, particle pair positions are updated by summing velocities iteratively and used for computing the objective function.

Two variants of PSO, Global best *(interval – GLbest)* PSO and Local best *(interval – LCbest)* PSO are considered for updating the velocities are presented below. In *interval – GLbest* PSO method, best position among all the particles in the swarm influences the position of every particle. The star topology is used to gather the best-known solutions from all the particles in the swarm. The *interval-LCbest* PSO method permits every particle's position to be governed by the best-known position of particles in the neighbourhood, and it resemble a ring topology. In both the methods, every particle pair has a current position $pos_{i(R,L)}^t$, current velocity $vel_{i(R,L)}^t$ and a personal best position $PS_{best, i(R, L)}$. The personal best position denotes largest value of a particle pair i from initialization through time t, as determined by the objective function for a maximization problem. The maximum value among all the $P_{best, i(R, L)}$ is called global best position denoted by $GL_{best(R, L)}$. In *LCbest* PSO, $LC_{best, i(R, L)}$ is the best solution or best position of any particle pair i that has had from initialization through time t. $PS_{best, i(R, L)}$, $GL_{best(R, L)}$, $LC_{best, i(R, L)}$ are updated using the Definition 1.3 (mentioned in Sect. 3) for optimistic decision making for maximization problems.

The governing equations for the velocities for a particle pair i in *interval – GLbest* PSO are given in Eqs. (32) and (33).

$$vel_{i(R)}^{t+1} = \omega vel_{i(R)}^t + \varphi_1 r_1^t \left[PS_{best,i(R)}^t - pos_{i(R)}^t \right] + \varphi_2 r_2^t \left[GL_{best(R)} - pos_{i(R)}^t \right] \tag{32}$$

$$vel_{i(L)}^{t+1} = \omega vel_{i(L)}^t + \varphi_1 r_1^t \left[PS_{best,i(L)}^t - pos_{i(L)}^t \right] + \varphi_2 r_2^t \left[GL_{best(L)} - pos_{i(L)}^t \right] \tag{33}$$

The governing equations for the velocities for a particle pair i in *interval – LCbest* PSO methods are given in Eqs. (34) and (35).

$$vel_{i(R)}^{t+1} = \omega vel_{i(R)}^{t} + \varphi_1 r_1^t \left[PS_{best,i(R)}^t - pos_{i(R)}^t \right] + \varphi_2 r_2^t \left[LC_{best,i(R)} - pos_{i(R)}^t \right] \quad (34)$$

$$vel_{i(L)}^{t+1} = \omega vel_{i(L)}^{t} + \varphi_1 r_1^t \left[PS_{best,i(L)}^t - pos_{i(L)}^t \right] + \varphi_2 r_2^t \left[LC_{best,i(L)} - pos_{i(L)}^t \right] \quad (35)$$

Interval arithmetic mentioned in the Definition 1.1. and 1.2 are used in evaluating the Eqs. (32), (33), (34) and (35). In the Eqs. (32), (33), (34) and (35), ω, time varying inertia weight is adopted here, and is found to improve the performance linearly and control the impact of previous velocity on the updated velocity.

Detailed description of all parameters used in the Eqs. (32), (33), (34) and (35) are presented below.

(a) $GL_{best(R, L)}$: is the global best position of a particle pair i from initialization through time t;

(b) $LC_{best, i(R, L)}$: is the best position of a particle pair i has had in the neighbourhood from initialization through time t;

(c) $PS_{best, i(R,L)}$: is the personal best position for a particle pair *i* from initialization through time t;

(d) $vel_{i(R,L)}^t$: velocity of a particle pair *i* at time t;

(e) $pos_{i(R,L)}^t$: is the position of a particle i at time t;

(f) ω: : is the inertia weight, is equal to $(w_1 - w_2) ((T_{max} - t)/T_{max}) + w_2$, where w1 and w2 are the initial and final weights respectively, t is the current iteration number and T_{max} is the number of iterations.

(g) φ_1 *and* φ_2: positive acceleration co-efficients, also called cognitive and social weights;

(h) r_1^t *and* r_2^t: random numbers from uniform distribution U (0,1) at time t.

Finally, the particle pair positions are updated with velocities for all particle pairs. The objective function is evaluated for every particle pair and using the same, convergence of the solutions is examined. Steps are repeated to compute $PS_{best, i(R, L)}$, $GL_{best(R, L)}$, $LC_{best, i(R, L)}$ in the next iteration. Stepwise description of *proposed interval – GLbest/LCbest* PSO algorithm is given below and pseudo code is presented in Fig. 8.

5.1 Stepwise Description of the Proposed Interval -GLbest/LCbest PSO Algorithms

The *interval – GLbest/LCbest* PSO algorithm suitably modified for interval RAP is implemented as follows.

1. Particle (pair) population is initialized. Every particle pair is evaluated using the objective function. Initially $PS_{best, i (R, L)}$ (Personal best) of a particle is the particle itself. Set of particles pairs are selected from a known size of particles pool. The interval numbers mentioned in the Table 1 are assigned to particle pairs such that

it maximizes the system reliability. Each particle is also associated with functions chosen with high wakeup probability to maximize system reliability as stated in Eq. (28).

2.a. $GL_{best\,(R,\,L)}$ is evaluated considering all the particle pairs.

2.b. $LC_{best\,i\,(R,\,L)}$ is evaluated from the particles in the neighborhood.

3.a. Velocities of the particle pairs are computed using Eqs. (32), (33) in *interval – GLbest PSO*.

3.b. Velocities of the particle pairs are computed using Eqs. (34), (35) in *interval – LCbest PSO*.

4.   Updated velocities for every particle are archived.

5. $PS_{best,\,i\,(R,\,L)}$, $GL_{best\,(R,\,L)}$, $LC_{best,\,i\,(R,\,L)}$ are updated using the Definition 1.3 for optimistic decision making for maximization problems.

6.   The iteration counter is incremented. Step 3 and 4 are repeated and the algorithm is terminated when the convergence in the solution occurs.

1. The particle positions $pos^0_{i(R,L)}$, velocities $vel^0_{i(R,L)}$, acceleration co-efficient φ_1, φ_2 are initialised. *system reliability* $^0_{i(R,L)}$ is computed using $pos^0_{i(R,L)}$ is computed at time t =0 using the Equation-(8). The number of particles (P) and iterations (N) are appropriately set. Each particle is selected and associated with known availability (A) of functions with wakeup probability as stated in Equation – (28) so that they maximize system reliability.

2. r^t_1 and r^t_2 are stochastically initialized.

Repeat

3. a. $vel^{t+1}_{i(R)} = \omega vel^t_{i(R)} + \varphi_1 r^t_1 [PS^t_{best.i(R)} - pos^t_{i(R)}] + \varphi_2 r^t_2 [GL_{best(R)} - pos^t_{i(R)}]$ and $vel^{t+1}_{i(L)} = \omega vel^t_{i(L)} + \varphi_1 r^t_1 [PS^t_{best.i(L)} - pos^t_{i(L)}] + \varphi_2 r^t_2 [GL_{best(L)} - pos^t_{i(L)}]$ are used to update velocities in *GLbest* algorithm.

3. b. $vel^{t+1}_{i(R)} = \omega vel^t_{i(R)} + \varphi_1 r^t_1 [PS^t_{best.i(R)} - pos^t_{i(R)}] + \varphi_2 r^t_2 [LC_{best.i(R)} - pos^t_{i(R)}]$ and $vel^{t+1}_{i(L)} = \omega vel^t_{i(L)} + \varphi_1 r^t_1 [PS^t_{best.i(L)} - pos^t_{i(L)}] + \varphi_2 r^t_1 [LC_{best.i(L)} - pos^t_{i(L)}]$ are used to update velocities in *LCbest* algorithm

3. c. r^t_1 and r^t_2 are randomly generated for each particle pair for every iteration.

4. $pos^{t+1}_{i(R,L)} = pos^t_{i(R,L)} + vel^{t+1}_{i(R,L)}$

While (i < P)

5. Compute the objective function *system relaibility* $^t_{i(R,L)}$ for every particle $pos^t_{i(R,L)}$ associated with set of available functions that maximize reliability. Convergence in the solution pairs is examined. The steps are repeated until solution converges.

6. If t < N goto step 2.

Fig. 8. Pseudo code for GLbest and LCbest PSO variants

5.2 Simulation Platform

The Borland C/C++ integrated edition platform is used to proposed interval-based PSO on multi-core system with quad-core i5 processor with clock frequency 2.5 Ghz. The system has 64-bit operating system namely WINDOWS PRO 10 with 8 GB DRAM. Both the problems, evaluation example-one and evaluation example-two large are evaluated in the system with configuration mentioned above.

5.3 Evaluation for Particle Swarm Optimization

Two problems are considered for evaluation – evaluation example-one and evaluation example-two as mentioned earlier. In evaluation example-one, six functions and three OICs is considered. In evaluation example-two, 10 functions and six OICs is considered. The initialization and evaluation of model parameters of OSS used in the estimation of system reliability is identical to usage in GA evaluation.

Evaluation Example-One

In evaluation example-one, interval RAP for multi-core system with three OICs each performing six functions is considered in the objective function (Eq. (8)) evaluated using *interval – LCbest* and *interval – GLbest PSO* algorithms. It has a population size of 30 with an archive size of 15 and 50 iterations. The values of φ_1, φ_2, w_1 and w_2 have been taken as 0.99876, 0.99678, 0.8999 and 0.2466 respectively. The wakeup probability and readiness parameters are tabulated in Table 2. The cost C_{ij}, the execution time in clock cycles for the function j on ith OIC is shown in Table 2. In Eq. (6), C is set to 50 clock cycles for the evaluation example one. The optimal solution given by *interval – LCbest* and *interval – GLbest PSO* algorithms are tabulated in Table 9. It is evident from the Table 8 both proposed *interval – LCbest* and *interval – GLbest PSO* algorithms has given better solutions than proposed GA and Regular GA for evaluation example-one problem under identical constraints. The best solution obtained for all the sets of interval numbers using *interval – LCbest* and *interval – GLbest PSO* algorithms are tabulated in

Table 9. Optimal solution for evaluation example-one with 3OICs and 6 functions using PSO

Description		Table 1 (set 1)	Table 1 (set 2)	Table 1 (set 3)	Table 1 (set 4)	Table 1 (set 5)
X		101000 000010 101101	110100 000111 011000	010000 000011 110111	111011 000110 001000	111110 001111 011110
A	U: OICs	2 2 2 3 3 3 3	2 2 2 3 3 3 3	2 2 2 3 3 3 3	2 2 2 3 3 3 3	2 2 3 3 3 2 3
Interval GLbest PSO System Reliability Lower/Upper		0.970276/ 0.970299	0.970281/ 0.970299	0.969060/ 0.970377	0.970274/ 0.970299	0.970276/ 0.970281
Interval LCbest PSO System Reliability Lower/Upper		0.969423/ 0.970289	0.968900/ 0.970282	0.968960/ 0.970282	0.969440/ 0.970283	0.970189/ 0.970281
Cost (in cycles)		44	40	46	49	41

Table 9. It is observed from Table 10, both the variants of PSO have produced solutions better than regular GA and proposed GA.

Table 10. Best solution for evaluation example-one with 3OICs and 6 functions using PSO

Description	Table 1 (set 1)	Table 1 (set 2)	Table 1 (set 3)	Table 1 (set 4)	Table 1 (set 5)
Interval GLbest PSO System Reliability Lower/Upper	0.970999/ 0.980377	0.970302/ 0.980599	0.979060/ 0.980687	0.980274/ 0.980999	0.980276/ 0.989999
Interval LCbest PSO System Reliability Lower/Upper	0.970823/ 0.980289	0.969999/ 0.979989	0.976699/ 0.980021	0.979840/ 0.980666	0.970856/ 0.988866

Evaluation Example-Two

In evaluation example-two, interval RAP for multi-core system with six OICs each performing ten functions is considered in the objective function (Eq. (8)) evaluated using interval – LCbest and interval – GLbest PSO algorithms. It has a population size of 50 with an archive size of 15 and 100 iterations. The values of φ_1, φ_2, w1 and w2 have been taken as 1.69876, 0.19678, 0.20 and 0.10 respectively. The 10 functions are designated as F1, F2, F3… F10. The wakeup probability, cost Cij (and C = 3000 cycles)

Table 11. Optimal solution for evaluation example-two with 6OICs and 10 functions using PSO

Description		Table 1(set 1)	Table 1(set 2)
X		1 0 0 0 0 0 1 1 1 0 0 0 0 0 0 0 1 1 0 0 0 0 0 0 0 0 0 0 0 1 0 1 0 0 0 0 0 0 0 0 0 1 0 0 1 1 0 1 1 0 0 0 0 0 1 0 0 0 0 1	0 1 0 0 0 1 0 0 1 0 0 1 0 0 0 0 1 1 0 0 0 0 1 0 1 0 1 0 0 0 0 0 0 0 0 0 0 0 0 1 1 0 0 0 1 1 0 0 1 0 0 0 0 1 0 0 0 0 0 0
A	U: OICs	3 3 3 1 3 3 3 3 4 4 6	5 2 4 2 3 2 4 3 3 2 6
Interval GLbest PSO System Reliability Lower/Upper		0.999977/0.999997	0.999945/0.999984
Interval LCbest PSO System Reliability Lower/Upper		0.999778/0.999913	0.999680/0.999883
Cost (in cycles)		2500	1900

Table 12. Optimal solution for evaluation example-two with 6OICs and 10 functions using PSO

Description	Table1 (set 3)	Table 1(set 4)	Table 1(set 5)
X	0 0 0 0 0 0 1 1 0 0 0 1 0 0 0 0 0 0 0 0 0 0 0 0 0 0 1 1 0 0 0 0 0 0 0 0 1 0 0 0 0 0 0 1 0 0 0 0 1 0 0 0 0 0 0 1 0 1 1 0	0 0 0 1 0 1 0 1 0 0 0 1 0 0 0 0 0 0 0 0 1 0 0 1 0 0 0 0 1 0 1 0 0 0 1 0 0 0 0 0 0 0 0 0 0 0 0 1 0 0 0 0 0 1 1 0 0 1 0 1	0 0 0 0 0 0 1 1 0 1 0 0 0 0 0 1 1 0 0 0 0 1 0 0 0 0 0 0 0 0 0 0 1 0 0 1 0 0 0 1 0 0 0 0 0 1 0 0 0 1 0 0 0 0 1 0 0 0 0 0
A U:/OICS	3 3 2 2 3 3 3 2 3 3 /6	4 3 3 3 3 2 3 3 3 4 /6	2 3 3 3 3 3 4 3 3 3 /6
Interval GLbest PSO System Reliability Lower/Upper	0.999984/0.999998	0.999955/0.999980	0.999989/0.999997
Interval LCbest PSO System Reliability Lower/Upper	0.999235/0.999766	0.999404/0.999592	0.999846/0.999947
Cost (in cycles)	1900	2150	2000

Table 13. Best solution for evaluation example-one with 6OICs and 10 functions using PSO

Description	Table 1 (set 1)	Table 1 (set 2)	Table 1 (set 3)	Table 1 (set 4)	Table 1 (set 5)
Interval GLbest PSO System Reliability Lower/Upper	0.999977/ 0.999999	0.999991/ 0.999999	0.999984/ 0.999999	0.999989/ 0.999999	0.999989/ 0.999999
Interval LCbest PSO System Reliability Lower/Upper	0.999899/ 0.999066	0.999901/ 0.999989	0.999834/ 0.999978	0.999560/ 0.999990	0.999956/ 0.999990

and readiness parameters are tabulated in the Table 5. The optimal solution given by interval – LCbest and interval – GLbest PSO algorithms are tabulated in Table 11 and 12. In both evaluation examples, GLbest PSO converges to a better solution than LCbest PSO. It is observed from Table 13, that PSO converges to better solutions faster when compared to regular GA and proposed GA. The conclusion for this paper is presented in the next section.

6 Conclusion

(1) A two-phase GA is used to solve Interval RAP. Optimal solutions for evaluation example-one and evaluation example-two are obtained. Results indicate that the proposed GA evolves better solution than regular GA. System reliability monotonically increasing with respect to function and component level redundancy is

proved. It is an inherent characteristic of the proposed Interval RAP. It is under-
stood that this property ensures enhancement of the system reliability for multi-core
systems with OICs.

(2) Results of sensitivity analysis indicate stability in the system. GA parameters are
fixed resulting in better solution for maximizing system reliability using sensitivity
analysis. It is observed that variations in GA parameters do not affect system stability
and the optimal solution.

(3) Two variants of PSO, Global best (GLbest) PSO and Local best (LCbest) are used to
solve Interval RAP. For evaluation example-one, results indicate proposed GLBest
and LCbest provide better results compared to proposed GA. In evaluation example-
two, insignificant difference in solutions given by PSO variants and GA is observed.
Results given by PSO also indicate system reliability increasing with respect to
function and component level redundancy.

(4) Considering GA and PSO evaluation of interval RAP, it is inferred that the system is stable and optimal solution does not change due to interval numbers, and
enhancement in the system reliability is ensured by the monotone property of the
Interval RAP.

References

1. Chiang, D.T., Niu, S.C.: Reliability of consecutive-k-out-of-n: F system. IEEE Trans. Reliab.
30(1), 87–89 (1981)
2. Coit, D.W., Smith, A.E.: Reliability optimization of series-parallel systems using a genetic
algorithm. IEEE Trans. Reliab. **45**(2), 254–260 (1996)
3. Coit, D.W., Liu, J.C.: System reliability optimization with k-out-of-n subsystems. Int. J.
Reliab. Qual. Saf. Eng. **7**(02), 129–142 (2000)
4. Aghaei, M., Zeinal Hamadani, A., Abouei Ardakan, M.: Redundancy allocation problem for
k-out-of-n systems with a choice of redundancy strategies. J. Ind. Eng. Int. **13**(1), 81–92
(2017)
5. Huang, L., Xu, Q.: Characterizing the lifetime reliability of manycore processors with core-
level redundancy. In: Proceedings of IEEE/ACM International Conference on Computer-
Aided Design, pp. 680–685. IEEE, San Jose (2010)
6. Fyffe, D.E., Hines, W.W., Lee, N.K.: System reliability allocation and a computational
algorithm. IEEE Trans. Reliab. **17**(2), 64–69 (1968)
7. Liang, Y.C., Smith, A.E.: An ant colony optimization algorithm for the redundancy allocation
problem. IEEE Trans. Reliab. **53**(3), 417–423 (2004)
8. Venkatesha, S., Parthasarathi, R.: 32-bit one instruction core: a low-cost, reliable, and fault-
tolerant core for multicore systems. J. Test. Eval. **47**(6), 20180492 (2019). https://doi.org/10.
1520/JTE20180492
9. Venkatesha, S., Parthasarathi, R.: design of low-cost reliable and fault-tolerant 32-bit one
instruction core for multi-core systems. In: Kounis, L.D. (ed.) Quality Control [Working
Title]. IntechOpen, London (2022)
10. Moore, R.E.: Interval Analysis. Prentice-Hall, USA (1966)
11. Pereira, L.E.S., Da Costa, V.M.: Interval analysis applied to the maximum loading point of
electric power systems considering load data uncertainties. Int. J. Electr. Power Energy Syst.
54, 334–340 (2014)

12. Kolev, L.V.: Interval Methods for Circuit Analysis. World Scientific, Singapore (1993)
13. Impollonia, N., Muscolino, G.: Interval analysis of structures with uncertain-but-bounded axial stiffness. Comput. Methods Appl. Mech. Eng. **200**(2), 1945–1962 (2011)
14. Wang, X., Yang, H., Wang, L., Qiu, Z.: Interval analysis method for structural damage identification based on multiple load cases. J. Appl. Mech. **79**(5), 051010 (2012)
15. Wang, W., Xiong, J., Xie, M.: A study of interval analysis for cold-standby system reliability optimization under parameter uncertainty. Comput. Ind. Eng. **97**, 93–100 (2016)
16. Bhunia, A.K., Samanta, S.S.: A study of interval metric and its application in multi-objective optimization with interval objectives. Comput. Ind. Eng. **74**, 169–178 (2014)
17. Gupta, R.K., Bhunia, A.K., Roy, D.: A GA based penalty function technique for solving constrained redundancy allocation problem of series system with interval valued reliability of components. J. Comput. Appl. Math. **232**(2), 275–284 (2009)
18. Mahato, S.K., Bhunia, A.K.: Interval-arithmetic-oriented interval computing technique for global optimization. Appl. Math. Res. eXpress **2006**, 1–19 (2006)
19. Roy, P., Mahapatra, B.S., Mahapatra, G.S., Roy, P.K.: Entropy based region reducing genetic algorithm for reliability redundancy allocation in interval environment. Expert Syst. Appl. **41**(14), 6147–6160 (2014)

Design of Low Powered and High Speed Compressor Based Multiplier

Narala Anudeep Reddy$^{(\boxtimes)}$ ⓘ, Chaitra Umesh ⓘ, Vishakha Harkood ⓘ,
and R. Marimuthu ⓘ

Vellore Institute of Technology, Vellore, Tamil Nadu 632014, India
rmarimuthu@vit.ac.in

Abstract. Multiplication is used in digital systems mostly because it is one of the main arithmetic functions. There are three steps for multiplication, which are partial product generation, partial product reduction to two rows and using a ripple carry adder (RCA) tree for final addition of the binary results. The second part mainly contributes to time delay, amount of power consumed and the complexity of the design. Hence, we enhance the efficiency of this stage by using proper arithmetic blocks, such as compressors, to directly improve the performance and energy efficiency of the multiplier. The goal of this paper is to introduce a few approximate 8x8 multipliers for low-powered and high-speed applications with a reasonable trade-off among accuracy, speed, area and power with the hybrid approach of inexact 4:2 compressors types.

Keywords: 4-2compressors · Approximate compressors · Approximate multipliers · Neighborhood processing · Unsigned 8×8 multipliers · Sharpening and smoothening

1 Introduction

Important emerging applications like machine learning, image processing etc., are all demanding in terms of power consumption and hardware. For these applications, it is necessary to obtain efficiency in terms of speed, power and area by approximate computing. Several models have been proposed for approximate computing to obtain highly efficient multipliers.

Multipliers are used in digital signal processors, microprocessors and many other applications, where the multiplications are abundant and the need of approximate computing like image processing is very much needed. Usually, they are located in critical paths of digital systems to improve the speed and multiplication is used for the internal processes.

As multiplication is important in various applications, it is executed in three main steps. These three steps are partial product generation, partial product reduction to two rows and Ripple Carry Adder (RCA) in the end for 2–1 compression. The second phase, that is, the reduction of partial products is the main contribution for overall power, area and speed.

© The Author(s), under exclusive license to Springer Nature Switzerland AG 2022
V. Arunachalam and K. Sivasankaran (Eds.): ICMDCS 2022, CCIS 1743, pp. 72–89, 2022.
https://doi.org/10.1007/978-3-031-23973-1_5

In [1], the authors proposed three designs for approximate compressors for error resilient multiplier design. The designs are referred to as Yang1, Yang2 and Yang3 respectively. Yang1 has 1/16 errors, Yang 2 has 2/16 errors and Yang 3 has 4/16 errors, all with a maximum deviation of error not more than 1. Here, approximate compressors were designed with low error rate constraint, which means accuracy is not compromised. Any of the three designs can be selected, based on the requirements. But with them being more accurate, design complexity of the compressors is increased, which in turn led to an increase in the use of other resources like power and area.

In [2], the paper presents a 4–2 compressor design, which can be used in binary multiplier in the partial product compression phase. It has also added an error recovery module to improve reducing errors. The proposed design was based on modifying an existing 4–2 compressor design that changes error profile. The resulting errors were located with a two-input AND gate. For design of 8-bit approximate multiplier, the partial product accumulation part is divided into three regions- a 7-bit accurate region, a 4-bit approximate region, and a 4-bit truncated region. Proposed design multipliers are more accurate because of the use of more accurate compressors for the most significant bits. It also consumes less power and area, which is a good balance of resources. But, the maximum error deviation from the accurate result is high.

In [3], the paper discussed about the various compressors and their comparisons along with its own proposed design which had 2/16 errors with maximum deviation of 1. It also introduced methods of stacking circuit technique and hybrid model, which used two different types of compressors. It used Lin compressor for the left side (more significant columns) and Ahma for the right side (less significant columns). Lin compressor was more accurate and consumes more power whereas Ahma compressor was less accurate and used less resources. The proposed design performed very well with good trade-offs between area, power and accuracy, but it was still slow compared to other designs which had less accuracy and were simpler.

In [5], the paper laid emphasis on multiplier use in place of XOR gates to utilize the outputs from previous stages efficiently and also because multiplier use in critical paths improves speed. There were 3 proposed designs- 3:2, 4:2, and 5:2 architectures. These compressors were very efficient and faster than traditional compressors. They were more accurate than approximate compressors and better than exact compressors in all aspects in the voltage range- 0.9 to 0.3. But the proposed designs were still not as fast and occupied more area than approximate compressors.

This paper presents a new proposed architecture for a low power and high-speed compressor-based multiplier.

2 4–2 Compressors

2.1 Exact 4–2 Compressor

An exact 4–2 compressor is compresses or adds all its input values and gives out a binary equivalent of that value, but for all 1s case at input, two output bits will not be sufficient as it requires 3 bits to give 100. By also considering CarryIn at the input, 4–2 compressor has in total 5,3 as inputs and outputs respectively. The design of an exact 4–2 compressor is shown in the Fig. 1.

2.2 Previous Works on Approximate and Efficient 4–2 Compressors

Studies of different compressors are considered and out of them, mainly 4 compressors are taken for the comparison studies. These 4–2 compressors are referred throughout the paper as Ahma [4], Yang1 [1], Ha [2] and Prop or Proposed(ref) [3]. Some of them are known for their accuracy and others for being very efficient in using the resources. Detailed designs and their truth tables are seen in Figs. 2, 3, 4 and 5 and Table 1.

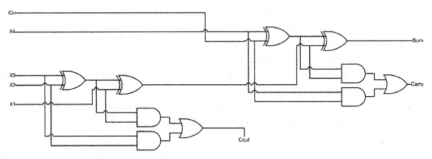

Fig. 1. Regular 4–2 compressor.

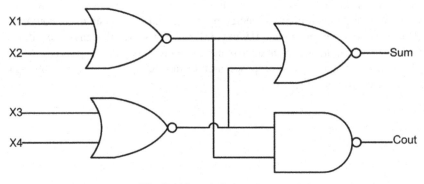

Fig. 2. Ahma 4–2 compressor.

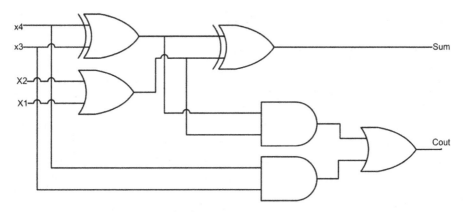

Fig. 3. Ha 4–2 compressor.

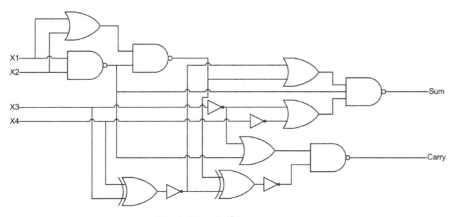

Fig. 4. Yang1 4–2 compressor.

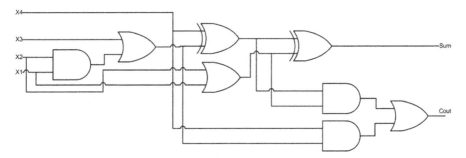

Fig. 5. Prop 4–2 compressor.

2.3 Approximate 4–2 Compressors Proposed by This Paper

This paper proposes two different compressor designs, Compressor(A) and Compressor(B), each ideally for slightly different use. Compressor(A) is more accurate than Compressor(B), but the latter is much better performing in area, power and delay.

The compressor design of Yang1 [1], Fig. 3, is considered for its accuracy and attempted to make it faster with less area. A technique of stacking circuit is used [3] as seen in the Fig. 3 and an efficient full adder design [5] is used. This efficient full adder design, helped in reducing the critical path and consequently the delay Fig. 6.

Compressor(B), Fig. 7, on the other hand focuses mainly on the performance like area, delay and power. This design trades some accuracy, effectively just becomes a full adder that doesn't take 4th input to consideration. This makes the compressor's error rate to be 50% but the error distance remains less than or equal to 1 and always negative. It has its advantages especially in the smoothening or blurring of an image.

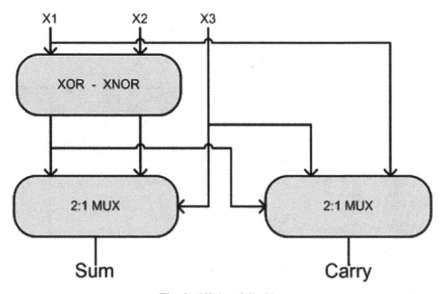

Fig. 6. Efficient full adder.

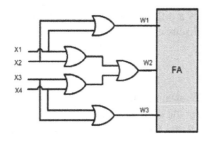

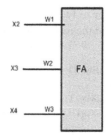

Proposed approximate 4-2
compressor

Proposed least approximate 4-2
compressor

Fig. 7. Proposed approximate compressors. (Compressor (A) on left and Compressor(B) on right)

Table 1. Truth-tables of approximate compressors.

X4X3X2X1	Yang1		Ha		Ahma		Prop		Compressor(A)		Compressor(B)	
	CS	E	CS	E	CS	E	CS	E	CS	E	CS	E
0000	00	0	00	0	00	0	00	0	00	0	00	0
0001	01	0	01	0	01	0	01	0	01	0	00	−1
0010	01	0	01	0	01	0	01	0	01	0	01	0
0011	10	0	10	0	01	−1	10	0	10	0	01	−1
0100	01	0	01	0	01	0	01	0	01	0	01	0
0101	10	0	10	0	11	+1	10	0	10	0	01	−1
0110	10	0	10	0	11	+1	10	0	10	0	10	0
0111	11	0	11	0	11	0	10	−1	11	0	10	−1
1000	01	0	01	0	01	0	01	0	01	0	01	0
1001	10	0	10	0	11	+1	10	0	10	0	01	−1
1010	10	0	10	0	11	+1	10	0	10	0	10	0
1011	11	0	11	0	11	0	11	0	11	0	10	−1
1100	10	0	01	−1	01	−1	10	0	10	0	10	0
1101	11	0	10	−1	11	0	11	0	11	0	10	−1
1110	11	0	10	−1	11	0	11	0	11	0	11	0
1111	11	−1	11	−1	11	−1	11	−1	11	−1	11	−1

3   8-Bit Multiplier Design

This paper mainly discusses the hybrid implementation of multipliers, where different types of compressors are used in the multiplier design, because it is proven to have better trade-offs than the conventional ones [3]. Hybrid designs are typically had divided the multiplier to two halves and each half utilizes a different type of compressor. The following are the multiplier designs this project discusses.

3.1 Multiplier Designs

Multiplier 1, also referred as Cap or Cap1 in some instances, has Compressor(A) on left and Compressor(B) on right. Compressor(B) being the least accurate is chosen to be on the right hand side because the closer to the LSB the better the overall accuracy and error distance when it comes to the output bits that are wrong after multiplication.

Multiplier 2, referred as Cap2 or CapHa is similar in construction to Multiplier 1 but uses compressor Ha instead of Compressor(B) resulting in even more accurate results compared to Multiplier 1 but only by using few more resources.

Multiplier 3 or Cap3, challenges the regular notion of using less accurate ones near LSB side and instead uses them on the left i.e. near the MSB side. This although seem counterintuitive as the error distance vary vastly, it is supposedly among the best multipliers especially for image processing when it comes to the multiplications with lower valued numbers. As the lower valued numbers rarely require the compressors on near MSB side apart from compressing all the zeros, using more resources for making them accurate is pointless (Figs. 8, 9 and 10).

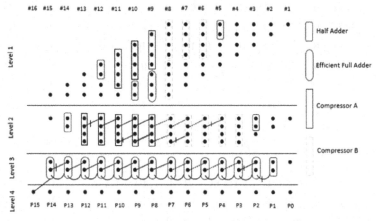

Fig. 8. Dot diagram representation of Multiplier 1 (Cap1). (*with Compressor(A) on left and (B) on right*).

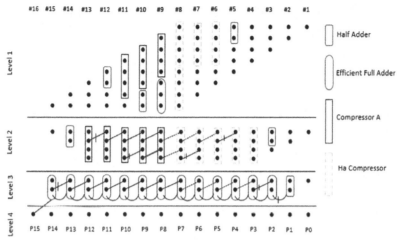

Fig. 9. Dot diagram representation of Multiplier 2 (CapHa/Cap2). *(with Compressor(A) on left and Ha on right).*

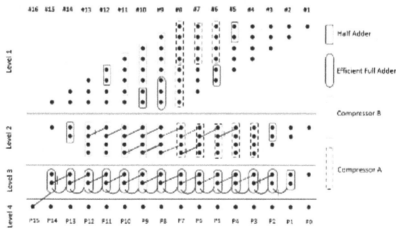

Fig. 10. Dot diagram representation of Multiplier 3(Cap3). (with Compressor(B) on left and Compressor(A) on right.

4 Results

The performance of the multipliers is measured mainly by three factors, its area, power consumption and delay.

4.1 Multiplier Performance

Cap1 is the multiplier with the designed compressors and it consumes less area and power when compared to others. The latency is also less. The multiplier is well balanced

Table 2. Delay, Area and Power results of the multipliers discussed (* Number of LUTs used is an area equivalent for an FPGA; + Power calulations are with respect to kirtex-7 and the rest are based on spartan-6).

Multiplier	Max delay(ns)	No of LUTs used *	Power(w)+
Cap1	22.6	137	13.35
Cap2(with Ha)	23.262	151	13.854
Yang1	24.399	164	14.314
Ha	22.710	140	13.527
Ahma	22.035	106	11.636
Proposed(ref)	23.142	150	13.953
Hybrid(prop-Ahma)	23.566	133	12.633
Accurate	25.126	215	14.798

in terms of consumption of resources and speed. Cap2 (with Ha) is the multiplier with the Ha compressor in place of the least approximate compressor. It is also well balanced in the use of resources and speed.

Table 3. Error analysis.

Multiplier	ER	NMED	MRED	NoEB	PRED
Cap1	0.93	1.58e−2	1.95e−1	5.98	6.25e−1
Cap2(with Ha)	0.61	1.45e−2	1.75e−1	6.11	4.58e−1
Yang1	0.44	1.42e−2	1.72e−1	6.13	4.15e−1
Ha	0.69	2.01e−2	1.85e−1	5.64	5.94e−1
Ahma	0.89	2.69e−2	2.19e−1	5.22	7.73e−1
Proposed(ref)	0.48	1.47e−2	1.73e−1	6.09	4.28e−1
Hybrid(prop-Ahma)	0.85	1.67e−2	1.83e−1	5.90	5.68e−1

Indicating as M and M' the results produced by an exact and an approximate multiplier, respectively;

- Error Distance: $ED = |M − M'|$
- Relative Error Distance: $RED = ED/|M|$ (for M not equal to 0).
- MaxOut, the maximum absolute value of the accurate multiplier: $MaxOut = (2n − 1)^2$ for unsigned multipliers.
- ERMS: Root mean Squared of ED
  The metrics considered in the following are:
- ER: The Error Rate, the percentage of multiplications that ED > 0.
- NMED: The Normalized Mean Error Distance = average(ED)/MaxOut.

- MRED: The Mean Relative Error Distance = average(RED).
- NoEB: The Number of Effective bits = $2n - \log2(1 + ERMS)$.
- PRED = the probability of having RED higher than 2 percent.

It is clearly evident from the Table 3 that Yang1 and Prop seems to be the best ones in the bunch, with the lowest of ER values. Which had been foreseen because Yang1 has 1 error in its 4–2 compressor truth table in Table 2, whereas the Proposed, only 2 errors in total out of 16. So, it is natural that the multipliers with these specific compressors are the best in regards to the error performance. Yang1 not only in the ER but also in every other error metric, did the best in comparison.

Cap1 has the worst Error Rate which is due to the fact 50% of the compressor(b) used in LSB side of Cap1 is prone to error. Ahma has 7/16 errors in its compressors, which explains why it right behind the cap1. Another reason for high ER in Cap1 is that all the error is due to not considering an input to the compressors which made it even more vulnerable to errors. But cap2 on the other hand managed to do pretty well on the error side with 3rd best ER and also every other metric, except the number of Effective bits, where in it is 2nd. As we know ER is not the whole story, it is merely a metric to know how many outputs from the multipliers are error prone whether the Error Distance is huge or small. So, considering other ones is always a better thing to do especially when small errors doesn't bother with compared to the accurate ones with inconsiderate resources allocated to it.

Therefore, the trade-off with the error in the two multipliers discussed is in two levels. Cap1 with extremely error prone all while being not the worst in the comparison, tends to beat Ahma and Hybrid in various metrics; Cap2 with reasonably good error, even comparable to the best one in the comparison the Yang1. These results have shown that Ahma and Hybrid have seemed to be doing not so good and the reason could be explained with a simple observation that the both multipliers use the same compressor, at least on the LSB side. As Ahma tends to also have errors that are positive. A positive error will usually have more effect on the Error Distance, which is the difference in values between accurate and the resultant output. For example, a positive error can make 4'b0100 to 4'b1000 a difference of 8 in decimal values, whereas a negative error can make 4'b0100 to 4'b0010 a difference of 4 ED in decimals.

Also, the reason behind using a hybrid solution is a bit faulty, considering the ER alone, but not the Error Distance, which is that a hybrid multiplier houses less approximate compressors on its LSB side and somewhat more approximate ones on its MSB side. With this whenever a multiplication takes place, since LSB side as its name suggest are less significant, they are less prone to swing the error too much. But a multiplication can result in higher values or lower values, depending on the inputs, and neither of them can escape from using less approximate compressors. Thus, a high Error Rate.

Most of the multiplications happen on the LSB side, especially the image processing application this project discusses about. This takes a heavy toll on the result. So, this project introduces a new multiplier specifically for multiplications with lower values numbers in mind.

4.2 Image Sharpening and Smoothening

Sharpening and Smoothening of an image can be achieved using the technique called Neighborhood Processing where the neighboring pixels also decide the output using a matrix called Kernel. Figure 11 has the kernels used for smoothening and sharpening respectively.

The following results are obtained when the image processing module is used for an accurate multiplier (Figs. 12, 13 and 14).

$$
\begin{bmatrix}
1 & 1 & 1 & 1 & 1 \\
1 & 4 & 4 & 4 & 1 \\
1 & 4 & 12 & 4 & 1 \\
1 & 4 & 4 & 4 & 1 \\
1 & 1 & 1 & 1 & 1
\end{bmatrix}
\quad
\begin{bmatrix}
0 & 0 & 0 & 0 & 0 \\
0 & 0 & -1 & 0 & 0 \\
0 & -1 & 5 & -1 & 0 \\
0 & 0 & -1 & 0 & 0 \\
0 & 0 & 0 & 0 & 0
\end{bmatrix}
$$

Fig. 11. Kernel used for image processing (For smoothening on left and sharpening on right).

Fig. 12. Original images (Lena on left and Boat on right).

Fig. 13. Smoothened images (Lena on left and Boat on right).

Fig. 14. Sharpened images (Lena on left and Boat on right).

4.3 Image Processing Results for Smoothening Using Approximate Multipliers

For the smoothening, the performance of each multiplier is hard to distinguish as these differences are very minute and yet the dissimilarities are a bit more pronounces when compared the images produced by less approximate multipliers.

For instance, here in the images Fig. 17, the top portions of the Smooth Lena on the top and Ahma Lena in the bottom. We can observe discolorations; a little patchy texture is seen on the right. A similar but slight texture are present in the Cap Lena.

The Boat pictures in Fig. 17 are Smooth Boat and Cap Smooth Boat to the left and right respectively. The major difference can be seen in the outline of the clouds, the image by the multiplier Cap seemed to blown out the whites in cloud. It's the same phenomenon as with the smoothening of Lena in effect but the fact that a lot of light area available in this picture made it possible for the blown-out clouds. The top of the image similar patches can also be seen.

The last image in Fig. 17 is from the multiplier Ahma with smoothened. Although it is able to maintain the clouds in a good enough manner, one of the corners is completely patchy. Also, the shadows casted by the boats. So, we can say the Ahma is struggling with darker shades and Cap with the lighter ones. One more thing to be aware of that, all the multipliers did very well in the smoothening and the errors can only be seen through pixel peeping, the PSNR and SSIM values can help with the performance even better (Table 4).

4.4 Image Processing Results for Sharpening Using Approximate Multipliers

Unlike smoothening the results with sharpening are clearly distinguishable. But only 3 out of 7 had shown any errors. One of the reasons for excellent performance of most multipliers is that they are accurate with multiplications that includes 1 or 5 as these are the numbers that make the sharpening kernel.

Cap tended to show worse PSNR values than Ahma and the Hybrid but the SSIM values are better for the Cap which can also be perceived from the pictures, the resultant pictures from Cap are much more original like than the others which had lost most of their details (Table 5).

Table 4. Image processing results for smoothening.

| | Smoothening | | | | | |
| | Lena | | Boat | | Average | |
	PSNR	SSIM	PSNR	SSIM	PSNR	SSIM
Cap1	34.8254	0.9819	34.7777	0.9821	34.8015	0.9820
Cap2(with Ha)	44.7346	0.9932	46.5583	0.9955	45.6464	0.9943
Ahma	31.9050	0.9559	35.4813	0.9703	33.6931	0.9631
Proposed(ref)	inf	1	inf	1	inf	1
Hybrid(prop-ahma)	47.5297	0.9957	49.8935	0.9970	48.7116	0.9963
Ha	44.7346	0.9932	46.5583	0.9955	45.6464	0.9943
Yang1	inf	1	inf	1	Inf	1

Table 5. Image processing results for sharpening.

| | Sharpening | | | | | |
| | Lena | | Boat | | Average | |
	PSNR	SSIM	PSNR	SSIM	PSNR	SSIM
Cap1	27.2558	0.6090	27.8402	0.6327	27.5480	0.6208
Cap2(with Ha)	inf	1	inf	1	inf	1
Ahma	29.1529	0.5422	29.4730	0.5686	29.3129	0.5554
Proposed(ref)	inf	1	inf	1	Inf	1
Hybrid(prop-ahma)	29.1529	0.5422	29.4730	0.5686	29.3129	0.5554
Ha	inf	1	inf	1	Inf	1
Yang1	inf	1	inf	1	inf	1

4.5 Observations

From both image sharpening and smoothening it can also be observed that Cap2(Cap Ha) and Ha pair, Hybrid and Ahma, both of these pairs tended to provide the same results, even in the PSNR and SSIM values and they both have LSB side compressor sides common. For cap2 and Ha it's the compressor Ha that on the LSB side and similarly for Hybrid and Ahma its the Ahma compressor.

The influence of compressors on LSB side is a lot more than previously expected. Especially for the lower valued numbers. Hence why the cap3 is introduced.

This new multiplier is created by swapping the compressors from LSB side to MSB and vice versa in order to make the LSB side less error prone compared to MSB.

This might result in drastic increase to the error distance when the overall performance of the multiplier is considered but just for the image processing, the sharpening and the smoothening, it is the perfect one and the results for the same are shown below (Figs. 15 and 16).

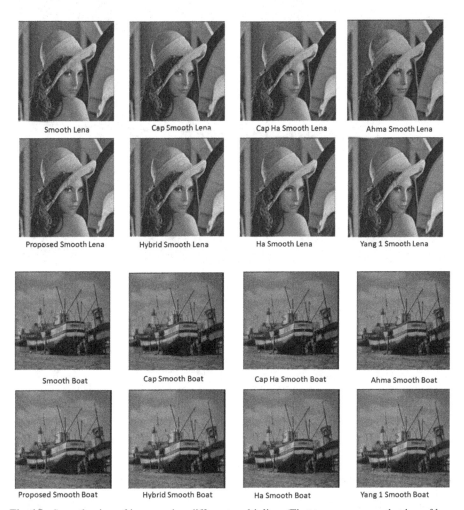

Fig. 15. Smoothening of image using different multipliers (First two rows smoothening of lena and the last two rows smoothening of boat; first image in row1 and row3 are the results using an exact multiplier).

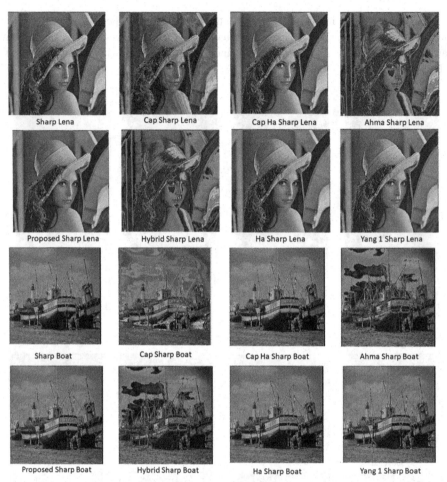

Fig. 16. Sharpening of image using different multipliers (First two rows sharpening of lena and the last two rows sharpening of boat; first image in row1 and row3 are the results using an exact multiplier).

4.6 Cap3 Multiplier

Cap3 in Table 6 is one of such multipliers and the difference is immediately noticeable. ER is relatively high. NMED, MRED and PRED got affected, as they are dependent on the Error Distance, due to the nature of the Cap3 design (Table 7).

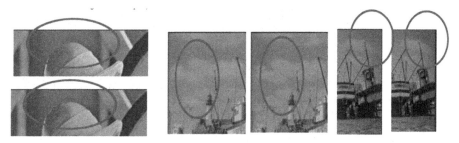

Fig. 17. Minute differences among smoothened images (first two lena exact on top and Ahma on bottom; next two, boat exact on left and cap boat on right; last two images Ahma Boat on right and Boat with exact multiplier on left).

Table 6. Error analysis of Cap3.

Multiplier	ER	NMED	MRED	NoEB	PRED
Cap3(swapped cap1)	0.606	1.97e−2	1.81e−1	5.67	5.58e−1

Fig. 18. Smoothened images with Cap3 (Lena on left and Boat on right).

Fig. 19. Sharpened images with Cap3 (Lena on left and Boat on right).

Table 7. Error analysis of Cap3 through image comparision.

Cap3 (swapped cap1)	Lena		Boat		Average	
	PSNR	SSIM	PSNR	SSIM	PSNR	SSIM
Smoothening	inf	1	inf	1	inf	1
Sharpening	inf	1	Inf	1	Inf	1

4.7 Error Analysis Charts

The graphs below help understand the multipliers depending on the input values. The x-axis is the number 0–255 y-axis is the average of absolute error distance for values in the x-axis as one of the inputs of the multiplier (Figs. 20, 21, 22, 23, 24, 25, 26 and 27).

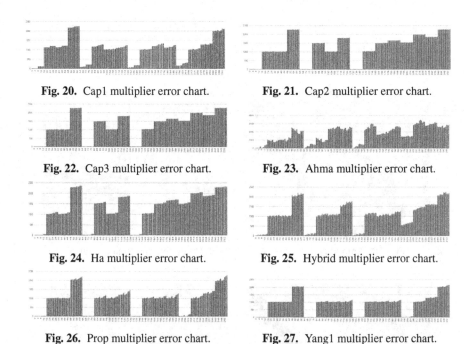

Fig. 20. Cap1 multiplier error chart.   **Fig. 21.** Cap2 multiplier error chart.

Fig. 22. Cap3 multiplier error chart.   **Fig. 23.** Ahma multiplier error chart.

Fig. 24. Ha multiplier error chart.   **Fig. 25.** Hybrid multiplier error chart.

Fig. 26. Prop multiplier error chart.   **Fig. 27.** Yang1 multiplier error chart.

5 Conclusion

Multiplication is one of the main arithmetic functions, which forms an important part of this project. It consists of three steps, which include partial product generation, partial product reduction to two rows and final addition. The second part contributes to delay, area and power. Hence, enhancing the efficiency of this stage through compressors can improve the performance of the multiplier. Multipliers that are designed with the intended purpose in mind can be very efficient in resources and delivers excellent accuracy (for that specific use case).

Optimal efficiency is hard to achieve; it varies depends on the use case. The definition of being optimal changes with every application. The best multiplier for a scenario may not hold its ground for another. But a careful design of multipliers is considered as part of the project which resulted in three different multipliers each are optimal for different use case scenarios. All of these designs are done with a hybrid approach which is believed to achieve closer to optimal performance and results clearly speak for themselves. The multipliers which the project had introduced, were designed not to compromise too much on the accuracy, for speed and power. Trade-offs among area, power, delay and accuracy are very well balanced, thanks to the hybrid approach.

References

1. Yang, Z., Han, J., Lombardi, F.: Approximate compressors for errorresilient multiplier design. In: Proc. IEEE Int. Symp. Defect Fault Tolerance VLSI Nanotechnol. Syst., pp. 183–186 (Oct. 2015)
2. Ha, M., Lee, S.: Multipliers with approximate 4–2 compressors and error recovery modules. IEEE Embedded Syst. Lett. **10**(1), 6–9 (Mar. 2018)
3. Strollo, A.G.M., Napoli, E., De Caro, D., Petra, N., Meo, G.D.: Comparison and extension of approximate 4-2 compressors for low-power approximate multipliers. In: IEEE Transactions on Circuits and Systems I: Regular Papers, vol. 67, no. 9, pp. 3021-3034 (Sept. 2020). https://doi.org/10.1109/TCSI.2020.2988353
4. Ahmadinejad, M., Moaiyeri, M.H., Sabetzadeh, F.: Energy and area efficient imprecise compressors for approximate multiplication at nanoscale. AEU-Int. J. Electron. Commun. 110 (Oct. 2019). Art. no. 152859
5. Veeramachaneni, S., Krishna, K.M., Avinash, L., Puppala, S.R., Srinivas, M.B.: Novel Architectures for High-Speed and Low-Power 3–2, 4–2 and 5–2 Compressors. In: 20th International Conference on VLSI Design held jointly with 6th International Conference on Embedded Systems (VLSID'07), pp. 324–329, Bangalore, India (2007). https://doi.org/10.1109/VLSID.2007.116
6. Venkata Ganesh, P., Jagadeeswara Rao, E., Nandan, D.: A Review of 4-2 Compressors: Based on Accuracy and Performance Analysis. In: Gunjan, V.K., Zurada, J.M. (eds.) Proceedings of International Conference on Recent Trends in Machine Learning, IoT, Smart Cities and Applications. AISC, vol. 1245, pp. 569–578. Springer, Singapore (2021). https://doi.org/10.1007/978-981-15-7234-0_53
7. Prasad, B.D.V., Sanjeev, N.S.S., Saladi, K., Nandan, D.: Review on Different Types of Multipliers and Its Performance Comparisons. In: Sherpa, K.S., Bhoi, A.K., Kalam, A., Mishra, M.K. (eds.) ETAEERE 2020. LNEE, vol. 691, pp. 329–339. Springer, Singapore (2021). https://doi.org/10.1007/978-981-15-7511-2_31

A Route Planning for Idyllic Coverage in Sensor Networks with Efficient Area Coverage

Kumar A. Shukla[1] , Debangan Mandal[1] , Ayush Thakur[1], Soham Adhikari[1],
and V. Vijayarajan[2]([✉])

[1] Department of Software Systems, Vellore Institute of Technology, Vellore, India
anik912345699@gmail.com
[2] Department of Internet of Things, SCOPE, Vellore Institute of Technology,
Vellore, India
virtual.viji@gmail.com

Abstract. Wireless sensor networks (WSNs) are often utilized to detect
the physical obstacles due to their heterogeneous movement and self-
organizing, and local cooperation capabilities. Meanwhile, with the
instantaneous growth of smart automobiles, mobile devices can be used
to collect data in WSNs. Although those mobile devices can consider-
ably improve network performance, it is difficult to create an appropriate trip path for efficient data collection. In this study, we provide an
itinerary planning schema (IPS- DM) to discover a route having minimum distance that passes through as multiple sensors as feasible. Sensor
nodes will probably refer to use a single-hop connection for networks, raw
data uploading in their transmission range to save energy usage. Monitor
nodes (MNs) are defined initially for the Data gathering module (DM) to
collect sensor basic metrics and then their quantity is establish found on
the absolute coverage rate. Finally, we use the route scheduling planning
module (RPM) model to organize the quickest loop for MNs.

Keywords: Sensor network · Route planning · Coverage
optimization · Wireless devices

1 Introduction

In the sensor network domain, nodes have newly been given rise to detect the real
world obstacles, especially in horrible circumstances, because they are ad hoc,
self-organize, and work together locally. WSN has received a lot of attention
in the last few decades as a way to connect the environment and computer
networks [1–3]. WSNs deploy sensors randomly via planes or other vehicles.
The locations are typically in severe environments, and if the sensors fail or
lose their charge, they are rendered useless due to the difficulty of repair or
battery replacement. Sensor nodes will share their basic network parameter like
distance, energy back up with their neighbors after deployment of the nodes

© The Author(s), under exclusive license to Springer Nature Switzerland AG 2022
V. Arunachalam and K. Sivasankaran (Eds.): ICMDCS 2022, CCIS 1743, pp. 90–104, 2022.
https://doi.org/10.1007/978-3-031-23973-1_6

in the application environment, and the network structure will be formed with full networks coverage. WSNs [4,5] may be found everywhere in our day today lives, such as in monitoring systems, because of their inherent advantages of easy deployment and self-organization [6], location vigilance [7], human health observation and smart systems [8]. Despite all the advantages of WSN, they have some difficulties in their implementation process and energy management strategies [9]. In most of the applications, sensor nodes are having in-built power units and the replacement of the unit was done manually. Replacing a battery unit in harsh environments manually is a difficult process. Hence, researchers concentrate on the energy management system of energy, deployment of efficient routing processes to improve the lifespan of a network [10]. In the past research, they deployed a network with static nodes. But in the current scenario, it has been changed with a moving node having multiple data collection points. As a result, we can collect various information about nodes simultaneously. Routing strategies broadly classified as:

1.1   Grouping Method

The network model under this concept is modeled as follows: From the above diagram, we may see that the network was grouped based on some predefined protocol. After the grouping was set up a supervisor node was defined among all the groups. With the help of that node, data was passed in a multi-hop manner. this was followed in the previous schema such as minimum Energy usage Clustered based methods, Dual structure Data transmission algorithm and Hybrid techniques with optimized Energy Distribution methods (Fig. 1).

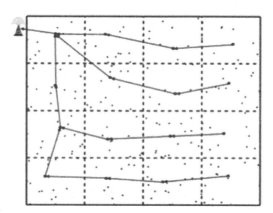

Fig. 1. Grouping strategy based network model [1]

1.2   Based on Data Gathering of Data

Here, the nodes in the transmission data network are being used to gather data for the processing of the transmission of data [10–13]. The network is configured as displayed below (Fig. 2).

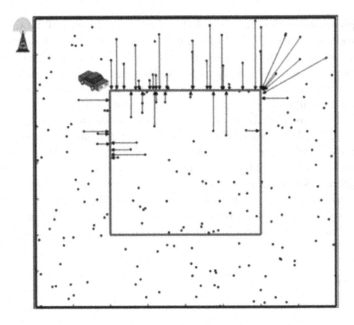

Fig. 2. Network setup with data gathering module [1]

The data transmitted may be done based on a predetermined data path or point was defined. The Data gathering module node collects the basic details from all the nodes. When it reaches a predefined path or point it stops the process of data collection from the sensor nodes. After that, the data transmission is started in the provided path described by the algorithms. Sometimes the path was defined as long travel or a long multi-hop process. The path may Passover Over many groups of nodes their supervisor node of the node may be defined as a Monitor node. The continuing part of the paper describes in Sect. 2 shows some of the methodologies provided in the previous years. Proposed model used in the technique is exemplified in section. The methodology is explained in detailed analysis corresponding to the intended mathematical model. Several comparisons have been made including the duration of the networks and the life span of various algorithms among others.

2   Link Between Proposed and Related Approaches

2.1   Node Clustering Using the Static Sink Node

The sensor nodes within the unit are grouped here, and a static sink node is installed in any of the network's corners. The multi-hop transmission was also used for packet communication. This was followed in LEACH [14], a cluster head that supports the data transmission inside a group of the nodes or between various groups in a varied-hop method. In PEGASIS [15], a link frame was built to pass the data in a multi-hop path to a cluster head at a long distance. At this time, data traffic may occur when a new hopping method was employed on the course. HEED [16] states a comprehensive method based on determining the source and range of residual batteries inside a cluster for specifying a hopping path. EEUC [17] categorized clusters into two groups of the cluster having small sizes nearer to the static sink for handling data transmission inside a group and higher can be used in forwarding data packets for multi-hop methods.

2.2   Information-Based Nodes Techniques

A node will get all the essential data from every other node during this process, including the amount of energy left, the distance from the static sink, and the number of packets that can be handled. With this, data will move forward from the moving node until it reaches the target node group.

3   Network Unit Model

3.1   Basic Factors

To obtain a clearer representation of our proposed IPS-DM and to execute the simulation and so conveniently, the following assumptions are presented.

1. After deployment, all sensors are immobile, and when their power is depleted, they become inactive. Sensors may modify their communication range within a preset distance, and data-hopping in the minimum hop is widely employed in the uploading of data.
2. Monitor nodes (MNs) are locations where the mobile collector collects information.
3. A stationary node is installed in the end area of the sensor deployment area, and Data gathering module approaches it once each round to upload the acquired data. Using a modified data collector, an intelligent automobile collects data. It traverses the sensor field, halting at MNs corresponding to data collection is predetermined.

3.2   Network Structure

This network model in the paper depicted in Fig. 3. For the analysis of network performance rectangular sized area with numerous sensors distributed throughout the network area. The data collector can gather data because the sensing field is unobstructed and has freedom for the free movement in deployment area. Timing metrics is calculated by the number of network rounds to pass over The MNs are all calibrated in rounds. Towards the data collected at the culmination of each round, each sensor transmits a data packet.

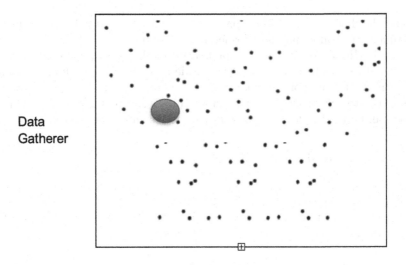

Data Gatherer

Fig. 3. Network model

3.3   Energy Illustration

In sensor networks, the energy of WSNs usage amalgamation of several components, including observing, data storage and their transmission. Data transmission, on the other hand, accounts for a significant share in total energy being
used. As a result, in this research, we exclusively address energy usage in transmission. We apply the same energy model that has been used in the literature
[18,19]. The energy usage for transferring kbit data is calculated using the formulas below:

$$F_{T_x}(k, dis(k_m, k_n)) = E_{elect}.k + \xi_{elect}.k \tag{1}$$

where $dis(k_m, k_n)$ shows the length of the neighboring nodes, it can be determined using m and n, as well as expression 2.

$$dis(k_m, k_n) = \sqrt{(x_m - x_n)^2 + (y_m - y_n)^2} \tag{2}$$

E_{elect} is the amount of electricity necessary to keep the distribution circuit operational. ξ_{elect} indicates energy.

$$\xi_{elect} = \begin{cases} \xi_{fs}.dis^2, & \text{if } dis<d_0 \\ \xi_{mp}.dis^4, & \text{if } dis>d_0 \end{cases} \tag{3}$$

Here ξ_{fs} conveys the nodes power for closest range of communication and
ξ_{mp} indicates the power usage of maximum of communication over a distance.
There are two schema: the open-space model and multi-path fading prototypes.
To make a choice, the threshold value d0 is employed for the classification to
adopt as shown by the relation given below:

$$d_0 = \sqrt{\frac{\xi_{fs}}{\xi_{mp}}} \tag{4}$$

$$E_{R_x} = E_{elect}.k \tag{5}$$

4 Our Proposed IPS-DM

4.1 Development of the Sensor Node's Coverage Capacity

In this part, we first adopt the Data gathering module's travel route planning problem into a MNs coverage problem. Neighboring sensors can merely transmit with each other. This will happens if both of the neighbor nodes in their communication range, as we all know. Even though the Data gathering module (DM) performs better than ordinary sensors, their acceptable transmission ranges will be in the similar manner. We presume that the Data gathering module only avoids in the collection of network information. As many nodes movement causes a huge rate of energy used for retransmission and packet loss.

In the above Fig. 4. **MN1**, **MN2**, and **MN3** correspond to three separate covered areas of MNs. As shown in the above Figure, the areas A1, A2, and A3 are covered by two MNs, whereas A4 is covered by three SPs at the same time. Covered areas are those that are covered by at least one MN, and overlapped covered areas are those that are covered by more than one MN. If a sensor is deployed in any of the MN's covered areas, it capable of communicating the data that it monitors to the Data gathering module whenever the sensor is put in any of the MN's covered regions. On the other hand, overlapping covered regions cause the Data gathering module's resources to be depleted, and they also increase the journey length that the Data gathering module must travel. The effectiveness of the Data gathering module will improve in proportion to

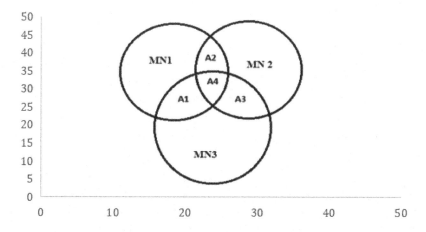

Fig. 4. Area of coverage of monitor node

the degree to which the overlapping coverage regions are cut back. Because of the circular nature in covered area of the sensor nodes. It is challenging in computation of the overlapping encircled regions, particularly those that are covered by a many of the MNs. As a direct consequence, the use of prop points has been made necessary to make it easier to calculate the coinciding coverage rate. The reinforcement points are fictitious junctures that are distributed identically within the sensor field and are a consistent distance apart from one another. Each prop point is able to calculate its distance from the MN in order to determine whether or not it is included in its coverage. As a result, we use Formula (6) & (7) to establish the communication scope rate and coinciding coverage rate:

$$K_{cover} = \frac{L_{cover}}{L} \tag{6}$$

$$K_{overlapcover} = \frac{L_{overlapcover}}{L_{cover}} \tag{7}$$

where L signifies the number of commentator points, Lcover and Loverlapcover denote the number of prop points covered by the minimum of one MN and more than one MN respectively. In our IPS-DM the sensor nodes are regarded as the prop points stated above. After all of the MNs have been chosen, the IPS-DM can be formalized. Sensors in the information distance of the DM will be referred to as adjacent of MNs when the DM stops at the MNs. Our goal is to cover as many sensors as possible with a certain number of MNs while keeping the overlapped coverage rate as low as possible. Formula (8)&(9) can be used to convert the IPS-DM object into mixed-integer programming:

$$L_{cover} = \frac{\sum_{i=1}^{n} C_i}{n} \tag{8}$$

$$L_{overlapcover} = \frac{\sum_{i=1}^{n} C_i}{\sum_{i=1}^{n} O_i} \tag{9}$$

where n indicates how many sensor nodes there are, Ci and Oi are characterized as follows,

$$C_i = \begin{cases} 1, & \text{if at least one MN covers sensor i} \\ 0, & \text{otherwise} \end{cases} \tag{10}$$

$$O_i = \begin{cases} 1, & \text{if more than one MN covers sensor i} \\ 0, & \text{otherwise} \end{cases} \tag{11}$$

4.2   Coverage Optimization Using IPS-DM

We propose an itinerary planning system (detailed plan) to find the MNs' ideal location that complies with the MN count limitations and the travelling in network route duration. This will be accomplished by finding the optimal position for each MN. Iteration is one method that may be used to get close to the ideal solution when looking for one. Finding the optimal solution might be challenging due to the fact that it has been established that the scheduling of routes for the

DM is an NP-hard problem. As a corollary, IPS is well suited to tour scheduling in WSNs. We employ easy accessibility nodes to indicate the placement of MNs, and each node represents a complete MNs selection solution. We must first validate the number of MNs due to the fixed dimension of nodes in IPS. Also, we assume that MNs can fully utilize the wirelessly transmission area, and we may determine the quantity of MNs using formula (12)

$$MN_n = \frac{S}{\pi r^2} \tag{12}$$

where S illustrates the whole region of the sensing region and r stands for sensor information distance.

For the formulation of the particles with the help of a matrix representation of the dimensions pn × (2 spn), as demonstrated below, where pn stands for the quantity of nodes.

$$P = \begin{bmatrix} P^1 \\ \cdots \\ P^n \end{bmatrix} \begin{pmatrix} \mathbf{x}^1{}_{\text{sp1}}, \mathbf{y}^1{}_{\text{sp1}} \cdots \cdots \cdots \cdots \mathbf{x}^1{}_{\text{spn}}, \mathbf{y}^1{}_{\text{spn}} \\ \cdots \cdots \cdots \cdots \cdots \cdots \cdots \cdots \cdots \cdots \cdots \cdots \\ \cdots \cdots \cdots \cdots \cdots \cdots \cdots \cdots \cdots \cdots \cdots \cdots \\ \mathbf{x}^{\text{pn}}{}_{\text{sp1}}, \mathbf{y}^{\text{pn}}{}_{\text{sp1}} \cdots \cdots \cdots \cdots \mathbf{x}^{\text{pn}}{}_{\text{spn}}, \mathbf{y}^{\text{pn}}{}_{\text{spn}} \end{pmatrix}$$

where the variables x^k_{spi}, y^k_{spi} signifies the direction of the i-th MN with the k-th node position. In each dimension, within the speed and stance limits of the node.

$$restriction(v^k_i) = (20, -20) \tag{13}$$

$$restriction(x^k_{spi}, y^k_{spi}) = (0, L) \tag{14}$$

v^k_i denotes the k-th and is particle speed and ith is dimension. While Formula (14) retains particles in the sensor field, Relation (13) suggests that nodes should not move too quickly. Define the fitness function for the IPS-DM. Positive numbers L_{cover} and $L_{overlapcover}$ cover. We adopt the fitness function as:

$$Fitness = \frac{L_{overlapcover}}{L_{cover}} \tag{15}$$

The execution steps are demonstrated using Algorithm 1.
Algorithm 1: Data gathering module (DM) execution steps
Step 1: Use random integers to initialise the virtual node and the velocity of the node.
Step 2: Calculating the fitness function using Formula 2 (15). The minor one is then selected as M_{best} after each node compares its new fitness cost to its old optimal fitness value. The minor is chosen as the common optimal result by correlating the prior ideal fitness price of each component with its most recent fitness cost, N_{best}.
Step 3: Utilizing formulas (16) and (17), revise particle position and velocity:

$$v(t+1) = \lambda v(t) + \alpha.\text{random}()(M_{best} - p(t)) + \beta.\text{random}()(N_{best} - p(t)) \tag{16}$$

$$p(t+1) = p(t) + v(t+1) \tag{17}$$

Finally, we arrive at the best approach for MN selection, as N_{best} indicates. As can be seen in Fig. 5, most sensor nodes are covered by a single MN, whereas a small number of sensor nodes are covered by many MNs. Undoubtedly, a few sensors won't be covered by any MN if they are outliers. For those uncovered sensors, we could only offer multihop transmission for data delivery. When a sensor realises that the nearest MN is not covering it. Even while multihop communication is still used by a small number of sensors, it has little effect on network performance.

4.3 Route Planning and Scheduling Module (RPM)

The Monitor Node (MN) is positioned in the deployed network to provide effective coverage. Using the Route Scheduling and Planner Module, a meta-heuristic methodology is used to plan the path for data going through the network (RPM) [19]. Initially, a travel agent (TA) was used in route planning to cover every node and create a matrix structure. at the beginning, we take the WSN as undirected graph as $G = <U, L > L$ indicates the link to virtually connect the closest MN where U specifies the collection of MNs. The matrix R representation used in this case was m $\times MN_n$, where m is the number of trips TA makes to reach each MN in the network, and MN_N is the total number of MNs. A matrix S of dimension $MN_n \times MN_n$ displays the number of virtual links that have been made between the MNs. The steps of the route planning algorithm as discussed in [19] are as follows:

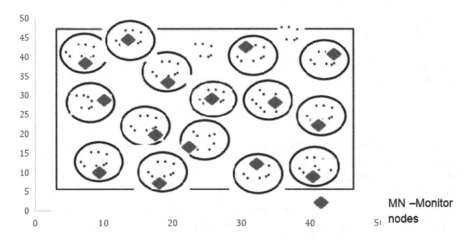

Fig. 5. MN selection using IPS-DM [1]

Algorithm 2: Route process scheduling steps

Step 1: For the initialization of Matrix R, TA traverse the network through each deployed node. The formula was used to calculate the unvisited node (18). Additionally, the matrix R contained records of the visited nodes.

$$p_{ij}^k(t) = \begin{cases} \dfrac{\phi_{ij}^{\propto}(t)*\delta_{ij}^{\beta}(t)}{\sum \text{m} \in \text{next}\phi_{im}^{\propto}(t)*\delta_{im}^{\beta}(t)}, & \text{if j} \in \text{next} \\ 0, & \text{otherwise} \end{cases} \tag{18}$$

where $p_{ij}^k(t)$ shows the chance of assigning path from MN_i to MN_j for the k-th TA in the t-th iterations. Also $\phi_{ij}^{\infty}(t)$ the utilisation of the relationship between MN_i to MN_j and $\delta_{ij}^{\beta}(t)$ depicts the separation between MN_i to MN_j which is reciprocal. $\propto$, β are taken into account when determining the link's use and inspiration. The factor determines the unvisited node by TA. *next*.

Step 2: The formula is used to determine the distance covered by TA between MNs. Since the TA must reduce the amount of travel time, we can use $x_{ij}* y_{ij}$

$$L(b^k) = \sum_{i,j \in MNs, i \neq j} x_{ij} * y_{ij} \tag{19}$$

In the calculation above, x_{ij} illustrates the separation between MN_i to MN_j whereas is illustrated by the given below equation (20).

$$y_{ij} = \begin{cases} 1, & \text{if link between } MN_i \text{ to } MN_j \text{ is covered by k-th unit} \\ 0, & \text{otherwise} \end{cases} \tag{20}$$

Step 3: The formula below was used to record the link count. The maximum number of times that steps 1–4 can be performed to visit every node is:

$$\phi_{ij}^{(t+1)} = (1 - \eta)\Delta\phi_{ij}^{(t)} + \phi_{ij}^{(t)} \tag{21}$$

$$\Delta\phi_{ij}^{(m)} = \sum_{k=1}^{m} \phi_{ij}^{(k)} \tag{22}$$

$$\phi_{ij}^{(k)} = \begin{cases} \frac{q}{L(b^k)}, & \text{if the m-TA crosses the } link_{ij} \\ 0, & \text{elsewhere} \end{cases} \tag{23}$$

here the cumulative count of the links travelled by one agent in a single travel is represented by q and the η exhibits the volatilization rate of the link count (Fig. 6).

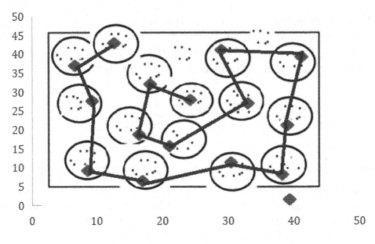

Fig. 6. Routing strategy using RPM [19]

5　Result and Comparision

5.1　Energy Usage of Various Methods

The network's energy usage is first compared using various ways. As shown in the graph below in Fig. 8, the energy consumption of the compared algorithms grows, but SHDGP with PSO (Particle Swarm Optimization) outperforms the other three methods. In comparison to TRPMC, SHDGP with PSO attains a slight improvement in energy consumption performance. SHDGP with PSO, on the other hand, has a faster rate of rising energy consumption than TRPMC. SHDGP with PSO spends the same amount of energy as IPS-DM after roughly 11000–13000 s, thus we can assume that it will outperform SHDGP with PSO in terms of energy usage after 10000 s. LEACH with GWO (Grey Wolf Optimization) uses the maximum energy since it is a hopping in multiple type of routing design that requires several cluster chiefs to send sensed data packets ages to a fixed sink over vast distances. Because MWR with ACO (Ant colony optimization), IPS-DM, and SHDGP with PSO all use mobile collectors to collect data, their energy usage is reduced to varying degrees as distinguished to LEACH with GWO.MWR with ACO specifies similar pairs for forwarding for data packets whereas LEACH with GWO requires significantly more transmission between the data collector and compatible pairings. Because IPS-DM and SHDGP with PSO are single-hop-based both conserve an amount of energy and accomplish likewise in terms of energy usage. The energy usage of mobile collectors however reduced significantly but as an alternative IPS-DM and SHDP will provide better value for the cost incurred on a real-time industrial system (Fig. 7).

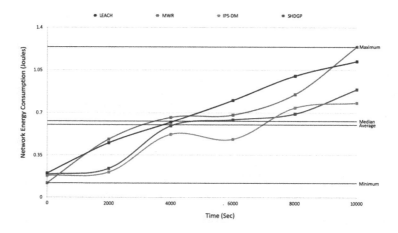

Fig. 7. Comparison energy usage

5.2 Lifespan of Network

After that, we check to see if the network can withstand many algorithms being performed on it. When a network's nodes begin to die, the network's lifespan is commonly determined. Figure 9 shows the simulation outcome. Because of this, LEACH with GWO's initial node dies after around 3200 s, whereas the other three algorithms all outlive LEACH with GWO. Cluster heads and long-distance transmission cause sensors in LEACH with GWO to fail prematurely because of unequal energy dissipation. The distance between the source node and the Data gathering module is greatly reduced when a Data gathering module is used. Due to the fact that these schemas use a mobile data collector, they have a longer network lifespan than LEACH with GWO. In MWR with ACO, the pressure on

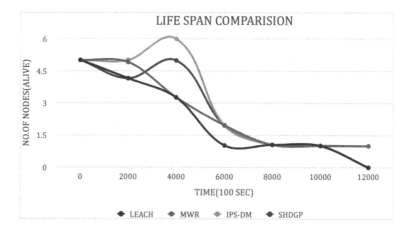

Fig. 8. Duration of the networks

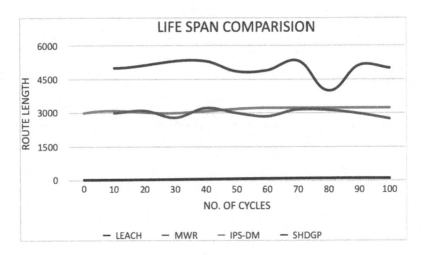

Fig. 9. Various Algorithm's life span

compatible pairs that operate as forwarders is one of the key causes for MWR with ACO's limited lifetime. Although both IPS-DM and SHDGP with PSO use single-hop communication, IPS-DM reduces the number of LMs that overlaps and enhances the mobile collector's gather efficiency.

5.3 Travel Routine Comparison

For network performance, particularly latency, route length has a significant influence. Rounds are measured by how long it takes a researcher to visit all of their local markets (LMs). Different algorithms are performed numerous times to compare the length of the planned route. Following is a diagram depicting the results of the simulation. To gather data, LEACH with GWO employs a static sink with a zero-length route. The trip route length in IPS-DM is constant since the coverage rate does not vary when the network model and transmission range are defined. Control message energy consumption has been greatly lowered as a result of this. Instead of using a loop, SHDGP with PSO creates a tree structure to tour all of the polling stations, which results in the longest possible route for each round, requiring many visits.

6   Conclusion

Route prediction in the shortest manner with a Data gathering module plays an important role in WSN applications. Here we discussed IPS-DM provided with a Data gathering module for getting the basic data of nodes. The route planning was handled by Route planning Manager which optimizes a Travel Agent to visit all the nodes deployed in the network. This makes it possible to join all of the nodes using the route with the least distance. A comparison is made between the performance of the suggested system in terms of network lifetime, energy usage, and coverage improvements.

References

1. Gao, Y., Wang, J., Wu, W., Sangaiah, A.K., Lim, S.J.: Travel route planning with optimal coverage in difficult wireless sensor network environment. Sensors **19**(8), 1838 (2019)
2. Zygowski, C., Jaekel, A.: Optimal path planning strategies for monitoring coverage holes in Wireless Sensor Networks. Ad Hoc Netw. **96**, 101990 (2020)
3. Yu, S., Zhang, B., Li, C., Mouftah, H.: Routing protocols for wireless sensor networks with mobile sinks: a survey. IEEE Commun. Mag. **52**, 150–157 (2014)
4. Galloway, B., Hancke, G.P.: Introduction to industrial control networks. IEEE Commun. Surv. Tutor. **15**, 860–880 (2012)
5. Ren, Y., Liu, Y., Ji, S., Sangaiah, A.K., Wang, J.: Incentive mechanism of data storage based on blockchain for wireless sensor networks. Mob. Inf. Syst. **2018**, 6874158 (2018)
6. Wang, J., Gao, J., Liu, W., Wu, W., Lim, J.: An asynchronous clustering and mobile data gathering schema based on timer mechanism in wireless sensor networks. Comput. Mater. Contin. **58**, 711–725 (2019)
7. Swaminathan, K., Ravindran, V., Ram Prakash, P., Satheesh, R.: A perceptive node transposition and network reformation in wireless sensor network. In: Iyer, B., Crick, T., Peng, SL. (eds.) ICCET 2022. SIST, vol. 303, pp. 623–634. Springer, Singapore (2022). https://doi.org/10.1007/978-981-19-2719-5_59
8. Butun, I., Morgera, S.D., Sankar, R.: A survey of intrusion detection systems in wireless sensor networks. IEEE Commun. Surv. Tutor. **16**, 266–282 (2014)
9. Krontiris, I., Langheinrich, M., Shilton, K.: Trust and privacy in mobile experience sharing: future challenges and avenues for research. IEEE Commun. Mag. **52**, 50–55 (2014)
10. Ravindran, V., Vennila, C.: An energy-efficient clustering protocol for IoT wireless sensor networks based on cluster supervisor management. Comptes rendus de l'Académie bulgare des Sciences **74**(12) (2021)
11. De, D., Mukherjee, A., Sau, A., Bhakta, I.: Design of smart neonatal health monitoring system using SMCC. Healthc. Technol. Lett. **4**, 13 (2016)
12. Wang, J., Zhang, Z., Li, B., Lee, S., Sherratt, R.S.: An enhanced fall detection system for elderly person monitoring using consumer home networks. IEEE Trans. Consum. Electron. **60**, 23–29 (2014)
13. Ya, T., Lin, Y., Wang, J., Kim, J.: Semi-supervised learning with generative adversarial networks on digital signal modulation classification. Comput. Mater. Contin. **55**, 243–254 (2018)
14. Ravindran, V., Vennila, C.: Energy consumption in cluster communication using MCSBCH approach in WSN. J. Intell. Fuzzy Syst. 1 (Preprint)
15. Swaminathan, K., Ravindran, V., Ponraj, R., Satheesh, R.: A smart energy optimization and collision avoidance routing strategy for IoT systems in the WSN domain. In: Iyer, B., Crick, T., Peng, S.L. (eds.) ICCET 2022. SIST, vol. 303, pp. 655–663. Springer, Singapore (2022). https://doi.org/10.1007/978-981-19-2719-5_62

16. Tirkolaee, E.B., Hosseinabadi, A.R., Soltani, M., Sangaiah, A.K., Wang, J.: A hybrid genetic algorithm for multi-trip green capacitated arc routing problem in the scope of urban services. Sustainability **10**, 1366 (2018)

17. Hu, X., Yang, L., Xiong, W.: A novel wireless sensor network frame for urban transportation. IEEE Internet Things J. **2**, 586–595 (2015)

18. Akyildiz, I.F., Sankarasubramaniam, W., Su, Y., Cayirci, E.: Wireless sensor networks: a survey. Comput. Netw. 393–422 (2002)

19. Padmapriya, S., Soundararajan, S., Arun, S., Su, Y.W., Krishnamoorthy, R.: Optimal route design for sensor network with effective area with coverage. Neuroquantology **2**, 3047–3059 (2022)

Low Power Mod 2 Synchronous Counter Design Using Modified Gate Diffusion Input Technique

Sanskriti Singh[1(⊠)], Sneha Kaushik[1], Anita Angeline Augustine[2],
and Sasipriya Palanisamy[2]

[1] School of Electronics Engineering, Vellore Institute of Technology, Chennai,
Tamil Nadu 600127, India
{sanskriti.singh2020,sneha.kaushik2020}@vitstudent.ac.in
[2] Centre for Nano-electronics and VLSI Design, VIT Chennai, Chennai, Tamil Nadu 600127,
India
{anitaangeline.a,sasipriya.p}@vit.ac.in

Abstract. The advancement in the VLSI field is more focused towards designing a low power digital system, which consumes less power and yields less power dissipation. Hence, the design of a low power sequential digital system demands low power consuming flip- flops. The use of Modified Gate Diffusion Input (MGDI) technique gets rid of the disadvantages of Pass Transistor Logic (PTL) and Complementary Metal Oxide Semiconductor (CMOS) design. In this paper the design of D flip-flop and JK flip flop using MGDI technique is performed, which demonstrates reduced power consumption and reduction in delay. Further, the same flip-flop designed using MGDI technique is being utilized to design Mod 2 synchronous counter with reduced transistor count. The simulations are performed using Cadence® Virtuoso tool with 180 nm technology library node. The performance of mod 2 synchronous counter design using MGDI technique is compared with CMOS logic style. The results demonstrate that the counter design using modified MGDI technique shows superior performance in terms of power, area and delay while compared to CMOS logic designs.

1 Introduction

In the world of sequential logic systems, flip-flops are the essential components for designing sequential circuits [1, 2]. In sequential circuit, the output at any time is dependent on the current input as well as the previous output. This makes the edge triggered memory element, the flip-flop, to be adopted widely. The combinational logic gates using various gates, CMOS latches, transmission gates etc., is utilized in configuring such a memory element [3–5]. Computers and other digital devices utilizes these circuits for storage operation and for counting events. It requires a memory element to recall its previous states. A counter architecture contains numerous flip flops [6, 7]. The number of flip-flops used and the interconnections determines the number of states and the order in which they occur for every cycle during the counter operation. In a synchronous counter, all the flip-flops are controlled by the same clock signal. As a result, all of the flip-flops change their states at the same time in a parallel fashion.

© The Author(s), under exclusive license to Springer Nature Switzerland AG 2022
V. Arunachalam and K. Sivasankaran (Eds.): ICMDCS 2022, CCIS 1743, pp. 105–113, 2022.
https://doi.org/10.1007/978-3-031-23973-1_7

Due to the increasing complexity of circuits, memory requirements are also expanding exponentially, and because of the large memory requirements in today's systems, flip-flop optimization is critical for the performance. The basic unit of data storage is the D-flip flop. Hence, this paper focuses on improving the D flip-flop speed performance and decreasing the power consumption. In general, power optimization results in increased delay, while delay optimization results in greater area. As a result, the circuit with the lowest power-delay product is regarded as the circuit with the best optimization. The literature reports various efforts being made to demonstrate D-FF implementation with the reduced power dissipation [8]. The GDI approach was chosen because it provided the best balance of power, delay, and area [9, 10].

A JK flip-flop is an important type of flip-flop since it is used to deduce all other flip-flops, such as RS, D, and T flip-flops. As a result, the JK flip-flop is also known as a Universal flip-flop. In addition the JK flip-flop also eliminates the issue of not-allowed input combinations, which is more pronounced in the case of an RS flip-flop, which pose a challenge with R = S = 1 input state by yielding inconsistent outputs. The forementioned problem is eliminated by having two feedback lines between the outputs and the inputs in the JK flip-flop. The JK flip-flop maintains its current state while the clock signal is not asserted. In addition, a JK flip-flop can be employed in designing a counter as a sequential element in data processors [3]. In today's real time applications, most of them are aimed towards battery-operated appliances, and hence it is imperative to reduce the power dissipation which is an important design limitation [4].

The ensuing sections of the paper is arranged as follows: Section II conveys a short description of GDI technique and MGDI technique circuit, Section III details mod 2 synchronous counter design, various gates and flip-flops utilized to configure it. Section IV exudes a comparative simulation result of the counter using modified GDI technique and CMOS design. Finally, Section VI concludes.

2 Gate Diffusion Input Technique

The GDI method is based on the utilization of a basic cell, as depicted in Fig. 1. The basic GDI cell resembles a CMOS inverter in appearance, and the notable few distinctions are:

- The GDI cell has four inputs: P (source/drain of pMOS), G (common gate input of nMOS and pMOS), N (source/drain of nMOS), and D (common gate input of nMOS and pMOS) (common diffusion node of both transistors).
- The bulk of nMOS is connected to N and the bulk of pMOS is connected to P.

Table 1 depicts the diverse operations performed by a single circuit by varying the input nodes. GDI technique designs require reduced transistor count; consume less power and offer increased speed of operation, but the major problem is the complexity in the fabrication process [10]. For fabricating a chip the GDI technique imposes the constraint of adopting a twin-well CMOS or Silicon on Insulator (SOI) process and not in traditional p-well process. This increases the complexity and hence, the fabrication cost. The twin well or triple well process demands increased area and separate wells for each transistor.

The modified GDI (MGDI) cell overcomes few constraints of the basic GDI cell, with the exception that the bulks of PMOS and NMOS transistors are permanently fixed

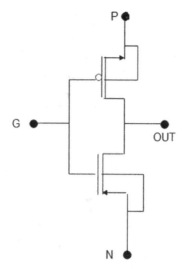

Fig. 1. Basic GDI cell

Table 1. Diverse operations of basic GDI cell

N	P	G	OUT	OPERATION
0	B	A	A'B	F1
B	1	A	A' + B	F2
1	B	A	A + B	OR
B	0	A	AB	AND
C	B	A	A'B + AC	MUX
0	1	A	A'	NOT
B'	B	A	A'B + AB'	XOR
B	B'	A	AB + A'B'	XNOR

to V_{DD} and GND respectively [9]. This allows the GDI gates to be easily realized using the standard CMOS processes. Further MGDI technique utilizes reduced transistor count as depicted in Fig. 2 and Table 2.

3   Proposed Mod 2 Synchronous Counter Design

The design of Mod 2 synchronous requires flip-flop and various other gates. Hence, various the design of gates such as AND, OR, NAND, NOR, EXOR, EXNOR etc. using MGDI technique is performed and is followed by the design of flipflops. Then, utilizing the same memory element, the counter design is performed.

Figure 3 depicts an AND gate using MGDI approach, where the port 'P' is linked to GND and the input 'B' is given to port 'N'. The input 'A' is given to port 'G'.

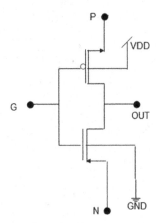

Fig. 2. Modified GDI cell

Table 2. Comparison of transistor count in modified GDI technique Vs static CMOS

FUNCTION	GDI	CMOS
INVERTER	2	2
FI	2	6
F2	2	6
OR	2	6
AND	2	6
MUX	2	12
XOR	4	16
XNOR	4	16
NAND	4	4
NOR	4	4

The NAND gate utilising a modified GDI approach is shown in Fig. 4. It comprises two modified GDI cells, with the first cell's port 'P' and gate 'G' terminal receiving an input 'A,' and the second cell's port 'N' receiving an input 'B.' The first cell's output is connected to port 'G' of the second cell, which serves as a basic inverter, complementing the first cell's output.

The NOR gate shown in Fig. 5 is made up of two modified GDI cells, with the first cell's port 'P' receiving an input of 'A' and the second cell's port 'G' receiving an input of 'B'. The first cell's port 'N' is supplied with Vdd, and the output 'nl' is linked to the second cell's port 'G,' which operates as a basic inverter, complementing the output received from the first cell.

The EXOR gate constructed with the modified GDI approach is shown in Fig. 6. It is made up of two modified GDI cells, with the first cell's port 'P' receiving an input of

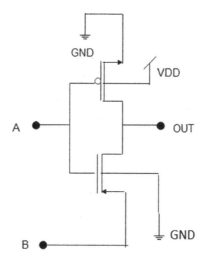

Fig. 3. AND gate using MGDI technique

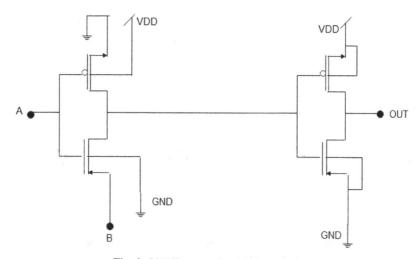

Fig. 4. NAND gate using MGDI technique

'A' and the second cell's port 'G' receiving an input of 'B'.. Port 'N' of the first cell is supplied with GND and the output 'nl' is connected to port 'N' of the second cell.

The Fig. 7 shows the logic diagram of D flip-flop which is made using four NAND gates of GDI technique and an inverter. Two NAND gates are connected in cross coupled fashion.

The logic diagram of the JK flip flop, using RS flip flop, is depicted in Fig. 8.The Boolean expressions of JK flip-flop derived from RS flip-flop are given as stated in Eq. 1

$$R = KQn; \ S = JQn \tag{1}$$

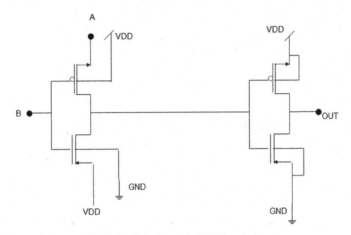

Fig. 5. NOR gate using MGDI technique

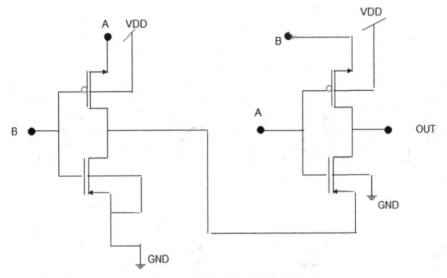

Fig. 6. Exor gate using MGDI technique

The modified GDI technique using synchronous NOR-based JK flip-flop operates at higher speed, consumes less power. Hence, offers reduced power delay product with reduced number of transistors. MGDI technique was utilized to design the NOR and AND gates.

Figure 9 depicts the Mod 2 synchronous counter, which is designed utilizing D flip-flop with modified GDI technique. It operates on the negative edge triggered clock and is connected to all the D flip flops simultaneously.

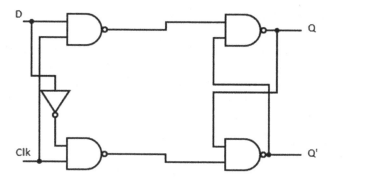

Fig. 7. Logic diagram of proposed D flip flop

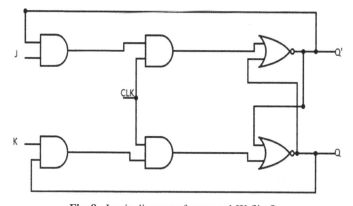

Fig. 8. Logic diagram of proposed JK flip flop

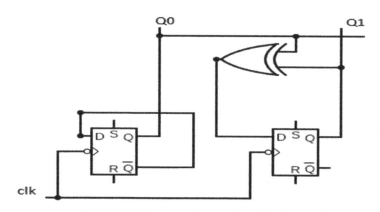

Fig. 9. MOD 2 counter design using D flip flop

4   Simulation and Analysis

The design and analysis are carried out using Cadence® Virtuoso tool with gpdk 180nm technology node. Table 3 shows the power delay and transistor count, power and delay analysis of various gates and flip-flops designed using MGDI technique Table 4 compares the performance of a counter using CMOS technology and modified GDI approach.

Table 3. Simulation results of gates and flip-flops using MGDI technique

Circuit	Transistor Count	Power(nW)	Delay (ns)
AND gate	2	32.94 nW	9.43
NAND gate	4	250.3 nW	40.05
NOR gate	4	288 nW	39.43
EXOR gate	4	272.4 nW	20.02
D flip flop	18	204.5 μW	60.25
JK flip flop	16	722.4 μW	25.53

Table 4. Performance comparison of counter designed using MGDI and static CMOS logical styles

Circuit	Mod 2 Counter using CMOS	Mod 2 Counter using MGDI
Transistor count	52	40
Power (mW)	1.39	0.8286
Delay (ns)	19.75	19.88

The design of the counter using MGDI technique demonstrates reduced transistor count of 23% over the CMOS logic style. Also, the power reduction Of 43% makes this MGDI technique an ideal choice in designing the memory elements.

5   Conclusion

The design of MOD 2 Synchronous counter using MGDI technique, for low power design is performed and analyzed. For designing the counter, various gates were designed using modified GDI technique and integrated. It is observed that the design of MOD 2 counter using MGDI technique reduces the transistor count by 43% and also offers a power reduction of 23% over the conventional CMOS design based MOD 2 Synchronous counter. The delay observation also demonstrates that the MGDI technique is faster than the typical CMOS based counter design.

References

1. DeMassa, T.A., Ciccone, Z.: Digital Integrated Circuits, Wiley Student ed., John Wiley & Sons (ASIA) Pte Ltd., p. 498
2. Morgenshtein, A., Fish, A., Wagner, I.A.: An efficient implementation of D-Flip-Flop using the GDI technique. In: 2004 IEEE International Symposium on Circuits and Systems (IEEE Cat. No. 04CH37512). Vol. 2. IEEE (2004). https://doi.org/10.1109/ISCAS.2004.132936
3. Morris Mano, M.: Digital Design. 3'd ed., Prentice Hall, pp. 272–279, 281–284,316–317
4. Sivakumar, M., Omkumar, S.: Implementation of Area & Power Optimized VLSI Circuits Using Logic Techniques. IOSR Journal of VLSI and Signal Processing (IOSR-JVSP) Vol. 7 (2017). https://doi.org/10.9790/4200-0704011523
5. Chandrakasan, A.P., Sheng, S., Brodersen, R.W.: Low- power CMOS digital design. IEEE J. Solid-State Circuits **27**, 473–484 (1992). Apr.
6. Chandrakasan, A.P., Brodersen, R.W.: Minimizing power consumption in digital CMOS circuits. Proc. IEEE **83**(4), 498–523 (1995). https://doi.org/10.1109/5.371964
7. Rabaey, J.: Low Power Design Essentials. Springer (2009)
8. Chiwandea, S.S., Keote, M.L., Katre, S.S., Bhagwate, S.H.: VLSI Design of Low Power 4 Bit Magnitude Comparator Using GDI Technique. In: Proceedings of 3rd International Conference on Internet of Things and Connected Technologies (ICIoTCT), pp. 26–27 (2018 April). https://doi.org/10.2139/ssrn.3166515
9. Patnala, T.R., Majji, S., Pasumarthi, G.K.: Optimization of CSA for low power and high speed using MTCMOS and GDI techniques. International Journal of Engineering and Advanced Technology (IJEAT) **8**(5S3) (2019). https://doi.org/10.35940/ijeat.E1062.0785S319
10. Sarkar, S., Chatterjee, H., Saha, P., Biswas, M.: 8-Bit ALU Design using m-GDI Technique. In: 2020 4th International Conference on Trends in Electronics and Informatics (ICOEI)(48184), pp. 17–22. IEEE (2020 June). https://doi.org/10.1109/ICOEI48184.2020.9142881

Analog, Mixed-Signal and RF Design

A Novel Blind Zone Free, Low Power Phase Frequency Detector for Fast Locking of Charge Pump Phase Locked Loops

Marichamy Divya⬡ and Kumaravel Sundaram[(✉)]⬡

Vellore Institute of Technology, Vellore, Tamilnadu, India
marichamy.divya2020@vitstudent.ac.in, kumaravel.s@vit.ac.in

Abstract. Phase Frequency Detector (PFD) being one of the important block of the high frequency clock generator encounters two major problems in its design. One being the dead zone and other is blind zone. The presence of the dead zone leads to phase noise. Blind zone increases the lock time of the clock generator. This paper presents a novel edge detector based PFD. In the proposed PFD, zero blind zone is achieved by eliminating the reset pulse beyond the dead zone region. The proposed PFD is designed in UMC 0.18 μm CMOS process. It consumes power of 648 μW at an operating frequency of 1 GHz. It is observed that the proposed PFD locks 43% faster than the conventional PFD.

Keywords: Phase frequency detector · Dead zone · Blind zone · Reset pulse · Clock generator

1 Introduction

High frequency clock generators commonly known as Phase Locked Loop (PLL) is being used in numerous applications across the globe that includes Wi-fi routers, televisions, Zigbee, etc. The widely used PLL is the charge pump based PLL. It consists of five blocks. PFD being the first block of the PLL detects the phase and frequency differences between the reference clock (REFCLK) generated by the crystal oscillator and the feedback clock (FBCLK) generated by the Frequency Divider (FD). It generates UP and DOWN (DN) signals. These signals are converted as a control signal (VCTRL) to the Voltage Controlled Oscillator(VCO) by the Charge pump (CP) and Loop filter (LF) which helps in the locking of the PLL loop. Thus, the ability of the PFD to detect all the phase differences in the range of $[-2\pi, 2\pi]$ is very essential as it helps in fast acquisition of the PLL and also helps in the generation of low phase noise, high frequency clock.

© The Author(s), under exclusive license to Springer Nature Switzerland AG 2022
V. Arunachalam and K. Sivasankaran (Eds.): ICMDCS 2022, CCIS 1743, pp. 117–128, 2022.
https://doi.org/10.1007/978-3-031-23973-1_8

1.1   Issues Related to Conventional PFD

Conventional PFD is shown in Fig. 1. The operation of the PFD can be easily visualised with the help of the state diagram as shown in Fig. 2.

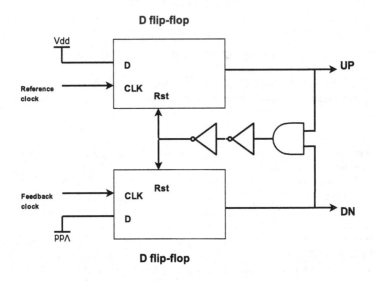

Fig. 1. Block diagram of Conventional PFD

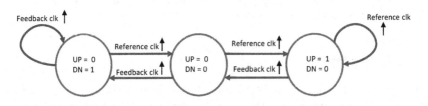

Fig. 2. State diagram

Conventional PFD encounters two issues in its architecture namely dead zone and blind zone that affects the linearity as presented in Fig. 3, thereby reducing the PFD operating range.

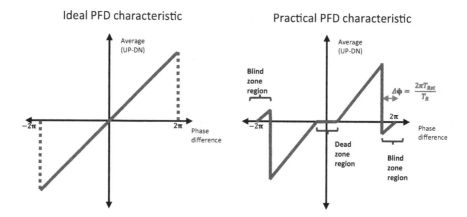

Fig. 3. PFD phase characteristic

In the PFD phase characteristics, dead zone occurs in the neighbourhood of zero phase difference. Due to the presence of finite parasitic capacitances, the PFD output doesn't have enough time to reach a particular logical level 0 or 1 (that is, 0 or Vdd) when small phase difference exists between the input clocks. Thus, PFD fails to trigger the CP leading to accumulation of static phase error until the PFD comes out of the dead zone region. This static phase error translates to phase noise in the PLL. Using finer and finer technology, the dead zone can be reduced but we cannot completely eliminate it. To eliminate completely we can add delay elements in the reset path of the PFD equal to the minimum ON time of the CP switches to turn ON. Hence, even for small phase difference, the charge pump will now be able to turn ON for correcting the phase error and making the PFD as a dead zone free circuit. Thus, increasing the delay in the reset path reduces the dead zone in the conventional PFD. As the delay in the reset path is increased, the highest frequency of operation of the PFD gets limited and also it leads to high blind zone.

The highest frequency of operation(f_{max}) of the PFD is inversely proportional to the reset path delay (T_{Rst}) and is given by [8],

$$f_{max} = \frac{1}{T_{Rst}} \tag{1}$$

Thus, high reset path delay limits the highest operating frequency of the PFD.

In the PFD phase characteristics, blind zone occurs in the neighbourhood of 2π phase difference. The PFD fails to detect the rising transition of the leading input clock signal due to high reset pulse. Thus, the PFD produces wrong output, misleading the PLL. This leads to increase in the lock acquisition of the PLL. Hence, need to eliminate the blind zone is necessary to reduce the lock acquisition which is a major concern for high speed applications. The PFD introduces wrong output for phase differences greater than $2\pi - \phi$ where,

$$\phi = \frac{2\pi T_{Rst}}{T_R} \tag{2}$$

Here, T_R = the reference clock time period.

As seen from the above equation, blind zone depends on the reset pulse. Blind zone is lower, when the reset path delay is lower. If reset path is zero, from the equation we obtain zero blind zone.

There are various PFD designs in the literature to overcome the problems of the PFD. In [5], PFD using transmission gate is designed. It is blind zone free but has an operating range of $[-\pi, \pi]$ severely affecting the PLL locking time. In [7], PFD using selective reset technique is designed to reduce the blind zone. It has a blind zone of 3 ps. In [1], differential PFD is designed. It is blind zone free but has an operating range of $[-\pi, \pi]$. In [3], composite PFD is implemented to eliminate blind zone. This leads to PLL design complexity as it requires two charge pumps and a switchable loop filter. In [9], delays were used to push the leading input clock signal edge out of the reset pulse to get the correct output to reduce the blind zone. The problem with such a design is that it may fail across process, temperature, voltage variations. In [2], edge detector is used to design the PFD. It has a reset pulse of 80 ps, thus introducing significant blind zone. In [6], latch based PFD is designed. The reset path is reduced to obtain high operating frequency and fast locking of the PLL. It has a highest operating frequency of 1.5 GHz. The presence of reset path indicates the presence of blind zone in the latch based PFD.

This paper introduces a novel blind zone free PFD using edge detector for fast locking of PLL. Section 2 introduces the proposed design. Section 3 and Sect. 4 presents the simulation results and the conclusion of the work respectively.

2   Proposed PFD

PFD requires reset pulse only in the dead zone region [4]. Thus, in the proposed circuit the reset pulse is eliminated after the dead zone region in the PFD. The circuit diagram of the novel PFD is presented in Fig. 4. In the PFD, REFCLKD and FBCLKD are the delayed version of the reference clock (REFCLK) and feedback clock (FBCLK) respectively, to completely eliminate the blind zone. RH and FH signals are generated using edge detectors. Edge detectors are used in the discharging path so as to get the correct output beyond the dead zone region. Transistors Mu4 and Md4 are used to ensure proper operation of the PFD.

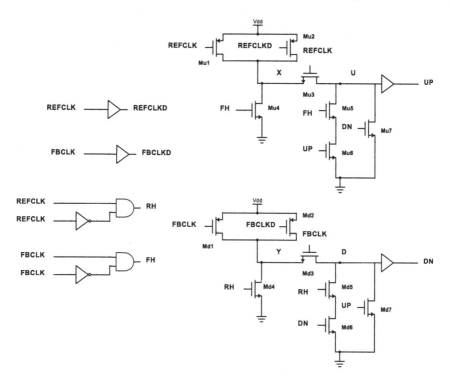

Fig. 4. Proposed PFD

2.1 PFD Operation

Let us assume REFCLK leads FBCLK. Initially node x and y are precharged to Vdd. Here, we consider two cases: (1) PFD operation beyond the dead zone region (2) PFD operation in the dead zone region.

Case 1. In Fig. 4, when REFCLK goes high, node U goes high. Thus, UP signal goes high. Transistor Md7 gets activated since, UP is high. Now, when FBCLK goes high, node D doesn't go high as it gets discharged through transistor Md7. Hence, DN is zero throughout the operation. FH gets activated since FBCLK is high. As both the transistors Mu5 and Mu6 are activated simultaneously, U is discharged to zero. Thus, UP goes low.

Hence, in the operation of PFD beyond the dead zone region, no reset pulse is generated making the PFD blind zone free.

Case 2. In Fig. 4, when REFCLK goes high, UP goes high. Since, in the dead zone region, the phase difference between REFCLK and FBCLK is small, transistor Md7 doesn't find enough time to discharge node D to zero. Thus, when FBCLK goes high, DN goes high. As the transistors Mu7 and Md7 are activated, UP and DN goes low.

Hence, in the operation of PFD in the dead zone region reset pulse is generated making PFD dead zone free.

3   Simulation Results

The proposed PFD is implemented in UMC 180 nm CMOS process. The proposed PFD consumes power of 65 μW at an operating frequency of 100 MHz and 648 μW when operated at frequency of 1 GHz. It is observed that the PFD is not sensitive to duty cycle variations of the REFCLK and FBCLK signals.

The timing diagram of the PFD is presented in Fig. 5 for a phase difference of 9.5 ns between the clocks.

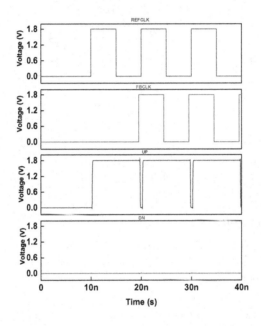

Fig. 5. PFD output when REFCLK leads FBCLK by 9.5 ns

It is observed that no signal is generated at the DN node as stated in the discussion.

The timing diagram of the PFD when REFCLK leads FBCLK by 2 ps is shown in Fig. 6. It is observed that the reset pulse is generated by the PFD when there is small phase difference.

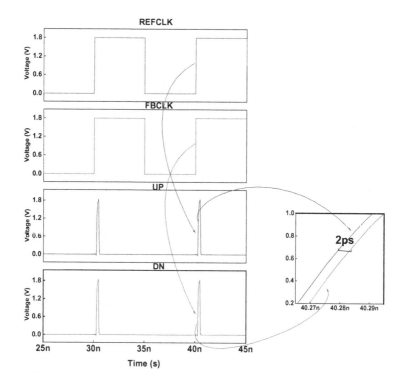

Fig. 6. PFD output when REFCLK leads FBCLK by 2 ps

In the proposed PFD, the reset pulse is generated within the dead zone region and is eliminated beyond the dead zone region. Thus, neither the dead zone nor the blind zone is present in the PFD designed in this work.

Figure 7 shows the PFD operation when REFCLK and FBCLK are in phase.

Figure 8 presents the UP and DN signals when REFCLK and FBCLK exhibits different frequencies.

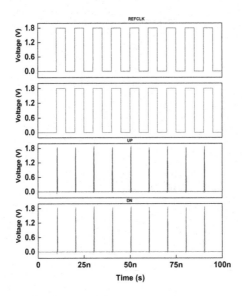

Fig. 7. PFD output when REFCLK and FBCLK are in phase

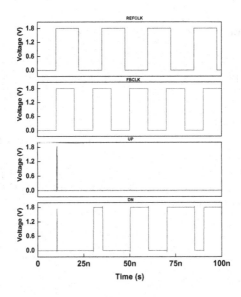

Fig. 8. PFD output when REFCLK and FBCLK signals have different frequencies

The PFD is simulated across different process corners to obtain the PFD transfer curves as shown in Fig. 9. It is found that the PFD maintains its linearity across different process corners.

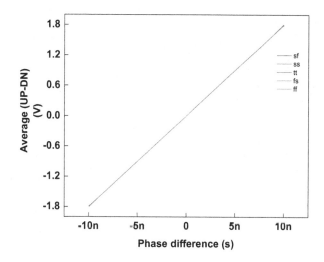

Fig. 9. PFD phase characteristic in various corners

To analyse the PFD performance in the PLL loop, it is important to design a PLL using the PFD designed in this work. The simulation setup is shown in Fig. 10.

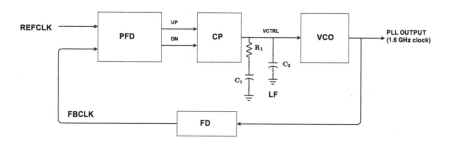

Fig. 10. Simulation setup

The PLL is designed to have an PLL OUTPUT of 1.6 GHz. The REFCLK frequency is considered as 100 MHz. The parameters of loop filter are chosen such that it has sufficient phase margin to maintain the stability of the overall PLL loop.

The conventional PFD is designed in UMC 180 nm process for the purpose of comparison. The locking of the PLL with the PFD designed in this work is shown in Fig. 11. It can be observed that the PLL locks with minimum steady state error between the UP and DN pulse which is caused due to the discrepancy between the source and sinking current of the next block, that is, CP.

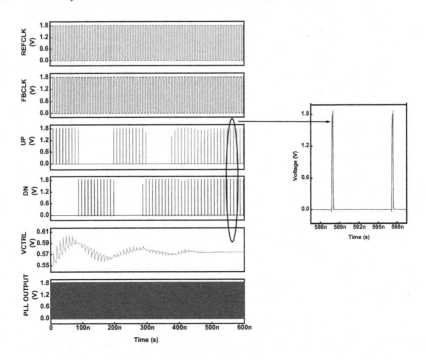

Fig. 11. PLL locking using the proposed PFD

The PLL is simulated using both the PFDs as shown in Fig. 12. It is observed that the PLL lock time using the novel PFD is 450 ns and using the conventional PFD is 790 ns.

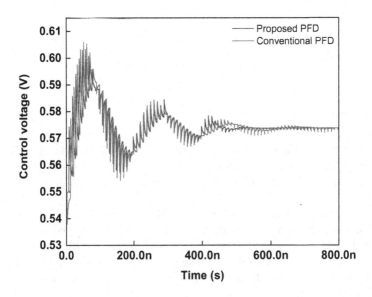

Fig. 12. Lock time of a 1.6 GHz PLL using different PFDs

The PFD designed in this paper is compared with the recent PFD designs as shown in Table 1. All the PFDs are operated at supply voltage of 1.8 V. It is observed that the PFD in [1] has an operating range of $[-\pi, \pi]$ which will severely affect the locking time of the PLL. Also, it has dead zone of 40 ps. Even though the PFD in [5] is free from dead zone and blind zone, it has an operating range of $[-\pi, \pi]$, thus leading to increase in lock time of the PLL.

Table 1. Comparison table

Designs	Technology (nm)	PFD ideal range	Blind zone (ps)	Dead zone (ps)	Power (μW)
[1]	180	$[-\pi, \pi]$	Free	40	107 @1 GHz
[7]	180	$[-2\pi, 2\pi]$	3	Free	2600 @100 MHz
[4]	180	$[-2\pi, 2\pi]$	Free	Free	1360 @1 GHz
[5]	90	$[-\pi, \pi]$	Free	Free	12.1 @100 MHz
This work	180	$[-2\pi, 2\pi]$	Free	Free	65 @100 MHz, 648 @1 GHz

In [7], the PFD architecture has an ideal operating range of $[-2\pi, 2\pi]$, but has a blind zone of 3 ps. The power consumed is 2600 μW when operated at frequency of 100 MHz which is 97.5% higher than that of the proposed PFD. In [4], the PFD is designed such that it is free from dead zone and blind zone. It has an operating range of $[-2\pi, 2\pi]$. The power consumed is 1.36 mW which is 52.3% higher than that of the proposed PFD. Thus, the PFD designed in this work has good performance when compared to the existing literatures.

4 Conclusion

In this paper, edge detector based PFD is designed and proposed. The reset pulse is not present in the PFD after the dead zone region, leading to a blind zone free PFD. The PLL using the proposed PFD acquires 43% faster locking than with the conventional PFD. The power consumption is significantly reduced when compared to the existing literatures. Thus, the designed PFD is suitable for low power high speed applications.

References

1. Abolhasani, A., Mousazadeh, M., Khoei, A.: A high-speed, power efficient, dead-zone-less phase frequency detector with differential structure. Microelectron. J. **97**, 104719 (2020)
2. Chen, W.H., Inerowicz, M.E., Jung, B.: Phase frequency detector with minimal blind zone for fast frequency acquisition. IEEE Trans. Circuits Syst. II: Express Briefs **57**(12), 936–940 (2010)
3. Abdul Majeed, K.K., Kailath, B.J.: PLL architecture with a composite PFD and variable loop filter. IET Circuits Devices Syst. **12**(3), 256–262 (2018)

4. Kuncham, S.S., Gadiyar, M., Sushmitha, D.K., Lad, K.K., Laxminidhi, T.: A novel zero blind zone phase frequency detector for fast acquisition in phase locked loops. In: 2018 31st International Conference on VLSI Design and 2018 17th International Conference on Embedded Systems (VLSID), pp. 167–170. IEEE (2018)
5. Majeed, K.A., Kailath, B.J.: Low power, high frequency, free dead zone PFD for a PLL design. In: 2013 IEEE Faible Tension Faible Consommation, pp. 1–4. IEEE (2013)
6. Mansuri, M., Liu, D., Yang, C.K.: Fast frequency acquisition phase-frequency detectors for Gsamples/s phase-locked loops. IEEE J. Solid-State Circuits **37**(10), 1331–1334 (2002). https://doi.org/10.1109/JSSC.2002.803048
7. Ravi, H., Mukherjee, J.: PFD with improved average gain and minimal blind zone combined with lock-in detection for fast settling PLLs. Microelectron. J. **116**, 105233 (2021)
8. Soyuer, M., Meyer, R.G.: Frequency limitations of a conventional phase-frequency detector. IEEE J. Solid-State Circuits **25**(4), 1019–1022 (1990)
9. Tak, G.Y., Hyun, S.B., Kang, T.Y., Choi, B.G., Park, S.S.: A 6.3-9-GHZ CMOS fast settling PLL for MB-OFDM UWB applications. IEEE J. Solid-State Circuits **40**(8), 1671–1679 (2005). https://doi.org/10.1109/JSSC.2005.852421

Performance Improvement of H-Shaped Antenna for Wireless Local Area Networks

S. Kannadhasan[1](✉) ⓘ and R. Nagarajan[2]

[1] Department of Electronics and Communication Engineering, Study World College of Engineering, Tamilnadu, India
kannadhasan.ece@gmail.com
[2] Department of Electrical and Electronics Engineering, Gnanamani College of Technology, Tamilnadu, India

Abstract. An H-shaped antenna with a clear and lightweight configuration is suggested for frequencies from 2.06 GHz to 5.0 GHz are used for wireless local area networks (WLAN) implementations. The first step in designing a microstrip antenna is deciding on a functioning frequency and a suitable substrate. The antenna's operating frequency must be carefully selected. The proposed antenna must operate inside the desired frequency range. The antenna structuring process continues with the selection of a suitable substrate. The electromagnetic characteristics of the antenna determine the height and dielectric of the substrate. FR4 was chosen as the dielectric material for the construction. Since the measurements of the antenna are inversely proportional to the dielectric constant, a high dielectric substrate limits the antenna's dimensions. Microstrip feedline is the feeding process used. The planned antenna estimated impedance bandwidths are 35.9% (742 MHz) based at 2.45 GHz and 9.2% (520 MHz) centered at 5.0 GHz. At 4.2 GHz and 5.0 GHz, the measured gain is 10.2 dBi and 8.2 dBi, respectively.

Keywords: H-Shaped · VSWR · WLAN · Gain and radiation pattern

1 Introduction

The Microstrip patch antenna has a dielectric layer on one side and a land plane on the other. The microstrip patch antenna is ideally suited for applications such as wireless communication systems, GPS, mobile phones, pagers, radar, and satellite communications systems due to advantages such as light weight, low profile flat configuration, lower production cost, and the potential to interface with microwave integrated circuit technologies. The exponential proliferation of military and commercial communications applications necessitates the construction of compact antennas that are interconnected. Interactive, data, and video services will be accessible voice anywhere, wherever, thanks to high-speed wireless. Recent developments in high-density RF and microwave circuit packaging have enabled the technologies to serve these applications. System specifications for faster data transfer in compact architectures with lighter drive technology, which often leads to increased design solutions Microwave modules, circuits, and radiating elements with high integration density, small scale, and optimal efficiency are needed for

© The Author(s), under exclusive license to Springer Nature Switzerland AG 2022
V. Arunachalam and K. Sivasankaran (Eds.): ICMDCS 2022, CCIS 1743, pp. 129–136, 2022.
https://doi.org/10.1007/978-3-031-23973-1_9

great designs [1–5]. Because of their compactness and other benefits, microstrip patch antennas have gotten a lot of coverage in the last two decades for use in personnel contact systems and synthetic aperture radar applications. The development of new strategies to address the shortcomings of patch microstrip antennas, the most limiting of which is narrowband, has become a major focus of study. Growing bandwidth and reducing return loss without increasing the antenna's size is critical to applying this antenna to modern mobile communications networks, and it must be done [6–10].

Many communications and radar applications need double circular or linear polarization, and the simplicity of microstrip antenna technology has resulted in a broad range of designs and techniques to meet this requirement. The market for small cell phone terminals has increased in recent years. Phones the size of a purse have started to emerge on the market, and as the need for increased electron mobility grows, so will the need for small phones. One of the most significant considerations of portable mobile communication systems is the antenna size. Because of its low volume and thin profile, Micro-strip Patch Antennas (MPA) are commonly used. The length and width resonance of an MPA decide its intensity. Patch size reduction may be accomplished by utilizing substrate content with a strong permittivity and a low substrate height. The antenna's gain is reduced in this case due to the poor radiation quality [11–15].

Because of its small footprint, low profile, and other characteristics, microstrip patch antennas can be used in a variety of wireless applications in the future. It's made up of a dielectric layer substance sandwiched between the radiating metal patch and the ground plane. Any conducting stone, such as copper, gold, or silver, may be used for the patch and the ground [16, 17]. They have a light weight planar frame, are mechanically stiff, and can be manufactured at a low cost using printed circuit board technology. Satellite, radar, MIC, and MMIC (Monolithic Microwave Integrated Circuits) are a few examples of microstrip antenna applications.

2   Development Stages of H-Shaped Structure

Micro-strip patch antennas have the physical features to be used for smart phones, Bluetooth device networks, and cellular local networking in the current scenario. Communication technology has been even faster, and has improved the efficiency of Smartphone apps. A micro strip patch antenna is presented in this article. The frequency spectrum of a given antenna is from 2.06 GHz to 5.0 GHz, with 2.45 GHz serving as an intermediate frequency between those frequencies. The antenna is built on a thin substrate with a thickness of 1.6mm and a dielectric constant of 4.4 is shown in Table 1. This dielectric constant is commonly used in high-pressure thermoplastics for strong strength-to-weight ratios. The return loss for frequencies 2.45 GHz is -20.02dB respectively. The antenna is low-cost, light-weight, and has a low profile, with a radiation efficiency of over 80%. This antenna meets all of the consistency criteria. The frequency spectrum mentioned above is suitable for telemetry, WI-max, and WLAN applications. With one feed stage, the H-shape micro strip dual band patch antenna is shown in Fig. 1. For improved return loss, we add a 50Ω load to one connector.

$$W = \frac{V_O}{2f_r} \sqrt{\frac{2}{\varepsilon_r + 1}} \tag{1}$$

$$L = \frac{V_o}{2f_r\sqrt{\varepsilon_{reff}}} - 2\Delta L \tag{2}$$

where

V_0 = Speed of Light

Δ_{reff} = Effective Permittivity

$2\Delta L$ = Extension in Length

$$f_c = \frac{c}{2L\sqrt{\varepsilon_r}} = \frac{1}{2L\sqrt{\varepsilon_0\varepsilon_r\mu_0}} \tag{3}$$

where

ε_0 = Permittivity of free space

ε_r = Permittivity of the dielectric substrate

μ_0 = Permeability of free space

The operating frequency of a patch antenna considering L and W is given by

$$f_r = \frac{c}{2\sqrt{\varepsilon_{reff}}}\left[(\frac{n}{L+2\Delta L})^2 + (\frac{m}{w+2\Delta w})^2\right]^{1/2} \tag{4}$$

Table 1. Design of antenna parameters

Sl. No	Parameters	Value
1	L	13.75 mm
2	W	18.2 mm
3	Substrate dielectric material	FR-4 epoxy
4	Substrate dielectric constant	$\varepsilon_r = 4.4$
5	Ground Plane	40 mm*40 mm
6	Thickness or Height	1.6 mm
7	Loss tangent (δ)	0.02
8	Operating frequencies	2.06 GHz, 2.45 GHz, 4.02 GHz and 5.0 GHz

The addition of Defected Ground Structure would undoubtedly improve the antenna's efficiency. DGS (Defected Ground Structure) is a defect or fractal form that is purposefully included in the ground plane. It may be non-periodic or periodic in nature. When it's applied, it alters the antenna's electrical and magnetic properties, making it easier to tune with lower frequencies while growing the antenna's scale. For low-frequency applications, the antenna scale would be bigger. Methods such as engraving slots in the field and patch usage of a dielectric substrate with a strong relative permittivity have been used to satisfy the criterion. However, the above results in the depletion of surface waves. The antenna often has slits and slots on the patch's radiating edges for two or three wavelengths of activity with reduced duration. To increase the characteristics of several frequencies of service, an H-shaped slot is typically used along the feed axis. With unequal weapons, the H-shaped strip line used as feeding has provided a high gain value with dual band frequency of activity and optimum scale. The microstrip patch antenna usually has a small bandwidth, which can be increased by adding stacked parasitic components. It not only increases the antenna's bandwidth, but also its gain performance.

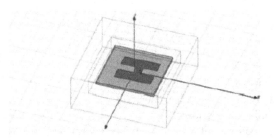

Fig. 1. H-shaped structure antenna

3 Results and Discussion

The return Loss effects are displayed in Fig. 2 for WLAN, Wi MAX, and telemetry applications. The light colour indicates a broad resonant current distribution, while the dark colour indicates a tiny one. This means that the proposed antenna is independent of the antenna radiator's resonant current route. The antenna to meet the bandwidth and frequency requirements thanks to the stated independence. The proposed antenna's simulated radiation pattern at each resonant frequency the suggested antenna is found to be suitable for telemetry applications with a bandwidth of 2.45 GHz, as well as WIMAX applications with a bandwidth of 5.0 GHz. The measurements of the planned antenna are 40 mm × 40 mm. It is small in scale and can be used for a variety of purposes. The antenna's gain would be less than −30 dB is shown in Fig. 3. The quality of the antenna is 80 %.

The following three parameters were chosen for this design: resonant frequency (fr) = 2.06 GHz, dielectric constant (r) = 4.4, and dielectric substrate height (h) = 1.6 mm. The first move is to choose a dielectric material, which in this case is FR4. After that, using measured mathematical proportions, the modelled patch was formed on the substrate content. Following that, a 50 micro strip feed line is drawn on the same substrate. The patch antenna was then slightly modified with a new inset gap with the same inset eating. This antenna's findings were also noted and are presented. Furthermore, the antenna effects were examined by cutting a notch in the patch antenna, which revealed a substantial increase in the patch antenna's return loss and bandwidth.

The resonant frequency of the Microstrip patch antenna is 2.45 GHz. The layer is made of FR4, which has a dielectric constant of 4.2. The substrate height is held at 1.6mm. The antenna input impedance of an inset fed microstrip patch antenna is determined by the direction of the feed. As a result, we use the connection to calculate the VSWR as

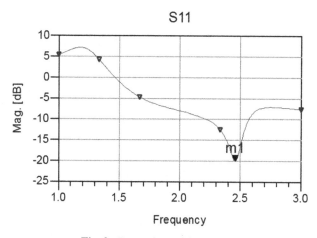

Fig. 2. Return loss of the antenna

seen in Fig. 4 to achieve 50 impedance. The Radiation pattern is shown in Fig. 5. The antenna is made up of three layers or blocks: the first is the radiating disc, the second is the microstrip line, and the third is the substrate.

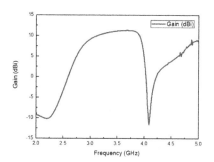

Fig. 3. Gain of the antenna

The difference of return loss versus frequency plot of a basic inset fed Microstrip antenna is seen in Fig. 2. The antenna has a frequency of 2.06 GHz. The return loss is -20.02 dB, and the average bandwidth is 9.95 percent at (2.067 GHz) (that is 42.9 MHz). The variance of VSWR versus frequency plot of a basic inset feed microstrip antenna is seen in Fig. 4. The antenna resonates at 2.06 GHz and has a VSWR of 1.6974 at the frequency (2.06 GHz).

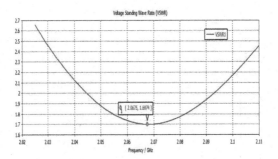

Fig. 4. VSWR of the antenna

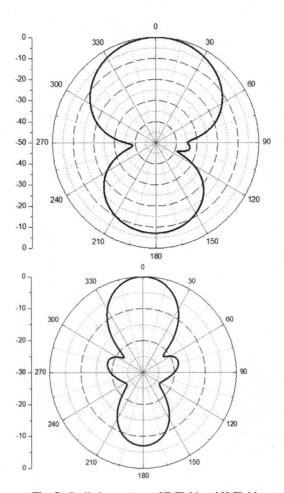

Fig. 5. Radiation pattern of E-Field and H-Field

4   Conclusion

The proper impedance balancing through stub feedline at the antenna's source point achieves the antenna's broadening. This strong return loss and decent bandwidth may be beneficial for a variety of wireless applications. For a successful broad band wireless use, a basic antenna will be useful. Because of their light weight, lightweight scale, and ease of manufacture, their uses are almost endless. One drawback is their inherently limited bandwidth. Latest research and trials, on the other hand, have discovered strategies to overcome this stumbling block. Modification of the patch form and experimenting with substrate parameters are among the methods that have been used. Bandwidth, gain, and VSWR are all critical characteristics for broadband applications. Other types of patch shapes could be used in the future to increase the antenna's overall efficiency without sacrificing the optimized parameters in the action.

References

1. Singh, I., Tripathi, V.S.: Micro strip Patch Antenna and its Applications: a Survey. Int. J. Comp. Tech. Appl. 2(5), 1595–1599
2. Basu, S., Abhishek Goswami, A.S.: Dual Frequency Hexagonal Microstrip Patch Antenna. International Journal of Scientific and Research Publications 3(11) (November 2013)
3. Keshav Gupta, K.J.: Different Substrates Use in Microstrip Patch Antenna-A Survey. International Journal of Science and Re-search (IJSR) ISSN (Online): 2319–7064 Impact Factor 3, 358 (2012)
4. Singh, S., Agarwal, N., Navendu Nitinand, A.K.J.: Design consideration of Microstrip Patch Antenna. International Journal of Electronics and Computer Science Engineering ISSN-2277–1956
5. Namrata Dewangan, R.V.: Equilateral Triangular Micro strip Patch Antenna Using Different Substrates. International Jour-nal of Advance Foundation and Research in Computer (IJAFRC) 1(3) (March 2014). ISSN 2348 –4853
6. Anscy, S.: Slot Microstrip Antenna for 2.4 GHz RFID Reader Application. Int. J. Adv. Res. Electro. Commu. Eng. 2(5), 527–531 (2013)
7. Bhardwaj, A.M., Yadav, A.K., Upmanu, V.: Design and simulation of U-shaped Microstrip patch antenna with bandwidth enhancement and size reduction. Int. J. Adv. Eng. Res. Technol. 4(2), 23-29 (2016)
8. Roy, A.A., Mom, J.M., Igwue, G.A.: Enhancing the bandwidth of a microstrip patch antenna using slots shaped patch. American Journal of Engineering Research 2(1), 33–37 (2011)
9. Ranjan Das, C., Sahoo, S.: Design of compact 1-slit microstrip patch antenna for wimax application. Int. J. Innov. Res. Technol. Sci. 2(1), 42-45 (2011)
10. Balanis, C.A.: Antenna Theory, Analysis and Design, 1st Edition. Wiley (1997)
11. Reja, A.H.: Study of micro strip feed line patch antenna. Antennas and Propagation International Symposium 27, 340–342 (December 2009)
12. Kraus, J.D., Marhefka, R.J.: Antennas for All applications, 5th Edition. Tata Mcgraw Hill (2005)
13. Kannadhasan, S., Shagar, .A.C.: Design and Analysis of U-Shaped Microstrip Patch Antenna. 3rd IEEE International Conference Advances in Electrical, Electronics, Information, Communication And Bio-Informatics, (AEEICB17), February 27-28 (2017). ISBN: 978-1-5090-5434-3©2017 IEEE Published for IEEE Digital Explore Libaray

14. Kumar, N., Parkash, D., Panwar, S., Khanna, R.: Design of a Compact U-shape Planar Antenna with Multiple Branches. 5th IEEE International conference
15. Kannadhasan, S., Nagarajan, R.: Performance improvement of antenna array element for mobile communication, Waves in Random and Complex Media (2022). https://doi.org/10.1080/17455030.2022.2036867
16. Keskin, N., Saka, U., Imeci, T.: U-Shaped Microstrip Patch Antenna. April 10–14, 2012 - Columbus, Ohio 2012 ACES
17. Robinson, J., Rahmat-Sami, Y.: Particle swarm optimization in electromagnetic. IEEE Transaction on antennas and propagation **52**(2), 397–407 (February 2004)

Emerging Technologies

Real-Time Rainfall Prediction System Using IoT and Machine Learning

Shreya Atul Sharma, Abantee Gangopadhyay, K. T. Koushik, K. C. Srihariapriya[✉],
and J. Christopher Clement

Department of Communication Engineering, School of Electronics Engineering, Vellore
Institute of Technology, Vellore, Tamil Nadu, India
srihariapriya.kc@vit.ac.in

Abstract. Predicting rainfall is a difficult and uncertain undertaking that has a big impact on civilization. Proactively reducing human and financial loss can be aided by timely and accurate projections. For nations like India, whose economy is heavily based on agriculture, accurate rainfall forecasting is crucial for the efficient use of water resources, crop productivity, and the early design of water structures.

In this paper, we have proposed a "SMART CAP", i.e. a wearable device for farmers. This will consist of a microcontroller (Arduino UNO) which will record atmosphere parameters with help of various sensors and other components while they are working on the field. These values will be logged into THINGSPEAK via the internet with help of a Wi-Fi module. The values recorded at various instants of time are then fed to the Machine Learning models used. The models have been trained using existing datasets. The input data is then processed by our trained prediction model and the predictions are shown on THINGSPEAK which can be accessed from anywhere in the world.

Keywords: Rainfall · Atmosphere · Machine learning · Sensors · Regression analysis

1 Introduction

Extreme variations in rainfall have a drastic effect on agriculture. Drought can kill crops while heavy rainfall can increase soil erosion and spoil the plantations. Because of how unpredictable the atmosphere is, statistical tools do not accurately predict rainfall. Droughts and floods affect our farmers significantly. Farming is a long process and depends majorly on the rainfall cycle which makes our main focus to be farmers of our nation. The optimum amount of water is required for the survival of crops. Since rainfall is a major factor affecting crop yield, there is a need to predict rainfall for potent use of water resources for crop productivity to give a better yield and decrease agricultural loss.

Existing rainfall prediction methods are large scale/locality based and don't sense atmospheric parameters for a specific place which can sometimes be a problem. Our project is essentially a wearable cap which can be worn by the farmer while working on

© The Author(s), under exclusive license to Springer Nature Switzerland AG 2022
V. Arunachalam and K. Sivasankaran (Eds.): ICMDCS 2022, CCIS 1743, pp. 139–158, 2022.
https://doi.org/10.1007/978-3-031-23973-1_10

the field and this device automatically logs atmospheric parameters to the THINGSPEAK cloud and predicts the rainfall for that day using its trained model.

This makes our device portable and specific to the farmer's location and hence eases the decision of the farmer of how much he has to water the plants and avoid agricultural loss. The main aim of our project is to predict the rainfall of a specific location by analysing the area"s atmospheric parameters like temperature, humidity, dew point, wind speed and alert the farmer about the type of rainfall to expect on that day and water his plants accordingly or at least be prepared and take preventive measures thereby decreasing agricultural loss to the farmers of or nation.

2 Literature Survey

In [1] B. Revathi et al., proposed a method that consists of two modules. The accuracy of CART is found to be much greater than that of IDA. Both the methods are completed and it is concluded that the CART is the most accurate algorithm, which achieves statistically and significantly higher predictive accuracy than IDA.

In [2] Ogochukwu Ejike et al. includes logistic regression-based models that predict the likelihood of rain occurring the following day using weather parameters that may be observed using inexpensive equipment. By selecting the relevant input variables (weather parameters), selecting acceptable model building approaches, and validating the best fit model using metrics like AUC and Hosmer-Lemeshow test, a logistic regression model analysis has been used to predict rainfall for the following day.

In [3] Mrinmoy Sadhukhan et al. utilized of inexpensive IOT gadgets with GPS. The server stores the sensed data in order to forecast meteorological variables for any location of interest, including temperature, humidity, air pressure, etc. SVM, KNN, DNN, Ridge, Linear Regression, and ANN are some of the computing tools that have been tested on supplied parameters and a correlation between conditions has been developed in a designated geographic area for the following days.

Wanie M Ridwan et al. [4] focuses on two techniques: (1) autocorrelation function (ACF)-based rainfall forecasting and (2) projected error-based forecasting of rainfall based on both historical and future rainfall data. Both approaches use several algorithms to find the best forecast for rainfall across various time frames. The results showed that cross-validation with BDTR improved the outcomes for Method 1. The model's performance will be more accurate the more input it receives. For approach 2, results varied while using various normalisation strategies, and it was determined that the best model was produced by utilising LogNormal normalisation in combination with BDTR and DFR.

Moulana Mohammed et al. [5] used a predictive model that is used for predicting precipitation amount. The project's main focus was on estimating rainfall, and it is believed that SVR is a useful and flexible strategy that can assist the client in overcoming challenges related to the distributional characteristics of fundamental factors, the geometry of the data, and the common problem of model overfitting. Finally, it was determined that SVR (Support vector regression) provides a superior expectation technique to MLR (Multiple Linear Regression). SVR can be useful in situations where MLR is unable to detect the non-linearity in a data set. In order to evaluate the models' execution, they also evaluated Mean Absolute Error (MAE) for both MLR and SVR models. The tuned SVR model provides the best expectation, as expected.

C. Z. Basha, N. Bhavana et al. [6] have used deep learning techniques to predict the rainfall. Multilayer Perceptron and Auto-Encoders are two deep learning methods that were employed. RMSE (Root MSE) and MSE are used to evaluate the effectiveness of the approach (Mean Square Error). The findings indicate that our suggested design performs better than alternative techniques in terms of MSE and RMSE. The MSE and RMSE comparisons to other models can be used to gauge accuracy. Artificial neural networks are better to all other methods because of the nonlinear correlations in rainfall datasets and their capacity to learn from the past.

In X, the system makes more precise rainfall predictions for the approach. The information set is gathered. Rainfall forecasting can be done using two methods. The first is a machine learning strategy called LASSO regression. The second method uses a neural network. This system compares both processes at first, and then it provides the outcome using the best algorithm. The correctness of both of these procedures was evaluated, and error types like MSE, MAE, R-SQUARED, and RSME were also taken into account. The system comes to the conclusion that LASSO regression is more accurate than artificial neural network regression. After comparison, LASSO's accuracy is approximately 94 percent, compared to ANN's accuracy of 77%.

Based on several weather characteristics considered as the independent variables, Hiyam Abobaker Yousif Ahmed et al. [8] employed a multivariate linear regression model to estimate the rate of precipitation (i.e., rainfall rate) for Khartoum state. The obtained data demonstrate that during the testing period, there was a considerable reduction in the mean square error between the actual and anticipated values of the rainfall precipitation rate (PRCP). According to research, it is 85 percent when using the same amount of test data as training data and 59 percent when using additional test data. Additional investigation is required for the explanation of this decline. It might suggest, for instance, that the model in use requires more training data.

Gaurav Verma et al. [9] measured temperature, humidity and light density. Using NodeMCU and the ESP8266-01 module, the sensors' detected data is uploaded to a ThingSpeak cloud server. A customised HTML webpage with the data is also used to monitor the current numbers. The machine learning environment is set up using a logistic regression model. Utilizing previously recorded sensor data values, this model is trained. Lastly, either logic "0" or "1" is sent as a predicted result. An LED is used for this purpose.

The research work carried out by M.K. Nallakaruppan et al. [10] revolves around understanding the weather prediction inconsistencies in linear regression algorithms and time series models. The goal of this research project is to develop a trustworthy decision tree and time series analysis-based weather prediction model.

Thirumalai, Chandrasegar, et al. [11] analyse past rainfall amounts in relation to growing seasons and forecast future rainfall. There are three plant seasons: Rabbi, Khalif, and Zaid. To anticipate early, the line regression method is applied. When one variation is known and the other can be anticipated using line regression, the Rabbi and the kharif are used as variables. Future agricultural seasons are forecast using the normal and mean deviations. These programmes will help farmers decide what crops to harvest based on the growing season.

Nikhil Tiwari, Anmol Singh et al. [12] used machine learning algorithms which include Neural Networks, Random Forests, XGBoost, Boosted Trees, and Support Vector Machines for predictive analysis and estimated them using the most widely used parameters i.e. MAE and r2 score. With the help of ensemble machine learning algorithms, an attempt was made to outperform the prior outcomes, and successful outcomes were attained utilising conventional techniques by fine-tuning various hyperparameters.

B.B. Meshram, Valmik B. Nikam et al. [13] Instead of being compute-intensive, the data mining strategy for rainfall prediction model is data-intensive. When compared to well-known compute-intensive models, the model shows to be the most accurate. Data mining promises to be extremely efficient since it reduces compute overhead, allowing for the analysis of very large amounts of data in comparably little time. The paradigm does not require a high-performance cluster or supercomputing environment; it can be implemented on commodity hardware. By creating a hybrid model using several data mining techniques, or even by merging computer-based models with the data mining models, the accuracy of the model can be improved.

Sunil Kaushik, Akashdeep Bhardwaj, Luxmi Sapra et al. [14] developed a study that analyses the three popular machine learning (ML) algorithms KNN, ELM, and SVM and looks for solutions to real-world issues. It is clear that SVM produced the best results with the lowest ET, MAE, and RMSE and predicted values that closely matched the observed rainfall curve. Due to the intricate weight calculation in the buried node, ELM had taken the longest. ELM was discovered to be CPU heavy; CPU consumption was seen to rise by 15–20% while running ELM, whilst CPU usage for KNN barely climbed by 5%. If the data collection had been larger and the number of parameters had been greater than tin, the KNN and ELM might have done better. If the data collection and the number of parameters had been larger than they were in the current study, the KNN and ELM might have performed better.

For the Indian dataset, R. Kingsy Grace, B. Suganya et al. [15] suggested a rainfall prediction model using Multiple Linear Regression (MLR). Multiple meteorological parameters are present in the input data, which allows for more accurate rainfall prediction. The parameters used to validate the suggested model are the Mean Square Error (MSE), accuracy, and correlation. The suggested machine learning model outperforms existing techniques in the literature, according to the results.

Moncef Bouaziz, Emna Medhioub, Elmar Csaplovisc et al. [16] proposed study, in which SPI used input from satellite CHIRPS precipitation data to track dryness from 1981 to 2019 over several time ranges (1, 3, 6, 9, 12, 15, 18, and 24 months). SPI was used as input for ELM algorithms in the forecasting of meteorological droughts.

An investigation of the effectiveness of rainfall rate and rainfall rate variability prediction systems has been presented by Pedro Garcia-del-Pino, Domingo Pimienta-del-Valle, Ana Benarroch, José M. Riera, et al. [17]. The approach to estimate inter-annual variability in Recommendation ITU-R P.678-3 has been evaluated against the experimental yearly variance of rainfall rate and has achieved a satisfactory coincidence. In various instances, this strategy has been used to explore the usefulness of monthly and seasonal variability, with generally positive results. The comparison of the model of inter-annual variability with the experimental variances of the yearly ECCDFs of rainfall rate determined from measurements in Spain likewise produced satisfactory findings.

L. Shaikh, K. Sawlani et al. [18] made a prediction, which was then used to study the Mumbai area using a feed-forward network. A three-layered network has been built to create artificial neural network-based predictive models. The experimental study yielded the following finding: An ANN's MSE falls as its number of neurons rises. Out of the three tested algorithms, BPA is the best. Performance-wise, the multi-layer approach outperforms the single-layer algorithm. Tools should be utilised to implement the prediction algorithms because they provide an alternative to BPA.

Aswin S, Geetha P, Vinayakumar R et al. [19] suggested modelling and predicting the Global Monthly Average Precipitation for 10368 Geographic Locations around the world for 468 Months using LSTM and ConvNet Architectures. RMSE and MAPE errors can still be decreased with fine accuracy by adding more hidden layers. The data projected for upcoming months would be accurate enough to be relied upon for meteorological purposes.

Manandhar S et al. [20] have used supervised machine learning techniques and downsampling techniques for rainfall prediction. They have determined the several ground-based weather characteristics that are crucial for the forecasting of rain events. To investigate the interdependency of these variables, a thorough analysis is conducted. They have included meteorological variables, seasonal and diurnal effects, and both in the model. All of the traits are important for classifying rainfall, and some of them have the ability to predict rainfall as well.

Akbari Ansanjan et al. [21] proposed a foundation in order to forecast precipitation in a short term (0–6 h).

The proposed framework comprises of a precipitation estimation method (termed as PERSIANN algorithm) to determine the anticipated rain rates and an enhanced deep learning model (termed LSTM) to forecast continuous CTBT images. Over the CONUS, three case studies are examined, including Florida, Oregon, and Oklahoma. The outcomes of our suggested model (LSTM/LSTM-PER) were contrasted with a number of baseline models in the initial phase of the evaluation of forecasting abilities. When compared to alternative extrapolation-based and numerical methods, the findings from LSTM/LSTM-PER show better statistics.

High quality SLR was employed by Aftab S et al. [22] to achieve their goal of presenting concise information on the needed research topic for a specific amount of time. For an effective SLR, a thorough research approach with step-by-step instructions is required. By focusing on data mining approaches, this study presented a thorough systematic mapping as well as a critical analysis of recent research in the field of rainfall prediction from 2013 to 2017. It was determined that improving, optimising, and integrating data mining techniques is essential to investigate and resolve these issues.

Liyew, C.M et al. [23] analyzed the existing machine learning algorithms suitable for accurate rainfall prediction. The data gathered from the meteorological station in Bahir Dar City, Ethiopia, was used to demonstrate and test tree machine learning techniques such MLR, FR, and XGBoost. Using the Pearson correlation coefficient, the pertinent environmental characteristics for rainfall prediction were chosen. The input variables for the machine learning model utilised in this paper were the chosen features. The three machine learning methods (MLR, RF, and XGBoost) were compared, and the findings indicated that the XGBoost was a superior fit for daily rainfall amount prediction utilising specific environmental data.

Radar observations of rainfall and their use in hydrological research are the main focus for the paper by W.F. Krajewski et al. [24]. Input to runoff and flood prediction models, validation of satellite remote sensing algorithms, and statistical characterization of extreme rainfall frequency all depend on radar-rainfall products. The framework for reflectivity-based rainfall estimation, including the assessment of radar-rainfall estimate uncertainty, is examined together with issues of radar-rainfall product development and the theoretical and practical needs of validating radar-rainfall maps and new radar technologies.

Nikhil Raj et al. [25] concentrated on learning the changes in the typical rainfall pattern of a river basin crucial to comprehending the hydrological cycle and water budget of the basin. The present study used monthly rainfall data for 34 years gathered from 28 rain gauge stations to evaluate the general rainfall pattern in the Bharathapuzha River basin of Kerala's Malabar coast. In the final years of the study, the basin's annual rainfall, southwest monsoon rainfall, and pre-monsoon rainfall all indicate a considerable decline. The main causes of the variance are thought to be changes in the local environment and the global climate.

A comparison of statistical and neuro-fuzzy network models for predicting the weather in Göztepe, Istanbul, Turkey, is presented in this publication by M. Tektaş et al. [26]. Nine years of data (2000–2008) containing daily average temperature (dry–wet), air pressure, and wind speed were utilised to create the models. They employed ARIMA models and the Adaptive Network Based Fuzzy Inference System (ANFIS). When comparing the performance of ANFIS with ARIMA models using the MAE, RMSE, and R2 criteria, it has been found that ANFIS produces better outcomes.

In this paper Enireddy.Vamsidhar et al. [27], based on humidity, dew point, and pressure, a back propagation neural network model was used to forecast rain in India. The data was split into two thirds for training and one third for testing. Rainfall is forecasted in the future using accuracy statistics.

The real-time dataset is used to test the hypothesis put forth by S. Santhosh Baboo et al. [28]. The comparison of the results with the actual operations of the meteorological department demonstrates that our model has the potential to be successfully applied to temperature forecasting. Real-time weather data processing suggests that the BPN-based weather forecast has outperformed official local weather service forecasts as well as guidance forecasts from numerical models.

In peninsular India, new rainfall intensity-duration-frequency (IDF) correlation were produced in the study by Daniel Dourte et al. [29]; the effects of runoff and groundwater recharging owing to changes in rainfall features are explored. In Hyderabad City, the capital of Andhra Pradesh, two data sets were used from a gauge: hourly rainfall data for the 19 years from 1993 to 2011 and daily rainfall data for the 30 years from 1982 to 2011. Daily data were used for trend analysis of threshold-based rainfall events, whereas hourly data were used to update rainfall IDF connections.

This paper by Mohini. P. Darji et al. [30] offers a thorough analysis and comparison of the many neural network topologies that scientists have employed to forecast rainfall.

The challenges with implementing various neural networks for yearly, monthly, and daily rainfall forecasts are also covered in the article. The publication also provides many accuracy metrics that academics use to assess the effectiveness of ANN.

In this research work by S. Narejo et al. [31], in order to discover the best network model for the intended forecasting task, various time series dependent Recurrent NARX-ANN models are built and trained with dynamic parameter settings. The Mean Square Error (MSE) value over training, validation, and test data sets is used to evaluate network performance.

In this paper by Sankhadeep Chatterjee et al. [32] a two-step procedure has been used. The feature collection is reduced and the most promising features for rainfall prediction are found using the Greedy forward selection technique. The data is first clustered during the training phase using the K-means algorithm, and then a distinct Neural Network (NN) is trained for each cluster. In terms of a number of statistical performance measuring criteria, the suggested two step prediction model (Hybrid Neural Network or HNN) has been contrasted with MLP-FFN classifier. The information needed for the experiment is acquired between 1989 and 1995 by the Dumdum Meteorological Station in West Bengal, India.

The project by Sunil Navadia et al. [33] uses Hadoop's predictive analysis to try and estimate the likelihood of rain. The suggested method works as a tool that effectively predicts the future rainfall with minimum, maximum, and average rainfall using rainfall data from a vast amount of data as input. In order to evaluate risk under a certain set of conditions and assign a score or weight, predictive analytic models identify correlations among numerous components in a data collection. These score/weight patterns in the history data can be used to forecast the future.

This paper by Sam Cramer et al. [34] outlines a novel approach for predicting rainfall using genetic programming (GP). A new GP that is specifically designed for this problem area analyses the effectiveness of the GP and MCRP on 21 different data sets of European cities. Results show that GP performs much better than MCRP overall.

This paper by Pratap Ganachari et al. [35] suggests a conventional neural network (CNN)-based rainfall prediction model for an Indian dataset. Multiple meteorological parameters are present in the input data, allowing for more accurate rainfall prediction. The parameters used to validate the suggested model are the Mean Square Error (MSE), accuracy, and correlation. The suggested machine learning model outperforms existing techniques in the literature, according to the results.

3 Proposed Methodologies

3.1 Multiple Linear Regression

Multiple linear regression (MLR is a statistical technique that uses several independent or explanatory variables to predict the value or response of output variable. Modeling the linear relationship between the response (dependent) variable and the explanatory (independent) variables is the objective. For our model the independent variable is precipitation level and dependent variables are temperature, humidity, wind speed, dew point and this model is trained with data of past 3–4 months. This is the training phase, after this our model is ready to take live input data of mentioned dependent variables and predict precipitation level.

$$yi = \beta 0 + \beta 1 x i 1 + \beta 2 x i 2 + \ldots + \beta p x i p + \epsilon \qquad (1)$$

where, for $i = n$ observations:

yi = dependent variable

xi = explanatory variables

$\beta 0$ = y-intercept (constant term)

βp = slope coefficients for each explanatory variable

ϵ = the model's error term (also known as the residuals)

3.2 Logistic Regression

A distinct approach to classification tasks is Multinomial logistic regression, which uses a linear combination of the observed features and some problem-specific factors to compute the probability of each possible value of the dependent variable. Hence applying this concept here can give us a categorical prediction depicting rainfall as "No Rain", "Drizzles", "Moderate Rains", "Heavy Rainfall". This can be easily understandable by farmers as it is in very simple terms. In the same way as linear regression, it is first trained and then ready for use and has the same variables as linear regression but the method is different as it uses a sigmoidal function and a cross entropy function.

$$P = \frac{1}{1 + e^{-(a+bX)}} \qquad (2)$$

P = probability of a 1

e = base of the natural logarithm

a, b = parameters of the model

X = independent variable

3.3 Block Diagram

In Fig. 6, we used an LM35 temperature sensor to get live inputs of temperature and humidity which were fed to the Arduino. The results obtained were converted into CSV files and later used for rainfall prediction using the algorithms mentioned above.

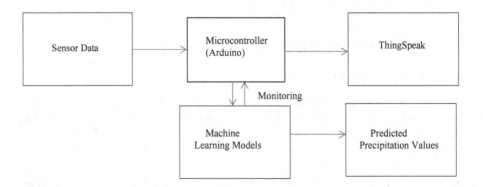

4 Results and Discussion

4.1 Machine Learning Results

Logistic Regression

Here we have used multinomial logistic regression in order to classify the rainfall level into one among "No Rain", "Drizzles", "Moderate Rains" and "Heavy Rainfall", after analyzing the parameters. Logistic regression based analysis of our dataset shows the below trends in each parameter.

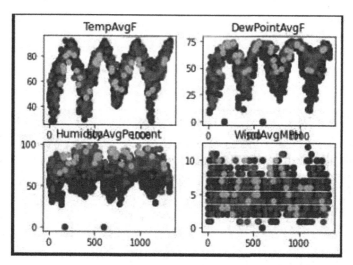

Fig. 1. Recorded parameters- average temperature, average dew point, average humidity and average wind speed

In Fig. 1, the parameters recorded have been plotted over a span of 1000+ days.

The following table shows the actual precipitation value vs. the predicted value. Values 1–4 correspond to the level of precipitation. 0 refers to No Rain and 4 means Heavy Rains (Table 1).

The accuracy score calculated between the test data and predicted data was found to **80.6%**.

Classification report and confusion matrix are metrics restricted to classification algorithms. The primary diagonal in the confusion matrix represents the true positives and negatives. In the proposed model, the values in the primary diagonal are found to be significantly higher than the secondary diagonal. In the classification report all the parameters were found to have satisfactory values as shown.

In Fig. 2, the confusion matrix summarizes the performance of the classification algorithm (Logistic Regression) by comparing the actual and predicted values with help

Table 1. Actual vs predicted values of logistic regression algorithm

Actual	Predicted
1	3
1	1
1	3
3	1
1	1
1	1
1	2
1	1
1	2
3	1

```
from sklearn.metrics import classification_report
from sklearn.metrics import confusion_matrix
print(confusion_matrix(Y_test,Y_pred))
print(classification_report(Y_test,Y_pred))

[[235    2    4    0]
 [ 20    3   17    0]
 [  7    2   27    1]
 [  0    0   11    1]]
               precision    recall  f1-score   support

           1       0.90      0.98      0.93       241
           2       0.43      0.07      0.13        40
           3       0.46      0.73      0.56        37
           4       0.50      0.08      0.14        12

    accuracy                           0.81       330
   macro avg       0.57      0.47      0.44       330
weighted avg       0.78      0.81      0.77       330
```

Fig. 2. Confusion matrix and classification report of logistic regression

of a matrix. The precision, recall, F1 Score, and support of the trained classification model are displayed in the classification report.

Linear Regression

Since this is a regression based model, we can determine the exact amount of rainfall after analyzing the recorded parameters for a particular day.

After feeding the training data into the model, for a set of custom input data it will generate the amount of precipitation (in inches) (Fig. 3).

```
inp = np.array([[85], [80], [77], [80], [77], [74], [85], [85],
[68], [29.68], [10], [7], [3], [2], [20], [4], [31]])
inp = inp.reshape(1, -1)

print( The precipitation in inches for the input is: , clf.predict(inp))
```

```
The precipitation in inches for the input is: [[0.9015007]]
```

Fig. 3. Precipitation level for custom inputs

Observed trends in precipitation level and other parameters were plotted for visualization of data.

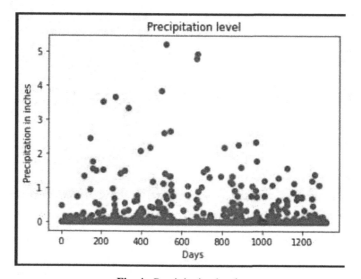

Fig. 4. Precipitation levels

In Fig. 4, precipitation level is observed over a span of 1000+ days. Precipitation level on the 1000th day was found to be nearly 0 (Fig. 5).

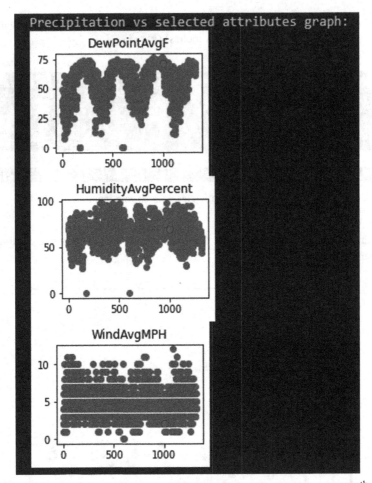

Fig. 5. Visualizing trends in other parameters. Their corresponding values for the 1000th day have been marked.

Some of the most commonly used performance metrics in regression algorithms are mean squared error, mean absolute error and R^2 error. Typically, values ranging from 0.2–0.5 are considered satisfactory (Figs. 7, 8 and 9).

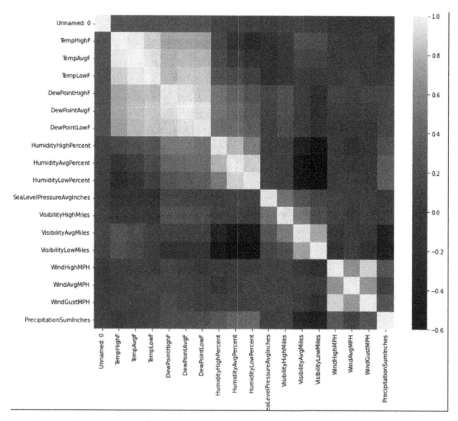

Fig. 6. Heatmap which shows the interdependence of the parameters on one another.

```
Mean absolute error = 0.18127552308397782
Mean squared error = 0.14022695383326256
R2 score = 0.23816537120308434
```

Fig. 7. Obtained values of the metrics

The following table shows the actual precipitation value vs. the predicted value of rainfall (in inches) (Table 2).

Table 2 Comparison of actual precipitation value and predicted precipitation value

	Actual	Predicted
0	0.00	-0.016891
1	0.67	0.680491
2	0.00	0.164693
3	0.00	0.074152
4	0.00	0.050031
...	...	...
325	0.00	-0.032371
326	0.00	0.123558
327	0.23	0.304002
328	0.00	0.062908
329	0.00	0.027698

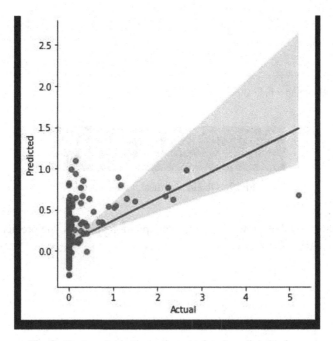

Fig. 8. Scatter plot between the actual and predicted values.

4.2   ThingSpeak Results

Sensor Values

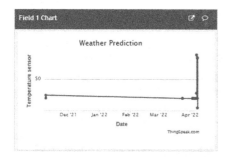
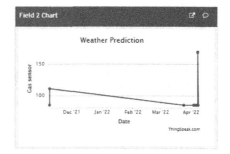
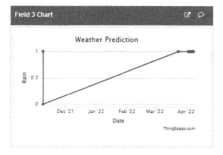

Fig. 9. Live values recorded by sensors over a period of time.

Precipitation Values
(Figures 10, 11 and 12, Table 3).

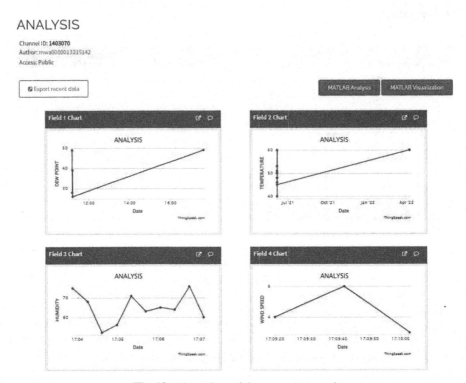

Fig. 10. Live values of the parameters used

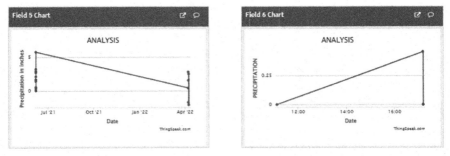

Fig. 11. Trends in precipitation levels over a period of time

Fig. 12. Exact amount of rainfall on the basis of a set of live measured values using linear regression.

5   Comparison

5.1   Linear Regression

Table 3. Comparison of

Proposed Model		Rainfall prediction using multiple linear regressions model by hiyam abobaker yousif ahmed	
Actual	Predicted	Actual	PREDICTED
0.07	0.181058	0.00	0.808
0.00	-0.1562002	0.00	0.800155
0.00	0.4223529	0.00	0.246736
0.00	0.015646	0.00	0.500647
0.00	0.052387	0.00	0.725022
0.00	0.000799	0.00	0.649510
0.00	0.04	0.00	0.3394
0.00	0.17	0.00	0.366929
0.00	0.14	0.00	-0.092754

5.2 Logistic Regression

Parameter	Proposed Model	Full	Lasso	AIC	BIC
Accuracy(%)	81	86.67	84.76	87.62	87.62
F1 score(%)	93	66.67	38.46	66.67	62.86

6 Extension of the Project

An advancement to this project would be to implement the hardware setup(cap) with wifi module to get live updates and further develop a smart band that can be worn by farmers to show the rainfall status of the day on their wearable smart band. As this status is already updating live on the ThingSpeak channel our next work to implement this would be to do web scraping and read this specific field and display it on this band.

7 Conclusion

The choice of algorithm ultimately depends on the nature of the prediction. For the above kind of input data and required output, linear regression gives more accurate results than logistic regression. A poor rainfall forecast might have an impact on agriculture, particularly farmers, whose entire harvest depends on the weather. Agriculture is always vital to every economy. Predicting the rain with some degree of accuracy is therefore possible. There are several machine learning approaches in use, however the accuracy of rainfall predictions is always a cause for concern. In the future, this system can be used to help in the agriculture and food industry as it will help farmers predict the outcome of their plot. It will also improve weather prediction systems and there might be personalized apps to regulate people in day to day life. These apps can be integrated into the working of organizations centred around agriculture and other businesses related to it. Since agriculture is often related to the economy of a country, accurate weather prediction will provide great help to the lives of those directly involved in the processing as well as most other citizens.

8 Comments/suggestions Made by the Session Chair

Since a selected amount of readings were taken and the rest were values based on the observed trend, the proposed model is not fully realistic or reliable. If we try and make a complete dataset out of sensor readings and then utilize it, it will be much more effective and helpful to people in real life.

References

1. Revathi, B., Usharani, C.: Rainfall prediction using machine learning classification algorithms. Int. J. Creat. Res. Thoughts (IJCRT) **9**(1) (Jan 2021)
2. Ejike, O., Ndzi, D.L., Al-Hassani, A.-H.: Logistic regression based next- day rain prediction model. In: International Conference on Communication and Information Technology (ICICT2021) – Basra – IRAQ (2021)
3. Sadhukhan, M., Dasgupta, S., Bhattacharya, I., An intelligent weather prediction system based on IoT. 2021 Devices for Integrated Circuit (DevIC). Kalyani, India (19–20 May 2021)
4. Ridwan, W.M., Sapitang, M., Aziz, A., Kushiar, K.F., Ahmad, A.N., El-Shafie, A.: Rainfall forecasting model using machine learning methods: case study Terengganu, Malaysia. Ain Shams Eng. J. (Jun 2021)
5. Mohammed, M., Kolapalli, R., Golla, N., Maturi, S.S.: Prediction of rainfall using machine learning techniques. Int. J. Sci. Technol. Res. **9**(01) (Jan 2020)
6. Basha, C. Z. , Bhavana, N. , Bhavya, P., Sowmya, V.: Rainfall prediction using machine learning and deep learning techniques. In: 2020 International Conference on Electronics and Sustainable Communication Systems (ICESC), pp. 92–97 (2020). https://doi.org/10.1109/ICESC48915.2020.9155896
7. Dutta, K., Gouthaman, P.: Rainfall Prediction using Machine Learning and Neural Network. Int. J. Recent Technol. Eng. (IJRTE) **9**(1) (May 2020). ISSN: 2277-3878
8. Ahmed, H.A.Y, Sondos, W.A.M.: Rainfall prediction using multiple linear regressions model. In: International Conference on Computer, Control, Electrical, and Electronics Engineering (ICCCEEE) (2020)
9. Verma, G., Mittal, P., Farheen, S.: Real time weather prediction system using IOT and machine learning, 978-1-7281-5493-0/20/$31.00 ©2020. IEEE
10. Nallakaruppan, M.K., Kumaran , U.S.: IoT based machine learning techniques for climate predictive analysis. Int. J. Recent Technol. Eng. (IJRTE) **7**(5S2), (January 2019). ISSN: 2277-3878
11. Thirumalai, C., et al.: Heuristic prediction of rainfall using machine learning techniques. In: 2017 International Conference on Trends in Electronics and Informatics (ICEI). IEEE (2017)
12. Tiwari, N., et al.: A novel study of rainfall in the indian states and predictive analysis using machine learning algorithms. In: 2020 International Conference on Computational Performance Evaluation. IEEE (2020)
13. Valmik, B., et al.: Modeling rainfall prediction using data mining method. In: 2013 Fifth International Conference on Computational Intelligence, Modelling and Simulation. IEEE (2013)
14. Kaushik, S., et al.: Predicting annual rainfall for the Indian state of Punjab using machine learning techniques. In: 2020 2nd International Conference on Advances in Computing, Communication Control and Networking (ICACCCN), 978-1-7281-8337-4/20/$31.00 ©2020. IEEE
15. Grace, R.K., et al.: Machine learning-based rainfall prediction. In: 020 2nd International Conference on Advanced Computing and Communication Systems (ICACCS), 978-1-7281-5197-7/20/$31.00 ©2020. IEEE
16. Bouaziz, M., et al.: A machine learning model for drought tracking and forecasting using remote precipitation data and a standardized precipitation index from arid regions. J. Arid Environ. **189**, 104478 (2021). Received 8 December 2020; Received in revised form 17 February 2021, Accepted 18 February 2021, 2021 Elsevier Ltd
17. Garcia-del-Pino, P., et al.: Evaluation of recent prediction models using a long-term database of rainfall rate data. In: 2017 11th European Conference on Antennas and Propagation (EUCAP), 978-88-907018-7-0/17/$31.00 ©2017. IEEE

18. Shaikh, L., et al.: A rainfall prediction model using Articial neural network. **5**(1) (Apr 2017). © 2017, IJSRNSC

19. Aswin, S., et al.: Deep learning models for the prediction of rainfall. In: 2018 International Conference on Communication and Signal Processing (ICCSP)

20. Manandhar, S., Dev, S., Lee, Y.H., Meng, Y.S., Winkler, S.: A data-driven approach for accurate rainfall prediction. IEEE Trans. Geosci. Remote Sens. **5**(11), 9323–9331 (2019)

21. Akbari, A.A., Yang, T., Hsu, K., Sorooshian, S., Lin, J., Peng, Q.: Short-term precipitation forecast based on the PERSIANN System and LSTM recurrent neural networks. J. Geophys. Res.: Atmos. **123**(22), 12–543 (2018)

22. Aftab, S., Ahmad, M., Hameed, N., Salman, M., Ali, I., Nawaz, Z.: Rainfall prediction using data mining techniques: a systematic literature review. Int. J. Adv. Comput. Sci. Appl. **9**(5), 143–150 (2018). https://doi.org/10.14569/IJACSA.2018.090518

23. Liyew, C.M., Melese, H.A.: Machine learning techniques to predict daily rainfall amount. J. Big Data **8**(1), 1–11 (2021). https://doi.org/10.1186/s40537-021-00545-4

24. Krajewski, W.F., Smith, J.A.: Radar hydrology: rainfall estimation. Advances in water resources, **25**(8–12), 1387–1394 (2002)

25. Nikhil Raj, P.P., Azeez, P.A.: Trend analysis of rainfall in Bharathapuzha river basin, Kerala. India. Int J Climatol **32**, 533–539 (2012)

26. Tektaş, M.: Weather forecasting using ANFIS and ARIMA models. Environ. Res. Eng. Manag. **51**(1), 5–10 (2010)

27. Vamsidhar, E.: Prediction of rainfall using backpropagation neural network model. Int. J. Comput. Sci. Eng. **02**(04), 1119–1121 (2010)

28. Baboo, S.S., Shareef, I.K.: An efficient weather model using artificial neural network. Int. J. Environ. Sci. Dev. **1**(4), 321–326 (2010)

29. Dourte, D., Shukla, S., Singh, P., Haman, D.: Rainfall intensity-duration- frequency relationships for Andhra Pradesh, India: changing rainfall patterns and implications for runoff and groundwater recharge. J. Hydrol. Eng. **18**(3), 324–330 (2013)

30. Darji, M.P., Dabhi, V.K., Prajapati, H.B.: Rainfall forecasting using neural network: a survey. In: 2015 International Conference on Advances in Computer Engineering and Applications (ICACEA), pp. 706–713. IMS Engineering College, Ghaziabad, India

31. Narejo, S., Pasero, E.: Time series forecasting for outdoor temperature using nonlinear autoregressive neural network models. J. Theor. Appl. Inf. Technol. **94**(2), 451–463 (2016)

32. Chatterjee, S., Datta, B., Sen, S., Dey, N.: Rainfall prediction using hybrid neural network approach. In: 2018 2nd International Conference on Recent Advances in Signal Processing, Telecommunications & Computing (SigTelCom), pp. 67–72

33. Navadia, S., Yadav, P., Thomas, J., Shaikh, S.: Weather prediction: a novel approach for measuring and analyzing weather data. In: International Conference on I-SMAC (IoT in Social, Mobile, Analytics and Cloud) (I-SMAC 2017), pp. 414–417

34. Cramer, S., Kampouridis, M., Freitas, A.A., Alexandridis, A.: Predicting rainfall in the context of rainfall derivatives using genetic programming. In: 2015 IEEE Symposium Series on Computational Intelligence, pp. 711–718

35. Ganachari, P., et al.: Int. J. Sci. Res. Comput. Sci. Eng. Inf. Technol. **7**(4), 208–212 (July–August 2021)

Performance Analysis of Image Caption Generation Using Deep Learning Techniques

Shweta S. Patil[1] , B. Srinivasa Varma[1] , G. Devadasu[2] ,
C. H. Hussaian Basha[3(✉)] , M. J. R. Inamdar[1] , and S. S. Salman[1]

[1] Department of E&TC, Nanasaheb Mahadik College of Engineering, Walwa, India
principal@nmcoe.org.in
[2] CMR College of Engineering and Technology (Autonomous), Hyderabad, India
[3] Nitte Meenakshi Institute of Technology (Autonomous), Bengaluru, India
sbasha238@gmail.com

Abstract. In recent years, Artificial Intelligent (AI) is rapidly developed. The image caption is attracting the attention of many scientists. It is very interesting work. Automatically generating image caption into the natural language description according to the objects observed in the image. This is the part of scene understanding. Since, understanding is the combination of computer vision and natural language processing. The text is processed by using Recurrent Neural Network (RNN) with clubbed single dimensional feature obtained from Convolutional Neural Network (CNN) model. Given the data is given to trained model and last output is predicted. For the experiment of image captioning Flickr8k dataset is used.

Keywords: Convolutional neural network · Image captioning · Rectifier Linear Unit (ReLU) · Recurrent Neural Network (RNN) · Visual Geometry Group (VGG16)

1 Introduction

The people use the languages for describing their opinions. Some are use the images and some are videos. The generation of sentences using the image is the biggest task in today's situation. But it can help in many applications. The image captioning takes double task. In image caption generation, the picture description is depend on the objects an also the relations between the image and situations. Both situations are most important for the image captioning.

The watching of the image can represent different ways like set of edges, shape of the object, and intensity of vector. In image captioning work first task is feature extraction for the given input image. Feature extraction is done by using the CNN model. The factures of CNN are spectral, shape feature, and texture feature. According to this parameters, the features extraction is done in CNN. In feature extraction reduce the numbers of features and create new features. For the feature extraction, the image size is 224 * 224. If any image size is different, first convert in it standard size and then features are extracted.

© The Author(s), under exclusive license to Springer Nature Switzerland AG 2022
V. Arunachalam and K. Sivasankaran (Eds.): ICMDCS 2022, CCIS 1743, pp. 159–170, 2022.
https://doi.org/10.1007/978-3-031-23973-1_11

Using the feature extraction system accuracy is increases and also increase the speed of system. In the CNN different models are present for feature extraction such as AlexNet, VGG16, and VGG19 etc.

In this work VGG16 is used. Using deep learning easily understand the unknown structures. For the good representation use the multi layered model. In this work, Flickr 8k data set is referred. The every image contains five tokens. This tokens are in understand language such as English. The image caption techniques has many applications such as image search tools where the automatic captions can help the searching for images based on the search string provided. So, here, captions can be generated first from images and ten searching can be done using search string is provided. The guidance device – the seen can be converted in text and the text is converted in to voice. This application is used for the blind people. The self-driving cars, it can boost the self-driving system. In web development, CCTV etc. Image captioning is the multi layered techniques in involves both convolutional and recurrent neural network. The encoder and decoder pipeline model is used in the natural machine translation. The input text or raw martial data is converted into the fixed length vector. This data is decoded to generate the output text. In the machine translation, the encoder and decoder can work parallel for the learning and evaluating the model.

The input and output sentence are similar in structure (order of the word is same). For the translation, the fixed length embedding is used. In this work, the CNN model is used for rich representation of the input image for embedding to fixed length vector. For this representation different many tasks are used. First pre-training image classification with hidden layers CNN model is used. CNN model and the hidden layer output is given to the RNN model is used for sentence generation. This model is also known as natural image caption. The sentence generation is start from image feature extraction. In python programming, data pre-processing is done. NLTK is used for the data pre-processing.

The natural language generation present one of the main issue in natural language processing. It is wide range in its applications and also the different task such like speech recognition (speech to text), word sense disambiguation, spam detection, named entity recognition, dialogue system, and machine translation etc. Natural language generation still the open research issue. The natural language processing mention the branch of artificial intelligence and computer science. It is the rule based (linguistics computational) model of human, and also including the machine learning and deep learning techniques. In the real time summarize the text, text generation, text translation in one language to another language is completely done in the NLP.

In python programming language more tools and libraries are present for the NLP. More programmers are found the NLTK or natural language toolkit. There are different dataset used in NLTK. Both libraries are open source. In this proposed work NLTK library is used. Word Embedding is the natural language processing (NLP) technique. In the word vectoring, the individual word are represented real valued vector. This vectors are pre-defined vector space. Each word is mapped with one new vector, this vectored value is assemble with the neural network. There are different steps in word embedding such as embedding layer, word2vec, and glove.

In embedding layer document text file is required. This layer is used in front of the neural network, and this network is used back propagation algorithm. Initially, the vector space is small. Second layer is word2vec. It is the statistical model for text corpus to word embedding. This method is developed in 2013 by Tomas Mikolov, et al. The response of this work was very effective. Third layer is Global Vector (GloVe), this is used for word representation. Learning representation of the data is based on the deep learning. The deep learning is the part of machine learning.

Bilingual Evaluation Understudy (BLEU) is the algorithm which is used for evaluating the quality of text. Depending on the BLEU score accuracy can be calculate. Score of BLEU in between zero and one. NLTK gives the implementation of BLEU score. In the dataset, the actual captions are present but after the image captioning model the predicted captions are generated. This two captions are compared and then BLEU score is generated. In this comparison each word is compared. NLTK library provides function called sentence BLEU which can be used to evaluate sentence in questions with one or more numbers of reference list of tokens. Here, the objectives are the first one is develop model for object classification from image using neural network, and second one is co-relate image feature and test description using neural network. The third, and fourth objectives are generate image captioning using trained model, and evaluate performance using user feedback test performance and validation test.

2   Literature Survey

Image Caption Generation is very important in today's situations. By using this there are many applications such as Image search, helping for blind people etc. In recent years many captioning techniques are developed by different scientist. They doing better results also. The ILSVRC is content many field. He et al. was proposed one architecture in 2014 [1]. Microsoft's AI Lab used the pipeline perspective to picture captioning in 2015 [2]. For the feature extraction, the CNN model is used. For the best word matches the Multiple Instance Learning (MIL) is used. The CNN highlights and RNN encoder are utilized in the PC vision assignments which is called Neural Image Caption (NIC).This is done by Vinyals et al. [3].

Correspondences among language and visual information. Their arrangement model depends on a novel blends of CNN over picture areas, Bidirectional Recurrent Neural Network (BRNN) over sentences, and an organized target to adjust the two modalities through a multimodal inserting. By utilizing state-of-the-art-method, the outcomes are equivalent in Flickr8k, Flickr30k and MSCOCO in databanks [4]. State-of-art-method model is more exchanged by Jonathan et al. [5] in 2015 when they proposed a thick inscribing task in which every locale of a picture was recognized and a bunch of portrayals produced. Another model which utilized a profound CNN and two separate LSTM networks was developed by Wang et al. [6] in 2016.

One of the most recent work was inspired by NIC model and was proposed by Xu et al. in 2016 [7]. They was inspired by the advancements in the field of object identification and machine translation. In the past few years, the progress is also done in image captioning. BLEU score is used for accuracy matrix [8]. Vedanta et al. was developed in 2015, the BLEU is gently changed by consensus-based image description evaluation [9]. Ali EI Housseini was proposed in 2017, automatic target recognition using the Synthetic Aperture Radar (SAR). In this work, convolutional auto encoder is used for image processing. The system accuracy become the 93% [10]. Kelvin Xu was developed in 2014, the attention based model that automatically learn to describe the content of the image. In the attention model both soft and hard attention model was generated. That validate using the state-of-the-art performance [11]. Junhua Mao was proposed in 2015, the multilevel Recurrent Neural Network (m-RNN). In this work, the two models was developed. The deep convolutional network is used for image and sentence generation deep recurrent neural network [12]. Benjamin Z. Yao is developed in 2010, the caption is generated from the image and video. In this work, they are using different stages. And-or-graph (AOG) is the heart of the work. AOG is represent the graphical representation. The AOG contains parts, objects, and sense [13].

Girish Kulkarni et al. was proposed in 2011, the automatically mining and huge text group to get statistical model for description language. The Conditional Random Fields (CRF) model is generated for sentence generation [14]. Binqiang Wang et al. was proposed remote sensing image (RSI) captioning in 2019. Five sentences are used for generating sentence dataset. But in the remote sensing the mainly objects are river, mountains etc. In RSI no daily life images are present they are completely different. Template based method is used for the sentence generation. It also include the retrial based method and RNN based method for sentence generation [15].

3 Proposed Methodology

The technique identify from the blind people. The features are extracted and trained using the CNN model. This training data is stored in the data bunch. There are two data bunch present. One for image data and another is text data bunch. The test images is compare to the trained model. Then the output sentence is generate in natural language. The caption generate in the command prompt window. Figure 1 shows the block diagram of the proposed work.

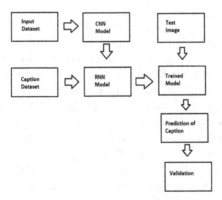

Fig. 1. Block diagram of proposed work

3.1 Convolutional Neural Network Model

In current situation for visual recognition CNN model is referred. CNN model present number of convolutional layer. CNN model is structured for 2D images. For training and processing less parameters are required this is the main advantage of CNN model. In CNN input layer, hidden layer and output layers are present. Input layer consist the input that gives the input in the form of image. Hidden layers are performed the calculation of the given input information and last output layer is generate the outcomes of the calculations and extractions. In all the layers neurons are present. Each neurons are interconnected with any another neurons. Each layer neurons are interconnected with privies neuron layers. The CNN model is used for the feature extraction. In CNN different stages are present. That are convolutional layer (kernel), max pooling, Padding, stride. In this work implement the CCN model for the feature extraction and this extracted features are feed to the LSTM Network for the sentence generation.

3.1.1 Convolutional Layer

In CNN, the convolutional is the heart of system. Convolutional layer is the first layer in the CNN. In image classification, the image size is in 224 * 224 * 3. The image size is compare with the h * w * d.

  Here, h = 224 height

  w = 224 = width

  d = 3 dimensions = RGB values.

3.1.2 Kernel

In the convolutional neural network consider as the 3 * 3 kernel size. Kernel is also the filter is used to extract the features from image. The kernel matrix is moves towards the input data. It provides the dot product operation for the kernel size and finally we can got output as the dot product matrix. For each kernel bias is present, bias is the scalar quantity. Figure 2 shows the operation of kernel to generate feature map output.

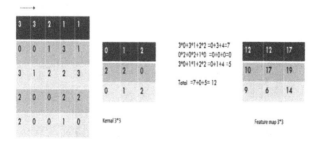

Fig. 2. Generation of feature map output

3.1.3 Activation Function

For every system generation activation function is most important. In this work, the ReLU activation function is used. Rectified linear activation function is the linear in nature. In the neural network, the activation function is used for transforming summed all weighted input from node into the output for that input. It overcome the vanishing gradient problem. Because of that the model because simple and faster. Figure 3 shows ReLU activation function.

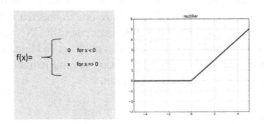

Fig. 3. ReLU activation function

3.1.4 Stride

Stride is also filter that moves across the image left to right and also the top to bottom. It also move one pixel column change on the horizontal direction and one pixel row on vertical direction. The movement direction of the filter is depend on the input image pixel size. Stride is always in symmetrical in height and width dimensions.

3.1.5 Pooling

Polling function is reduce the spatial size of given input pixel value according with the stride. Here stride is 2 * 2. Figure 4 shows the pooling operation. There are two types of pooling such as max pooling and average pooling. In most of the applications, max pooling is used. Figure 4 shows the Pooling operation. In this example the stride is consider as 2 * 2.

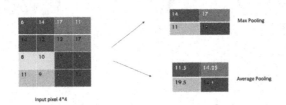

Fig. 4. Pooling operation (max pooling and average pooling)

3.1.6 Padding

Padding we cannot lose the information. If padding is 1 then add 1 row in top and bottom of the matrix and 1 column is in right and left side of the matrix. After adding this row and columns then operation is performed. There are two types of padding one is Zero padding. In this padding insert all the zeros in the all rows and columns. This technique is commonly used. In another techniques add the nearing of the matrix that is zero or one. Using the padding operation we can get the same size of the matrix as the output side also.

3.1.7 Fully Connected Layer

Large data perform the classification on dataset. The fully connected layer is the feed forward network. The output of the pooling layer or convolutional layer is given to the fully connected layer. This output is in the form of flattened (the output is in the form of matrix in any layer or final layer of the network). It also called as the flattened vector. This output is given to the fully connected layer. The flattened layer is connected to the fully connected layer is similar to the artificial intelligent network and also perform the mathematical operations. Next layer is the softmax activation function. In the softmax layer, the mathematical operation is done.

3.1.8 Recurrent Neural Network Model

RNN model is mainly used for the natural language processing. RNN or LSTM is the sequence processer which is actually uses embedding layer which is the kind of word representation which allows words with similar meaning to have similar representation. That is identifying the context of the words. Using word embedding word are represent in the form of vectors. There are different RNN application in natural language processing and also in other domains. One of the best example of RNN model is Google mail - Gmail. Here, when you type in a sentence it will auto complete it. In RNN also the input layer, hidden layer and output layer is present. The input layer of the data is in the form of the vector. Each neuron has the activation function. RNN process word by word. Once generate the output then go back and this generated output is given to hidden layer because of the sequentially generating the captions or sentence.

3.1.9 VGG16

The VGG16 is the advanced model of ResNet and AlexNet. This is pre-trained model. In this work VGG16 model is used. It is deep CNN for large scale image recognition. VGG16 model is used as the feature extraction. VGG stands for Visual Geometry Group (VGG). It gives the image as the input and image features as the output. And 16 stands for 16 layers presents in model. After every layer, the output is generated. Figure 4 shows the input image and the extracted image output.

3.1.10 LSTM

LSTM is the special kind of the RNN model used is deep learning. LSTM layer is utilize to process to text data which is in the form of vector data after is passed through embedding layer. To preserve the sequence information of text. LSTM is solve the memory problem. LSTM model is deal with vanishing gradient problem. Here, the LSTM model is used for the sentence generation. It is the feedback based device. It can process sing point data as well as sequence of the data. LSTM model contains Cell, input gate, output gate, forget gate. Each are interconnected with each other.

3.1.11 Dataset

Image caption generation is most important part is dataset. In this work Flickr8k Image data set. The dataset consist of 8000. For the Training and development purpose 1000 images are used. For the flickr8k dataset the time compensate is less. Each image has 5 Captions at each image contains unique ID. Training pictures are 6000. Training pictures are used for the train the model. This is the main task of system. Testing pictures are 1000. After the training go for the testing the model. Using this system we can calculate the accuracy of the model. Flickr8k.token - in this file tokens are present which are used for RNN model for the sentence generation. Each image contains the 5 captions based on this dataset the output sentence is generated. Expert annotations.txt. This is the expert judgment file. File contents different columns. First column is image Id, Second contains the Token ID. Next three columns are the expert judgments. The scores ranges are 1 to 4.

Fig. 5. Input image dataset

According to above Fig. 5 following captions are present in dataset in token file. Five tokens are present. That are as follows,

- A blonde boy wearing a blue life vest and camo shorts jumps off a diving backward into a blue lake.
- A boy diving backward off a pier in a large lake.
- Boy in a blue life jacket jumps into the water.
- A boy in a blue life jacket jumps off a board into the lake.
- A boy is holding his nose and jumping off a diving board backwards into a lake.

3.1.12 Data Pre-processing

It is the process making the given input data is converted in to the machine language. This language is easily understand by machine. It is better for the accuracy of the system. This is because the data is mostly noisy, and it sometimes missing the value or also the false values. The feature extraction and feature selection are two methods of data pre-processing. Which is directly impact on the accuracy of the mode. In the feature selection is the method of selecting some features of data and discarded irrelevant feature.

4 Experimental Results

4.1 Python Environment

In proposed work install python 3.7.1. We must have to install tensor flow, keras, Pandas, pillow etc. In additional Matplot and NLTK is also installed for caption generation.

4.2 Tokenization

Tokenization is the first step in the natural language processing. In natural language processing tokenization is main task. First separate the words of the sentence. This words means tokens are used for text processing. There are main two types of tokenization.

4.2.1 Character Level Tokenization

Character level tokenization is first introduced in 2015 by Karpathy. In this tokenization, the characters are separating using space.

4.2.2 Word Tokenization

In the word level tokenization consist of the splitting the sentence by whitespace and punctuation marks. In the python NLTK library is used for the tokenization. This tokenization is commonly used. In our work also used word tokenization. The work result as follow the given input sentence.

"It originated from the idea that there are readers who prefer learning new skills from the comforts of their drawing rooms".

Tokenization output-

['It', 'originated', 'from', 'the', 'idea', 'that', 'there', 'are', 'readers', 'who', 'prefer', 'learning', 'new', 'skills', 'from', 'the', 'comforts', 'of', 'their', 'drawing', 'rooms'].

4.3 LSTM Captioning Model

The captioning model in commend prompt, this is the summery of the captioning work. In the summery of the work different layers are present such as input layer, embedding layer, dropout, and dense layer and LSTM model. Some parameters are explained brief. Here the Dropout is consider as the 50% that means the 0.5. The dropout value is present between o and 1. Dense layer is regular deeply connected neural network. This is frequently used layer. Bias, activation function, this are the supporting argument of the dense layer. Figure 6 shows the result of captioning model layers.

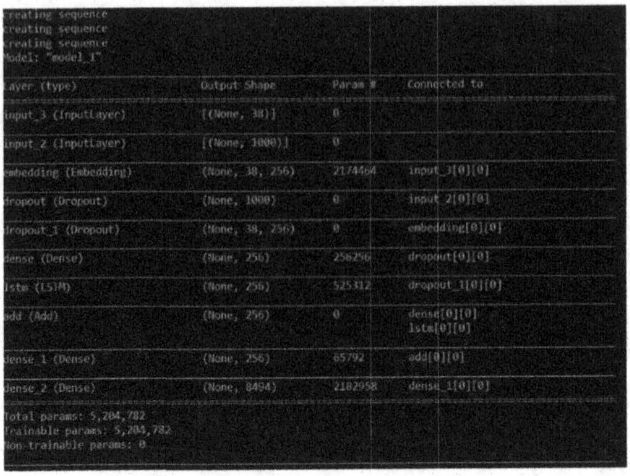

Fig. 6. Result of LSTM model layers

5 RNN

In the RNN decoder we uses the 50 epoch for the iteration. More literation's the accuracy is better and also the execution time is also more. The number of Epoch is also depends on the configuration of the PC. Accuracy of the system is increases with increasing the number of epoch and loss is decreases. Figure 7 shows the accuracy and loss of the system. One Input image is given to the Command Prompt and sentence is generated. Figure 8 shows the input image of system and Fig. 9 is the output of the system generated in the command prompt.

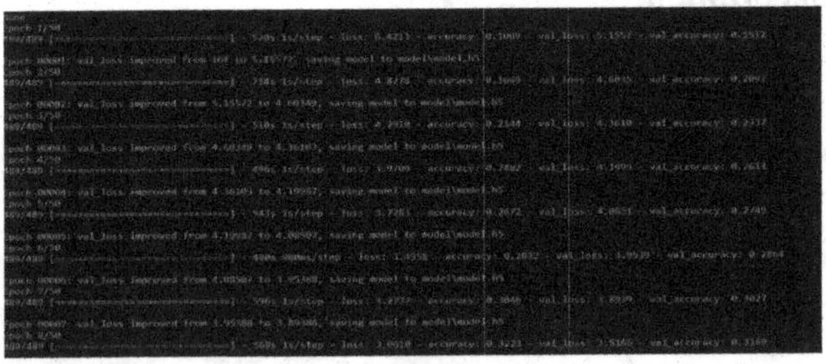

Fig. 7. Accuracy and loss of system

Fig. 8. Input image

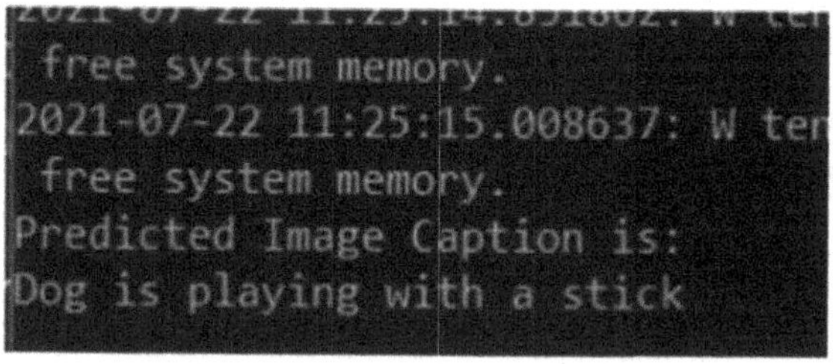

Fig. 9. Output of the system

6 Conclusion

In this work, we present the image captions are generated using the CNN and RNN model in Python 3.7.1 using command prompt. All the steps are easily written and executed. The Flickr8k dataset are used for testing and training of the model. The captions are created using the token dataset. The VGG16 model, data pre-processing (Tokenization), LSTM captioning model and CNN model is generated.

References

1. Vinyals, O., et al.: Show and tell: a neural image caption generator. In: Proceedings of the IEEE Conference on Computer Vision and Pattern Recognition (2015)
2. Simonyan, K., Zisserman, A.: Very deep convolutional networks for large-scale image recognition. arXiv preprint arXiv: 1409.1556 (2014)
3. Fang, H., et al.: From captions to visual concepts and back. In: Proceedings of the IEEE Conference on Computer Vision and Pattern Recognition (2015)
4. Basha, C.H., Rani, C.: Different conventional and soft computing MPPT techniques for solar PV systems with high step-up boost converters: a comprehensive analysis. Energies **13**(2), 371 (2020)
5. Johnson, J., Karpathy, A., Li, F.-F.: Densecap: fully convolutional localization networks for dense captioning. In: Proceedings of the IEEE Conference on Computer Vision and Pattern Recognition (2016)

6. Hussaian Basha, C.H., Rani, C.: Performance analysis of MPPT techniques for dynamic irradiation condition of solar PV. Int. J. Fuzzy Syst. **22**(8), 2577–2598 (2020)
7. Basha, C.H., Rani, C.: Design and analysis of transformerless, high step-up, boost DC-DC converter with an improved VSS-RBFA based MPPT controller. Int. Trans. Electr. Energy Syst. **30**(12), e12633 (2020)
8. Papineni, K., et al.: BLEU: a method for automatic evaluation of machine translation. In: Proceedings of the 40th Annual Meeting on Association for Computational Linguistics. Association for Computational Linguistics (2002)
9. Vedantam, R., Lawrence Zitnick, C., Parikh, D.: Cider: consensus-based image description evaluation. In: Proceedings of the IEEE Conference on Computer Vision and Pattern Recognition (2015)
10. El Housseini, A., Toumi, A., Khenchaf, A.: Deep learning for target precognition from SAR images. In: 7th Seminar on Detection System Processing IEEE Conference Paper (2017)
11. Xu, K., Ba, J., Kiros, R.: Show, attend and tell: neural image caption generation with visual attention (2016)
12. Mao, J., Xu, W., Yang, Y., Wang, J., Huang, Z.: Deep captioning with multimodal Recurrent Neural Network (M-RNN). Published as a conference paper at ICLR 2015 (2015)
13. Yao, B.Z., Yang, X., Lin, L., Lee, M.W., Zhu, S.-C.: I2T: image parsing to text description. Proc. IEEE **98**(8), 1485–1508 (2010)
14. Kulkarni, G., et al.: Baby talk: understanding and generating simple image descriptions. In: Processing of the IEEE Conference Paper (2011)
15. Wang, B., Zheng, X.: Retrieval topic recurrent memory network for remote sensing image captioning. IEEE J. Sel. Top. Appl. Earth Obs. Remote Sens. **13**, 256–270 (2020)

The Heroes and Villains of the Mix Zone: The Preservation and Leaking of USer's Privacy in Future Vehicles

A. V. Shreyas Madhav[1], A. K. Ilavarasi[2] , and Amit Kumar Tyagi[3]([✉])

[1] School of Computer Science and Engineering, Vellore Institute of Technology, Chennai, India
[2] Centre for Healthcare Advancement, Innovation and Research/SCOPE, Vellore Institute of Technology, Chennai, India
[3] Department of Fashion Technology, National Institute of Fashion Technology, New Delhi, Delhi, India
amitkrtyagi025@gmail.com

Abstract. The privacy of computer users has become more important over the last decade considering the rapid advances that have occurred in the technological industry. Cloud computing, distributed computing, the future internet network, sensor networks, and ad hoc networks, to name a few, are now under assault from a variety of sources, putting the data of millions of users (car users) at jeopardy. Vehicular Adhoc Network (VANET) is a type of Mobile Adhoc Network, having low security infrastructure, faces many serious concerns like security, privacy and trust, etc., over the road network (during travelling). In the last decade, several researchers/scientists have come up with various solutions to these essential concerns. In spite of this, many studies concentrate exclusively on data privacy or identity privacy, and not on location privacy. In 2003, the Mix Zone idea was established to address the issue of privacy for drivers and passengers on highways. When it comes to mixing zones, there are a variety of options, but they all fail due to various benefits and downsides. The main objective of this article is to act as a comprehensive information repository of mix-zones in order to protect the privacy of vehicle occupants from a variety of angles. This paper also discusses a number of interesting concepts, such as prospective improvements or research gaps in the mix zone.

Keywords: Mix-zone · Privacy preservation · Vehicular ad-hoc network · Leaking information · Route confusion · Security issues

1 Introduction

Moving automobiles serve as nodes in a mobile network called the Vehicular Ad-Hoc Network (VANET). In order to broadcast data to the network, each car serves as a transmitter, receiver, and router. Once this data is collected, it is put to good use in order to maintain a smooth flow of traffic. For connection with other cars and roadside units, automobiles include a radio interface termed On Board Unit. The Global Positioning

© The Author(s), under exclusive license to Springer Nature Switzerland AG 2022
V. Arunachalam and K. Sivasankaran (Eds.): ICMDCS 2022, CCIS 1743, pp. 171–184, 2022.
https://doi.org/10.1007/978-3-031-23973-1_12

System and other similar technologies are standard equipment in modern vehicles (GPS). In the near future, VANETs will alter the way people drive, but whether or not they do so for the better or worse is totally dependent on the security measures that are put in place. VANETs may aid with traffic flow and roadside safety by reducing congestion. A VANET, on the other hand, has its own set of problems, especially in terms of security and privacy. A VANET is particularly vulnerable to the security risks that come with mobile ad hoc networks, making it a prime target for attacks and service abuse. It's possible that an attacker might manipulate traffic apps and convince people to take another route, thereby freeing up the original route for the attacker's advantage. Using a phoney identity to sign culpability statements would be a more serious example of an attacker trying to avoid being tied to an automobile accident scene. Other less obvious, but no less criminal, uses of network apps include following individuals in their cars. So, there is a clear need for security methods, particularly those that preserve the user's privacy. One of the security aspects of VANET is against its malicious software. In order to execute harmful assaults, the attacker employs malicious viruses to access the vehicle's network through wireless connection. As a result, the Internet of Vehicles' security will be gravely jeopardised since these harmful viruses will disrupt routine vehicle connection while also deceiving or altering data. Figure 1 depicts the architecture of VANETs involved in this process.

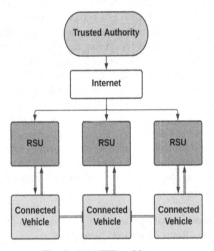

Fig. 1. VANET architecture

Radio communications interfaces are planned to be added to automobiles in the near future as they become more sophisticated systems. As a result, mobile ad hoc networks may be used to create vehicular networks, often known as VANETs (Vehicular Ad hoc NETworks). Conventional security techniques are not always successful in VANETs because of their mobility, short connection periods, and other unique aspects. The inherent properties of vehicle communication have thus prompted a broad range of research contributions to be lately made available. Data transmission through VANETs relies heavily on its authentication method for both security and privacy. In other cases, such as cloud computing, the abundance of storage and processing resources boosts efficiency. OBUs that store sensitive data must typically validate between 1000 and 5000 messages per second with a network of 100 to 500 cars. Due to the increased computational load and improved traffic flow, cloud-assisted VANET has been a huge asset for OBUs. The metadata stored by cloud providers is often stored in relational databases, which leaves the data privacy of users open to attack.

Using pseudonyms to communicate with each other and the roadside units, VANETs authenticate their vehicles and hide their real identities by using these pseudonyms, which are frequently changed so that the pseudonyms cannot be easily linked together and thus reveal the real identities of the vehicles. A pseudonym change will be of little benefit if past and present pseudonyms are connected in any way. Because of this, a variety of approaches have been suggested to obscure the pseudonym reforms to make it impossible to connect pseudonyms together. When changing your pseudonym in a low-traffic setting, many of these solutions don't completely protect your anonymity.

2 Motivation

VANETs demand a unique grade of requirements to maintain responsibility and account-ability of drivers engaged in accidents, traffic infractions, emission standards and anomalies in order to conduct punitive steps if a driver commits any crime. Besides that, location and context-aware services must pin-point user location and preferences to deliver the most detailed, accurate and complete list of customised information. Despite such, sharing of such information presents serious privacy considerations that cannot be overlooked. Also, privacy considerations in vehicular communications are important to give security for the user data from profiling and monitoring. Several aspects effect on the success of mix-zone method, such as user population, mix-zones shape, location sensing rate and spatial resolution, as well as geographical and temporal limits on user movement patterns. None of the current mix-zone techniques address all these aspects properly. Most of the previous mix-zone ideas fail to offer effective mix-zone creation algorithms that are effective for mobile users moving on road networks and yet impervious to timing and transition assaults [27]. The objective of this article is to present a detailed explanation of mix-zones in order to safeguard the privacy of vehicle passengers from a range of aspects. This study also explores a variety of fascinating issues, such as possible enhancements or research gaps in the mix zone [28–31].

3 Privacy Preservation in Autonomous Vehicles

A system for protecting the privacy of one's whereabouts Obfuscation, anonymization, and the addition of fake events are all examples of primitives. Users' paths are obscured and events are mapped with various timings while concealing events. Additional events, such as those of a typical user, are included while creating mock events. It's possible to obfuscate locations by adding noise. Cloaking in space and time are two examples of this. Unlinkability between a place and a user's identity ensures anonymity in anonymization. For example, pseudonymous or pseudonymous identification may be performed via the use of pseudonyms, mix zones, group signatures, and silent periods. In order to keep track of upcoming events, users must register their interest in the application zone. This helps the consumer stay up to speed on the latest product information. A user's location may be readily tracked when they connect directly with an application. Communication between car and application is done through middleware, which prevents a direct link between a vehicle and the network. When a vehicle is in the mix zone, it comes into contact with a vehicle that does not have an application callback. Store and forward networks, such as Mix networks, are used to allow anonymous communication. Prior to transmission, the messages are rearranged based on several variables. As a result, there is no way to connect the two messages that were sent and received. Users' location privacy is protected via a variety of mix zone strategies. Geometry, population, spatial and time resolution, and spatial restrictions in road networks all have a role in how effective a mix zone is. Due to the lack of a location-based service connection and an application call back, it is not possible to link a place to a vehicle's identity in the mix zone. An individual's identity is readily discernible when they communicate with the app in this manner. Middleware acts as a go-between between the car and the application, keeping the user's identity private. The use of middleware protects the confidentiality of the data and the anonymity of the user. The previous and new pseudonyms of a user in a regular traffic environment are simply connected. When a person switches pseudonyms in the mix zone, their identity can no longer be tied to their current location, allowing for unlinkability.

4 Necessity of Mix-Zone

We have identified three main avenues for an attacker to connect pseudonyms:

- The use of non-volatile data (such as unencrypted upper layer identifiers or the radio fingerprint of a unit) to infer a relationship between two messages is an example of an attack based on non-volatile data.
- Use of protocol knowledge (e.g., a vehicle consistently transmits in one time slot, regardless of its pseudonym) to connect messages is an example of a protocol-based attack.
- This kind of attack relies on physical factors and limitations to determine a node's present location, which may then be used to establish a connection between two messages as being from the same node. The perpetrators of this assault have characterised it as a straightforward tracking operation.

As a starting point, we have identified three main avenues for an attacker to connect pseudonyms:

- The use of non-volatile data (such as unencrypted upper layer identifiers or the radio fingerprint of a unit) to infer a relationship between two messages is an example of an attack based on non-volatile data.
- To connect communications, attackers utilise attacks based on protocol information (for example, a car consistently communicates within a certain time slot, regardless of its pseudonym).

- This kind of attack relies on physical factors and limitations to determine a node's present location, which may then be used to establish a connection between two messages as being from the same node. Simple tracking has been used to characterise this attack.

In order to connect a pseudonym, there are three main ways an attacker may go about it. Extra data, such as unencrypted upper layer IDs, or the radio fingerprint of a unit (such as the radio fingerprint of a unit), are utilised to infer a link between two messages. Protocol-based attacks, in which knowledge of the proto-col (e.g., a vehicle consistently transmits at a given time-slot, regardless of its pseudonym) is used to connect messages, notwithstanding the pseudonym's anonymity [6]. The physical parameters and restrictions are used to infer the current location and connect two messages as belonging to the same node, for example, by using the estimated distance travelled and the previous position. The term "simpletracking" has been used to characterise this attack. An attacker might take one of three routes, which we've identified. Pseudonyms for links are as follows: Based on non-volatile data, where extra information is required for an attack. Such as an unencrypted upper layer) does not alter the radio fingerprint of a device, which is used as an identifier [7, 8].

A method known as mix-zone was devised to ensure that past and new pseudonyms could not be linked. This kind of zone allows unlinkability by having a large number of users enter in a random sequence, adjust their pseudonyms, and then leave the zone in a different order. The mix-zone concept makes the following assumptions to preserve privacy: k participants must arrive in a mix zone area before any participant may exit the territory. Each participant in the zone spends an unspecified amount of time in the territory, beginning and ending at various points. Transition probabilities follow a uniform distribution. Methods for constructing mixed zones: Based on the mix-zone paradigm [9–14], three building methods have been devised for the development of functional mix-zones. The time window limited method defines a rectangle at the centre of the intersection in a predetermined size. On the basis of this assumption, an anonymity set is created depending on how many people enter the mix-zone at a given moment. There should be a relatively short time frame in which to conduct the experiment. The size of the window is determined by criteria such as the size of the zone, the anonymity level of the user, and the speed of the user. TWB shifted Rectangular Mix-zones include two additional features: First, the rectangle is defined in a shifted manner. A non-rectangular size is described in the TWB NonRectangular mix-zones as well. Using a non-rectangular method eliminates the risk of timing attacks.

To maintain their anonymity, each user talks with the network infrastructure using a pseudonym or their actual name and device number. In order to access location-based services, users first get their location through a positioning system, and then submit this information to the LBS application server. Although pseudonyms may protect a user's true identity, the LBS application server may deduce a user's position or movement path from this information, resulting in a breach of location privacy.

5 Variants of Mix-Zone

The position of a car in a vehicular network is a critical piece of information. It is possible to safeguard vehicle privacy by using a technique known as "pseudonym change," in which a large number of cars collectively adopt different pseudonyms in order to create a "mix zone." But the number of collaborators in the spatiotemporal environment is a factor. Figure 2 showcases the mixzones and their visualization.

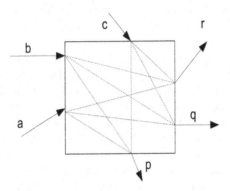

Fig. 2. Mixzone visualization

MobiMix is a mix-zone architecture for road networks focused on the protection of mobile users' location privacy. MobiMix's solution to location privacy protection is to employ mix-zones, where no programmes may track user movement, in place of spatial cloaking. Certification issuance and pseudonym issuance methods are included in indMZ's pseudonym scheme for vehicular networks. When a vehicle joins a roadside unit, its pseudonym will be L. When a pseudonym is about to expire, the car may create a mix zone by broadcasting beacon signals to the area. The independent mix zone implies that each of the collaborating vehicles will generate some randomised pseudonyms and contribute to the required k-anonymous mix zone. It is possible for the vehicle to create a k-anonymous pseudonym change region even if there is no input from anybody else.

In [31], time-window-based options for protecting location privacy in mix zones are discussed. Based on the mix-zone paradigm, three building methods have been devised for the development of functional mix-zones. The time window limited method defines a rectangle at the centre of the intersection in a predetermined size. On the basis of this assumption, an anonymity set is created depending on how many people enter the mix-zone at a given moment. There should be a relatively short time frame in which to conduct the experiment. The size of the window is determined by criteria such as the size of the zone, the anonymity level of the user, and the speed of the user. TWB shifted Rectangular Mix-zones include two additional features: First, the rectangle is defined in a shifted manner. A non-rectangular size is described in the TWB NonRectangular mix-zones as well.

6 Background Work

Using pseudonyms to hide one's identity in a dedicated infrastructure (DI) system has been suggested by Raya et al. Pseudonyms are fictitious names that are only valid for a short period of time. VANET pseudonyms may be used in a variety of ways [24, 25]. For the time being, it has been proved that pseudonyms may be tracked and their genuine identities revealed using various probabilistic models as stated in [5]. Mix zones were a popular way to connect pseudonyms. To describe mix zones, a group of people may alter their pseudonyms together at a secret location, without being connected to each other. Pseudonyms will be harder to connect if the pseudonym shift is concealed in this manner. Dedicated Infrastructures could benefit from the usage of pseudonyms and mix zones (VANETs). There are no significant deployments of the DI technique at this time [1, 4, 13, 14, 26]. Online privacy preservation is an important method for safeguarding the private of moving things. There are a variety of ways to keep location data private. Cloaking, either in time or space, is a common method [3, 10, 12]. Generalization, in this case, is the process of expanding in both time and space in order to meet the k-anonymity level [17]. k-anonymity refers to the condition of being anonymous among other k things. On the basis of the quality of the data, cloaking can ensure k-anonymity. If you want to hide your position, you'll have to utilise one of two methods: a trusted third party or a group of people updating their locations simultaneously [11, 12]. The latter depends on open and honest communication among the group's members, which calls for mutual trust. Virtual trip lines (VTLs) were introduced by Hoh and Gruteser [3]. Vehicles must update their position when they pass a VTL border, which is sent to the client programme. Because cars do not update their whereabouts outside of VTL areas, the system is unable to collect traffic conditions. Pseudonyms may easily be linked to hacked VTLs if any of the lines are compromised. As a result of the considerable time and effort put into selecting VTLs and making them available to users, the system is not suitable for usage by a large number of people [16]. Location cloaking is used in [11] by the writers to obscure the location of users. As a result, the precise position of the data is obscured by a jumble of temporal and geographical parameters. It ensures k-anonymity in terms of both the temporal and spatial aspects. However, it still depends on a trustworthy third party and reduces the data quality. Using [8], the authors propose a two-way cloaking technique, in which a user submits her cloaked position to an anonymization server, which in turn produces an anonymous cloaking rectangle with k users inside of it [17]. By generalising location to the safe zone, cloaking depends on an untrusted third party to determine the safe region. It is comparable to the technique used by [12] in which users collaborate to construct a secure zone without the assistance of a trusted third party [18–24]. In this approach, users are presumed to be honest and trust each other to determine the safe region.

7 The Mix Zone Network Model

There are two basic kinds of designs for the anonymization methods used in Location Based Services (LBS) to improve privacy [24]. Peer to peer and a Trustworthy Third-Party (TTP) server are two different ways of doing this. Mix-Zones [19] may be used to create a real-time anonymity system based on the previous design. Third-party trustworthy servers are the trusted servers of the telecom operator linked with the Location Based Services server and the end user. The anonymization method will be performed only by the TTP, which is expected to maintain complete security over the data it processes [25]. In order for this technique to be effective, the MO's routes must cross. Generally, these intersections are traffic signal junctions on the road networks [26]. Because of this, the intersections of traffic lights are known as Mix-Zones. According to the trusted third-party server that links the MOs with the Location Based Service providers, a Mix-Zone is a particular region. LBS application servers connecting to this trusted server must know the identities of the appropriate MOs. Pseudonyms, rather than real names, should be used for this purpose. Anonymizing all users inside the Mix-Zone further enhances the MO's real-time privacy. A period of time will be set aside for this anonymization to take effect, which corresponds to the length of time it takes for the TTP server to activate the Mix-Zone. In addition, the existing MOs will be reseudonymized in order to confuse the user's privacy thief. The TTP server informs MOs in advance of their entering the network about the Mix-location Zone's and duration. Figure 3 depicts composition of a gate in a mixzone.

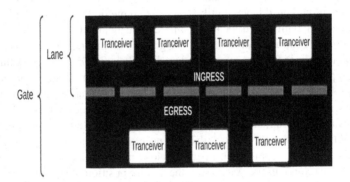

Fig. 3. Gate composition in a mix zone

7.1 Confidentiality Threats

The security of communications in a vehicle network is especially jeopardised by methods like as eavesdropping and broadcast messaging, which may be used to gain position data and read private messages. An insider or an outsider may eavesdrop on other drivers' conversations without their consent, and then utilise that information for their own purposes without the drivers' knowledge. For drivers, privacy and anonymity are critical considerations. Protecting users' privacy by hiding their precise spatial and temporal position is a kind of location privacy. Anonymity may be obtained by making a user's request indistinguishable from those of other users.

7.2 Pseudonym Switching

Location privacy, the capacity to keep others from knowing one's present or previous location, is crucial in VANETs. Whenever vehicles exchange data across communication channels, such data may be uniquely identified by the other cars in the system as originating from that specific car. To be clear: If this identification were to stay constant, other external users might de-anonymize individuals via broadcast messages that correlate to this constant ID, which could be used by other users to identify them. When it comes to location privacy, an adversary would be able to follow the vehicle's position and movement over a period of time if they detected that the same identification was being broadcast along a route. The method VANETs interact must be changed to avoid this breach of privacy.

7.3 Pseudonym Scheme Change Effectiveness

Pseudonyms are being studied for their usefulness in altering schemes, which is a major focus of the study. An adversary's ability to link changes in pseudonyms to the appropriate user is often used to assess this. The pseudonym changing technique is insecure if an attacker is able to determine the connection. Although this thesis does not concentrate on the details of a pseudonym-changing strategy, numerous previous publications have analysed various strategies and their usefulness. The degree of privacy acquired is one of the key issues that will be examined in this thesis. Entering and departing a mix zone affects how much location privacy an individual user has. Pseudonym-changing schemes are necessary for assessing the severity of any other attack threat models that might compromise the system's location privacy [37, 38].

7.4 VANET Cryptographic Mix Zones

To make it more difficult for the enemy to determine who performed a certain action, Chaum [5] proposes anonymous systems. Anonymizing areas in virtual networks (VNs) may be created using a cryptographic approach known as mix-zones [2]. Adversaries can't read communications containing sensitive information, such as vehicle signatures, if they use a pseudonym that can be easily linked to it. This means they can't link two different pseudonyms that are used by the same vehicle at the same time. In order to provide location privacy, anonymizing zones need to be densely populated with cars and unpredictable in their movements. We suggest that preset areas be designated as "mix zones," in which pseudonym modifications must be enforced. Because road crossings are where traffic's speed and direction fluctuate the greatest, the most cars are mixed together.

7.5 CMIX Protocol

The opponent may readily identify mix-zones due to their fixed locations. As a result, communications emanating from the mix-zone region might be intercepted. While in a cryptographic MIX zone (CMIX), all valid cars are given a symmetric key by a roadside unit (RSU) of the mix-zone, and they use this key to encrypt all communications sent and received while in the zone. Once the symmetric key has been established, it may be used. It is possible for nodes entering the mix-zone via a key forwarding technique to acquire the mix-zone key, and then the RSU may switch to a new key using a key update mechanism.

7.6 Private Pseudonym Change Chaff Mechanisms

Cooperative awareness messages are vital for safety and efficiency applications in vehicle communication systems. Passenger privacy may be compromised if these conversations are not properly designed. For this reason, the use of ephemeral credentials such as pseudonyms was recommended, in order to divide up an excursion into unlinkable sections. Encrypted mix-zones allow vehicles to covertly change their pseudonyms during segment transitions. In spite of previous attempts to address the location, design, and procedures of mix zones, attacks on cars entering and existing these zones remain a problem. Earlier techniques primarily looked at homogeneous traffic, ignoring variations in vehicle density caused by changes in the population of drivers, the shape of the route, and even the time of the day. It is dangerous to draw conclusions about the practicality of a new technology based just on anecdotal information. As a result, a unique method that works regardless of vehicle movement patterns has been developed. If there are a sufficient number of fictive chaff vehicles present, the system will create them and broadcast their traces, but otherwise it will remain undetectable. This greatly enhances privacy protection in low-traffic areas, such as suburban areas, and during low traffic times. Since chaff vehicles (and messages) must not interfere with the proper operation of safety applications, the new method ensures that an external attacker cannot tell the difference between real and chaff vehicles.

8 Problem, Issues, and Challenges Today in Mix Zone Network Model

Despite the present tendency, future VANETs and their applications will include new developing technologies that bring new capabilities. Future VANETs face a number of difficult difficulties, some of which are listed below: Control and management of vehicle-to-infrastructure communication networks is a major problem. Vehicular networks should not have intermittent connections owing to high vehicle mobility or significant packet loss. Future VANETs will need vehicles that are both mobile and cognizant of their surroundings in order to function properly. In the event of an emergency, each car in the network should be aware of the location of the other vehicles. Management of heterogeneous smart cars will be necessary in the future, since there will be many of these types of vehicles on the road. Another problem of future VANETs is the management of diverse vehicles and their erratic connectivity. The content and location of a user's data are constantly at danger [32–37]. When automobiles talk to one other, users should be able to choose what information they want to give and what information they don't. Instead of transmitting sensitive data to the cloud for analysis, local examination may ensure privacy. Future VANETs have the task of supporting network intelligence, which is one of the most pressing issues. The edge cloud receives and preprocesses the data acquired by cars in future VANETs before sharing it with other portions of the network, such as standard cloud servers.

9 Possible Enhancement in Near Future Towards Mix Zone

The edge cloud receives and preprocesses the data acquired by cars in future VANETs before sharing it with other portions of the network, such as standard cloud servers. In the same way that we're all accustomed with and rely on mobile phones in our daily lives, VANETs have a bright future ahead of them. It's now a component of the government's overall plan. A new form of laser speed camera is being considered by NSW and Victoria police in Australia. This camera can detect mobile phone use and speeding cars from half a mile away [13–15]. As part of a zero-tolerance campaign against driving crimes, Dorset police in the United Kingdom are using cameras developed by Tele-Traffic UK branded as Concept II. Numerous VANET traffic safety and reliability initiatives are now underway in nations throughout the world. Because of the potential of associating prior and current pseudonyms, privacy-preserving approaches that use shifting pseudonyms might result in privacy leakage and disclose true identities [38–41]. Users may change their pseudonyms in secret by using mix zones, however it has been shown that statistical algorithms can trace this pseudonym change under certain conditions.

10 Conclusion

VANETs are a new kind of ad hoc network that establishes communications between smart vehicles, devices and associated infrastructure. Drivers and passengers alike benefit from VANET's enhanced safety and entertainment features. There are a wide variety of threats and assaults that may be launched against automobiles using wireless communication technology. As a result, protecting VANETs is more difficult than securing any other kind of network. In order to maintain one's privacy, this research examines alternative pseudonym tactics and mix zone formation methods. A review of recent studies dealing with VANET privacy, authentication, and secure message distribution was provided in this presentation. We categorised the publications based on the tools and strategies employed in them. We compared and contrasted the procedures in each area and evaluated the benefits and limitations of each. After that, we spoke about some of the difficulties that still need to be resolved. With any luck, the results of this poll will be useful to others doing similar work and will help to clarify some of the remaining questions.

References

1. Dotzer, F.: Privacy issues in vehicular ad hoc networks. In: Proceedings of the Workshop on Privacy Enhancing Technologies (2006)
2. Amro, B., Saygin, Y., Levi, A.: PA-CTM: privacy aware collaborative traffic monitoring system using autonomous location update mechanism. In: 4th ACM SIGSPATIAL International Workshop on Security and Privacy in GIS and LBS SPRINGL 11, Chicago, USA (2011)

3. Hoh, B., et al.: Virtual trip lines for distributed privacy-preserving traffic monitoring. In: Proceedings of the Sixth International Conference on Mobile Systems, Applications, and Services, Mobisys 2008, pp. 15–28 (2008)

4. Calandriello, G., Papadimitratos, P., Hubaux, J.P., Lioy, A.: Efficient and robust pseudonymous authentication in VANET. In: Proceedings of the Fourth ACM International Workshop on Vehicular Ad Hoc Networks Vanet 2007, New York, NY, USA, pp. 19–27 (2007)

5. Buttyán, L., Holczer, T., Vajda, I.: On the effectiveness of changing pseudonyms to provide location privacy in VANETs. In: Stajano, F., Meadows, C., Capkun, S., Moore, T. (eds.) ESAS 2007. LNCS, vol. 4572, pp. 129–141. Springer, Heidelberg (2007). https://doi.org/10.1007/978-3-540-73275-4_10

6. Fonseca, E., Festag, A., Baldessari, R., Aguiar, R.: Support of anonymity in VANETs - putting pseudonymity into practice. In: 2007 IEEE Wireless Communications & Networking Conference, WCNC, pp. 3402–3407. IEEE, Hong Kong (2007). International Journal of Network Security & Its Applications (IJNSA) Vol. 10, No.1, January 2018 20

7. Varsha, R., et al.: Deep learning based blockchain solution for preserving privacy in future vehicles. Int. J. Hybrid Intell. Syst. **16**(4), 223–236 (2020)

8. Hu, H.B., Xu, J.L., Lee, D.L.: PAM: an efficient and privacy-aware monitoring framework for continuously moving objects. IEEE Trans. Knowl. Data Eng. **22**, 404–419 (2010)

9. Hoh, B., Gruteser, M.: Protecting location privacy through path confusion. In: Proceedings of First International Conference on Security and Privacy for Emerging Areas in Communications Networks, pp. 194–205 (2005)

10. Zhang, C.Y., Huang, Y.: Cloaking locations for anonymous location-based services: a hybrid approach. GeoInformatica **13**, 159–182 (2009)

11. Gedik, B., Liu, L.: Protecting location privacy with personalized k-anonymity: architecture and algorithms. IEEE Trans. Mob. Comput. **7**, 1–18 (2008)

12. Chow, C.Y., Mokbel, M., Liu, X.: A peer-to-peer spatial cloaking algorithm for anonymous location-based service. In: Proceedings of the 14th Annual ACM International Symposium on Advances in Geographic Information Systems. ACM, Arlington (2006)

13. Gerlach, M., Guttler, F.: Privacy in VANETs using changing pseudonyms - ideal and real. In: IEEE 65th Vehicular Technology Conference, pp. 2521–2525 (2007)

14. Tyagi, A.K., Agarwal, D., Sreenath, N.: SecVT: Securing the Vehicles of Tomorrow using blockchain technology. In: 2022 International Conference on Computer Communication and Informatics (ICCCI), pp. 1–6 (2022). https://doi.org/10.1109/ICCCI54379.2022.9740965

15. Raya, M., Papadimitratos, P., Hubaux, J.P.: Securing vehicular communications. IEEE Wirel. Commun. **13**, 8–15 (2006)

16. Samarati, P.: Protecting respondents' identities in microdata release. IEEE Trans. Knowl. Data Eng. **13**, 1010–1027 (2001)

17. Beresford, A.R., Stajano, F.: Location privacy in pervasive computing. IEEE Perv. Comput. **2**, 46–55 (2003)

18. Tyagi, A.K., Aswathy, S.U.: Autonomous Intelligent Vehicles (AIV): research statements, open issues, challenges and road for future. Int. J. Intell. Netw. **2**, 83–102 (2021). https://doi.org/10.1016/j.ijin.2021.07.002, ISSN 2666-6030

19. Sampigethaya, K., Huang, L., Li, M., Poovendran, R., Matsuura, K., Sezaki, K.: Caravan: providing location privacy for VANET. In: Proceedings of 3rd Workshop on Embedded Security in Cars, Cologne, Germany, ESCAR 2005 (2005)

20. Nair, M.M., Tyagi, A.K.: Preserving privacy using blockchain technology in autonomous vehicles. In: Giri, D., Mandal, J.K., Sakurai, K., De, D. (eds.) ICNSBT 2021. LNNS, vol. 481, pp. 237–248. Springer, Singapore (2022). https://doi.org/10.1007/978-981-19-3182-6_19

21. Xu, Q., Zheng, R., Saad, W., Han, Z.: Device fingerprinting in wireless networks: challenges and opportunities. IEEE Commun. Surv. Tutor. **18**(1), 94–104 (2016). International Journal of Network Security & Its Applications (IJNSA) Vol. 10, No.1, January 2018

22. Freudiger, J., Shokri, R., Hubaux, J.-P.: On the optimal placement of mix zones. In: Goldberg, I., Atallah, M.J. (eds.) PETS 2009. LNCS, vol. 5672, pp. 216–234. Springer, Heidelberg (2009). https://doi.org/10.1007/978-3-642-03168-7_13

23. Zhu, X., Lu, Y., Zhang, B., Hou, Z.: A distributed pseudonym management scheme in VANETs. Int. J. Distrib. Sensor Netw. **9**, 615906 (2013). https://doi.org/10.1155/2013/615906

24. Vasudevan, H., Joshi, A.R., Shekokar, N.M., Patel, N.J., Jhaveri, R.H.: International Conference on Advanced Computing Technologies and Applications (ICACTA) Trust Based Approaches for Secure Routing in VANET: A Survey, Procedia Computer Science, vol. 45, pp. 592–601 (2015). ISSN 1877–0509, http://dx.doi.org/10.1016/j.procs.2015.03.112

25. Madhav, A.V.S., Tyagi, A.K.: Explainable Artificial Intelligence (XAI): connecting artificial decision-making and human trust in autonomous vehicles. In: Singh, P.K., Wierzchoń, S.T., Tanwar, S., Rodrigues, J.J.P.C., Ganzha, M. (eds.) Proceedings of Third International Conference on Computing, Communications, and Cyber-Security. LNNS, vol. 421, pp. 123–136. Springer, Singapore (2023). https://doi.org/10.1007/978-981-19-1142-2_10

26. Tyagi, A.K., Sreenath, N.: A comparative study on privacy preserving techniques for location based services. Br. J. Math. Comput. Sci. **10**(4), 1–25 (2015)

27. Freudiger, J., Raya, M., Félegyházi, M., et al.: Mix-zones for location privacy in vehicular networks. In: ACM Workshop on Wireless Networking for Intelligent Transportation Systems (WiN-ITS), pp. 1–7 (2007)

28. Carianha, A.M., Barreto, L.P., Lima, G.: Improving location privacy in mixzones for VANETs. In: IEEE 30th International Performance Computing and Communications Conference (IPCCC), pp. 1–6 (2011)

29. Palanisamy, B., Ravichandran, S., Liu, L., et al.: Road network mix-zones for anonymous location based services. In: IEEE 29th International Conference on Data Engineering (ICDE), pp. 1300–1303 (2013)

30. Ying, B., Makrakis, D., Mouftah, H.T.: Dynamic mix-zone for location privacy in vehicular networks. IEEE Commun. Lett. **17**(8), 1524–1527 (2013)

31. Li, X., Liu, P., Zhang, S., Xie, Y.: An improved secure and efficient group key agreement scheme in VANETs. Int. J. Commun. Syst. **35**(3), e5025 (2022)

32. Didouh, A., El Hillali, Y., Rivenq, A., Labiod, H.: Novel centralized pseudonym changing scheme for location privacy in V2X communication. Energies **15**(3), 692 (2022)

33. Imran, M., Memon, H., Arain, Q.A.: Pseudonym changing strategy with mix zones based authentication protocol for location privacy in road networks. Wirel. Pers. Commun. **116**(4), 3309–3329 (2021)

34. Al-Marshoud, M.S., Al-Bayatti, A.H., Kiraz, M.S.: Improved chaff-based CMIX for solving location privacy issues in VANETs. Electronics **10**(11), 1302 (2021)

35. Jan, S.A., Amin, N.U., Othman, M., Ali, M., Umar, A.I., Basir, A.: A survey on privacy-preserving authentication schemes in VANETs: attacks, challenges and open issues. IEEE Access **9**, 153701–153726 (2021)

36. Sen, A., et al.: Fog mix-zone approach for preserving privacy in IoT. In: 2021 8th International Conference on Computing for Sustainable Global Development (INDIACom), pp. 405–408. IEEE (2021)

37. Nair, M.M., Tyagi, A.K.: Privacy: history, statistics, policy, laws, preservation and threat analysis. J. Inf. Assur. Secur. **16**(1), p24–34. 11p. (2021)

38. Tyagi, A.K., Nair, M.M., Niladhuri, S., Abraham, A.: Security, privacy research issues in various computing platforms: a survey and the road ahead. J. Inf. Assur. Secur. **15**(1), p1–16. 16p. (2020)

39. Tyagi, A.K., Kumari, S., Fernandez, T.F., Aravindan, C.: P3 block: privacy preserved, trusted smart parking allotment for future vehicles of tomorrow. In: Gervasi, O., et al. (eds.) ICCSA 2020. LNCS, vol. 12254, pp. 783–796. Springer, Cham (2020). https://doi.org/10.1007/978-3-030-58817-5_56

40. Krishna, A.M., Tyagi, A.K., Prasad, S.V.A.V.: Preserving privacy in future vehicles of tomorrow. JCR **7**(19), 6675–6684 (2020). https://doi.org/10.31838/jcr.07.19.768
41. Nair, M.M., Tyagi, A.K.: Preserving privacy using blockchain technology in autonomous vehicles. In: Giri, D., Mandal, J.K., Sakurai, K., De, D. (eds.) Proceedings of International Conference on Network Security and Blockchain Technology. ICNSBT 2021. Lecture Notes in Networks and Systems, vol. 481. Springer, Singapore (2022). https://doi.org/10.1007/978-981-19-3182-6_19

Analysis and Design of High Speed and Low Power Finite Impulse Response Filter Using Different Types of Multipliers

K. T. Kavyadevi[1] ⓘ, Apurva Saindane[1(✉)] ⓘ, and T. Vigneswaran[2] ⓘ

[1] M.Tech VLSI Design, School of Electronics Engineering, VIT Chennai, Chennai, Tamil Nadu, India
{kavyadevi.kt2020,saindaneapurva.nitin2020}@vitstudent.ac.in
[2] School of Electronics Engineering, VIT Chennai, Chennai, Tamil Nadu, India
vigneswaran.t@vit.ac.in

Abstract. Filters with a finite impulse response (FIR) are widely utilized in high-speed digital signal processing (DSP) applications. Digital filters have a spectacular contribution in several applications related to signals. Filtering is a technique for obtaining the desired output by manipulating the input data. This paper proposes the FIR filter using different types of multipliers. The proposed FIR filter is made up of a combination of multipliers and adders. The Dadda multiplier has three multiplication steps for partial product reduction and has specific methods to minimize the parameters. To minimize the delay and lower the area, the Dadda multiplier is used together with the exact compressor. This paper compares performance parameters of the FIR filter, which contains various multiplier architectures like the Dadda multiplier with exact compressor, Wallace tree multiplier, and Baugh Wooley multiplier. Dadda multiplier with exact compressor provides reduced 27.27% delay as compared to Wallace tree multiplier and 18.9% compared to Baugh Wooley multiplier. LUTs are 14.28% minimized as compared to other multipliers. Synthesis and simulations are done using Xilinx ISE 14.7.

Keywords: Exact compressor · Dadda multiplier · Approximate compressor · Wallace tree multiplier · Baugh wooley multiplier

1 Introduction

The role of DSP has been increased excessively. It has many applications, including biomedical signal processing, speech processing, loudspeaker equalization, echo cancellation, adaptive noise cancellation, and several communication applications, including software-defined radio (SDR). Large-order [2–6] to achieve rigorous frequency specifications. Filters carry out two other vital functions. The separation of the signal is the first step, and the restoration of the signal is the second. A finite amount of time has taken to settle to zero. A multiplier block is used in the FIR filter for area reduction of the block. It is used to lower the power consumption of high throughput FIR filters with low delay and high speed. [8]. The backbone of DSP systems is FIR filters. If the impulse is distorted,

© The Author(s), under exclusive license to Springer Nature Switzerland AG 2022
V. Arunachalam and K. Sivasankaran (Eds.): ICMDCS 2022, CCIS 1743, pp. 185–197, 2022.
https://doi.org/10.1007/978-3-031-23973-1_13

that is, if a Signal "1" sample is followed by several "zero" samples, the result will be 0 after the "one" sample has passed through the filter's delay line. The impulse response is finite since there is no feedback in the FIR. However, if feedback is implemented, the filter is still an FIR, yet the impulse response is finite. The structure of the FIR filter contains a series of delays, which is followed by a group of multipliers and adders. The multiplier is a vital component of the FIR filter. Multipliers are used to reduce computational stages and increase the FIR filters' overall performance [9]. Sequential multiplier architectures have low power. The speed of parallel multipliers is high while having high power consumption as compared to sequential multiplier architectures. There are four main multipliers Wallace tree, Dadda multiplier, Baugh Wooley multiplier, and Booth multiplier. Wallace tree and Dadda are the types of parallel architecture. Parallel multiplier architectures are used in numerous applications where computation speed concerns more than power consumption. The drawbacks of booth multiplier are it requires high power consumption and more area due to the high complexity of the circuit. Energy and area-efficient systems are executed by accurateness and reliability of the system. Since power speed and delay are the crucial design parameters of the multiplier, the optimization of design parameters is crucial. Compressors are used to reduce power consumption in multipliers. Generally, compressors provide high speed along with low power consumption. Compressors are used to reduce the delay associated with the summation of partial products.

The frequently used compressors are 3:2, 4:2, 5:2, 5:3, and 7:3. A 4:2 compressor topology is preferred over others because it achieves regularity while cascading. Dadda multiplier is designed substantially to enhance the accurateness of an approximate compressor output while allowing less capacity of destruction in the metrics of hardware in comparison with existing compressors. The Dadda multiplier is designed using the 4:2 compressor and the Parallel Prefix Adder (PPA). The Dadda multiplier makes use of fewer gates than the Wallace tree multiplier and Baugh-Wooley multiplier, increasing its performance [14]. Adder is a primary component in an FIR filter. The speed of computing becomes the most considerable condition for a designer.

Depending on criteria like space usage, power dissipation, and adder delay, adders are chosen for various applications based on criteria like space usage, power dissipation, and adder delay. Nowadays, the parallel prefix adder is the fastest adder to perform an efficient addition, a Parallel prefix adder (PPA) employs a prefix operation. These adders make binary addition with a comprehensive word simple. The carry look-ahead adder is the source of Parallel prefix adders.

The speed of the FIR filter is increased by the parallel prefix adder. High-speed arithmetic circuits contain a parallel prefix adder because the operation is carried out in a parallel manner [15]. Parallel prefix adder has a comparatively lesser delay and low power consumption. The overall performance and the speed of the FIR filter increased with the use of the Dadda multiplier and parallel prefix adder. This paper deals with a comparative analysis of the FIR filters with different types of multipliers.

2   Related Work

A signal processing application utilizes a radix-8-based modified booth multiplier. The carry look-ahead adder algorithm is implemented to improve the performance of the booth multiplier. The circuit's inefficiency when isolated 1's are encountered, as well as the difficulty in creating parallel multipliers, are the main disadvantages of the booth multiplier [1]. Hardware architecture of FIR filter using fine-grained seamless pipelining is implemented. Wallace tree multiplier and ripple carry adder is used to implement seamless pipelining. The main drawback of ripple carry adder is it does not allow to use of all the full adders simultaneously [2]. Dadda multiplier is used to implement the FIR filter. The main disadvantages of the Dadda multiplier are, that it is less regular and more complex and it reduces a smaller number of bits at the early stages of reductions [3]. A bit-level multiplier less FIR filter has been implemented using the sparse filter. The main disadvantages of the sparse matrix are it can contain a lot less information and every information cannot be modeled by a sparse matrix [4]. For a low-power, area-efficient FIR filter, a multiplier with a binary common subexpression elimination technique is used. The sub-expression algorithm's main disadvantage is that it takes longer to recompute an arithmetic result when it is needed [5].

3 Proposed Design of Finite Impulse Response

In most cases, the FIR filter calculates the weighted sum of an input signal. The FIR filter examines the many multiplies and adds operations utilized in various applications [2]. The differential equation describes the structure of the filter. The required elements such as adders, multipliers, and time delays are represented in the filter structure.

As demonstrated below, the conventional FIR filter equation is:

$$y[n] = h0x[n] + h1x[n-1] + h2x[n-2] + \ldots + hNx[n-N] \tag{1}$$

The PPA is given the product of the input sample and the coefficient, and the products are summed consistently.

3.1 Dadda Multiplier

Any multiplier's primary function is to offer a high-speed unit that is physically compact and consumes less power. The Dadda multiplier offers a high-speed unit with great accuracy while taking up less space [2]. Because it uses a lesser number of gates than the Wallace tree multiplier, the Dadda multiplier's operation is fast. Dadda multiplier, Wallace tree multipliers, and Baugh-Wooley multiplier are the types of parallel multipliers. The Wallace tree multiplier and the Dadda multiplier are equivalent. The Dadda multiplier is a type of design that requires less area than the Wallace tree multiplier and Baugh-Wooley multiplier. As well as, Dadda multipliers are slightly faster than the other two multipliers. In a multiplier, the coefficient values are utilized to reduce partial products [10].

The architecture of the Dadda multiplier is shown in Fig. 1. Dadda multiplier uses half adders and full adders in its stages. Parallel multipliers are fast and consume less power. A multiplier normally has three stages: the first is to generate partial products, the second is to add the generated partial products, and the third stage is to put them all together i.e. addition of the partial products. The overall addition of the partial products

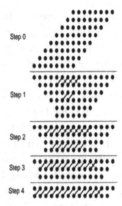

Fig. 1. The architecture of the Dadda multiplier

is used to generate delay, area, and power. Due to this, the demand for high-performance compressors is increasing day by day. This paper deals with a comparative study analysis of the Dadda multiplier with the Exact 4:2 compressor [2].

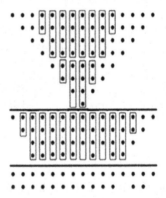

Fig. 2. 8 × 8 Dadda multiplier with compressors.

Figure 2 Shows reduction circuitry of 8 × 8 bit Dadda multiplier with compressors. Compressors are used in the Dadda multiplier stage. Exact and approximate compressors are used. This paper proposes a comparative analysis of the Dadda multiplier with an exact 4:2 compressor, Wallace tree multiplier, and Baugh Wooley multiplier architecture present in the FIR filters. The proposed multiplier structure requirements are low power consumption, high speed, minor delay, and lesser area. Partial product summation stage reduction is made by using compressors. To reduce the required design parameters of the multiplier, compressors are used. The compressor reduces area, delay, and power consumption. It is also used to increase the speed of the multiplier by reducing the number of stages.

3.2 Exact Compressor

Compressors can help reduce delays in the final stage of the Dadda multiplier. The 4:2 compressors and 5:2 compressors are frequently used to eliminate the delay. Some compressor architectures are employed in the optimization of design factors such as delay, power consumption, and area. Figure 3 shows the structure of an Exact compressor.

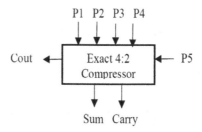

Fig. 3. Block diagram of 4:2 compressor

It has four inputs (P1, P2, P3, P4) along with an input carry (P5) and two outputs, i.e., sum and carry along with an output (Cout). The internal structure of the compressor is shown in Fig. 4. In an internal structure of an exact compressor, the weights of all the inputs (P1, P2, P3, P4) and the sum output are the same. In contrast, the weights of the carry and Cout outputs are higher than the sum output, and input weights of Output signal Cout. The output equations of an exact compressor are shown below. Sum, carry, and Cout equations are given below.

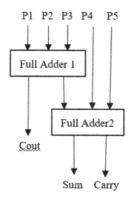

Fig. 4. The internal structure of the 4:2 compressor

The following equations are used to obtain output signals -Sum, Carry, and Cout (Table 1).

$$Sum = P1 \oplus P2 \oplus P3 \oplus P4 \oplus P5 \tag{2}$$

$$Carry = cin(P1 \oplus P2 \oplus P3 \oplus P4) + P4(P1 \oplus P2 \oplus P3 \oplus P4) \qquad (3)$$

$$Cout = (P1 \oplus P2)P1 + (P1 \oplus P2)P3 \qquad (4)$$

Table 1. The truth table for the exact 4:2 compressor

P1	P2	P3	P4	P5	Sum	Carry	Cout
0	0	0	0	0	0	0	0
0	0	0	0	1	1	0	0
0	0	0	1	0	1	0	0
0	0	0	1	1	0	1	0
0	0	1	0	0	1	0	0
0	0	1	0	1	0	1	0
0	0	1	1	0	0	1	0
0	0	1	1	1	1	1	0
0	1	0	0	0	1	0	0
0	1	0	0	1	0	1	0
0	1	0	1	0	0	1	0
0	1	0	1	1	1	1	0
0	1	1	0	0	0	0	1
0	1	1	0	1	0	0	1
0	1	1	1	0	1	0	1
0	1	1	1	1	0	1	1
1	0	0	0	0	1	0	0
1	0	0	0	1	0	1	0
1	0	0	1	0	0	1	0
1	0	0	1	1	1	1	0
1	0	1	0	0	0	0	1
1	0	1	0	1	1	0	1
1	0	1	1	0	1	0	1
1	0	1	1	1	0	1	1
1	1	0	0	0	0	0	1
1	1	0	0	1	1	0	1
1	1	0	1	0	1	0	1
1	1	0	1	1	0	1	1
1	1	1	0	0	1	0	1
1	1	1	0	1	0	1	1
1	1	1	1	0	0	1	1
1	1	1	1	1	1	1	1

3.3 Approximate Compressor

The approximate circuit design is an advanced prototype for the applications like digital signal processing. Multiplication is generally used arithmetic function for multiple applications related to high speed and performance. Figure 5 shows the approximate compressor. The approximate compressor has four inputs (P1, P2, P3, and P4) and two outputs (carry and sum). The approximate compressor uses P5 internally so, P5 input is neglected. The approximate compressor has a high speed of operation.

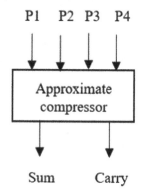

Fig. 5. Approximate compressor

Accuracy is the main prerequisite in traditional arithmetic circuits. An approximate compressor is used to increase the speed of the multiplier circuit with area reduction. The internal structure of an approximate compressor is shown in Fig. 6.

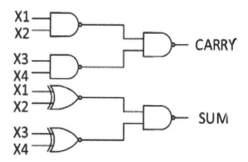

Fig. 6. Approximate compressor internal structure

Truth table of an Approximate compressor is shown in Table 2.

Table 2. The truth table for the approximate compressor

P1	P2	P3	P4	Sum	Carry	Difference
0	0	0	0	0	0	0
0	0	0	1	1	0	0
0	0	1	0	1	0	0
0	0	1	1	0	1	0
0	1	0	0	1	0	0
0	1	0	1	1	0	1
0	1	1	0	1	0	1
0	1	1	1	1	1	0
1	0	0	0	1	0	0
1	0	0	1	1	0	1
1	0	1	0	1	0	1
1	0	1	1	1	1	0
1	1	0	0	0	1	0
1	1	0	1	1	1	0
1	1	1	0	1	1	0
1	1	1	1	1	1	1

3.4 Parallel Prefix Adder

A Parallel prefix adder is used to boost the performance of the DSP processor when performing addition. Because the operation takes place in a parallel manner, the Parallel Prefix Adder is commonly utilized in the fastest arithmetic circuits [2]. The Parallel prefix adder works in the same way as the Carry Look Ahead Adder. Parallel prefix adders are utilized in high-performance arithmetic circuits. Figure 7 shows the parallel prefix adder method.

The parallel prefix adder has the following steps:

1. The pre-processing stage
2. The carrier generation network
3. The post-processing stage

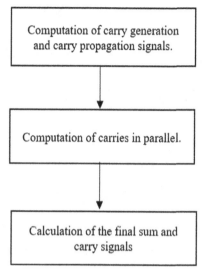

Fig. 7. Parallel prefix adder structure

The parallel prefix adder mechanism is shown in Fig. 7. It consists of 3 stages. The main functionality of each stage is shown in a parallel prefix adder mechanism.

1. Pre-processing stage.

In this stage carry input for each adder is generated and propagate signals are used in this stage. The propagate and carry signals are given by Eqs. 5 and 6.

$$Pi = Ai \cdot Bi \tag{5}$$

$$Gi = Ai \cdot Bi \tag{6}$$

In this stage computation of input bits, carry generation, and carry propagation is done.

2. Carry generation network

In this stage of the carry generation network, calculating carries according to each bit is done. Execution is done in parallel form. Carries are divided into smaller groups of pieces after the computation stage, carry operator contains two AND gates, and one OR gate. Equation 7 and 8 gives the representation of intermediate signals of propagating and generating (Fig. 8).

$$A(i : k) = A(i : j) \cdot A(i) \tag{7}$$

$$B(i : k) = B(i : j) + (B(j - 1 : k \cdot A(i : j))) \tag{8}$$

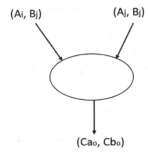

(Ai, Bj)   (Aj, Bj)

(Cao, Cbo)

Fig. 8. Carry operator

In this stage, the carry signals in parallel are calculated, also known as prefix computation.

3. Post-processing stage

In the parallel prefix adder mechanism, the post-processing phase is the final step. The final sum and carry are computed at this point. This stage is the same for all adders, and the sum and carry equations are represented as follows:

$$Si = Xi \cdot Zi \tag{9}$$

$$Zi + 1 = (Xi \cdot Z0) + Yi \tag{10}$$

The post-processing stage involves the analysis of the sum obtained for the given inputs.

4 Performance Analysis and Results

FIR filter is a vital component in DSP processors. For the high throughput of the FIR filter, high-speed multipliers and adders are required. Multipliers are used to minimize power consumption and to increase the speed of FIR filters. The multiplier is an essential component in digital circuits. The Dadda multiplier is utilized with the exact compressor to minimize the computation time.

Table 3 shows an 8×8 Dadda multiplier with compressors. Delay, area, power consumption, and memory utilization is reduced in an 8×8 Dadda multiplier with an approximate compressor. Though the approximate compressor gives inexact results for some input combinations, the Approximate compressor has high speed than the exact compressor. The area is reduced by 1% in an approximate compressor.

The delay is reduced by 29.31%, and power consumption by 2.8% compared to the Dadda multiplier with an exact compressor; the design parameters have been reduced to an approximate compressor.

Table 4 shows a comparative analysis of the 16×16 Dadda multiplier with exact and approximate compressor. Delay is minimized by 29.31%, power has been reduced by 2.8%, and the area is reduced by 2% in the 16×16 Dadda multiplier with an approximate compressor. The above table shows that the delay, power consumption, area utilization, and memory utilization have been reduced in the approximate compressor.

Table 3. Comparative analysis of 8 × 8 Dadda multiplier with exact and approximate compressor

8 × 8 Dadda multiplier with	Area	Delay	Power	Memory (in KB)
Exact compressor	Used LUTs: 145 Total: 1920 Utilized: 7%	29.248 ns	33.59 mW	4509832
Approximate compresor	Used LUTs: 130 Total: 1536 Utilized: 6%	20.673 ns	32.65 mW	4509576

Table 4. Comparative analysis of 16 × 16 Dadda multiplier with exact and approximate compressor

16 × 16 Dadda multiplier	Area	Delay	Power	Memory (in KB)
Exact compressor	Used LUTs: 290 Total: 1920 Utilized: 15%	29.248 ns	33.59 mW	4511240
With Approximate compressor	Used LUTs: 260 Total: 1920 Utilized: 13%	20.673 ns	32.65 mW	4511240

In the Dadda multiplier with an approximate compressor, the delay has been reduced, so the speed is increasing simultaneously.

Table 5. Comparative analysis of 32 × 32 Dadda multiplier with exact and approximate compressor

32 × 32 Dadda multiplier with	Area	Delay	Power	Memory (in KB)
Exact compressor	Used LUTs: 580 Total: 1920 Utilized: 30%	29.248 ns	33.59 mW	4517360
Approximate compressor	Used LUTs: 520 Total: 1536 Utilized: 27%	20.673 ns	32.65 mW	4516192

Table 5 shows the comparative analysis for the 32 × 32 Dadda multiplier with exact and approximate compressors. Delay is minimized by 29.31%, and power has been reduced by 2.8%. Furthermore, the area is reduced by 3% in the 32 × 32 Dadda multiplier with an approximate compressor. Thus, the Dadda multiplier with an approximate compressor is used to reduce design parameters. Memory utilization is an important design parameter. Memory utilization is reduced in the Dadda multiplier with an approximate compressor.

Design parameters (delay, power, area, and memory) of FIR filters vary according to the type of multipliers. The Dadda multiplier with the exact compressor gives an accurate output. Dadda multiplier is comparatively faster than Wallace tree and Baugh-Wooley multiplier. In the parallel prefix adder, the addition operation has been performed in a parallel manner which results from the faster circuit operation of the FIR filter. A comparative analysis of the FIR filter with different multipliers is shown in the given parameter comparison tables.

Table 6. Comparative analysis of 8-tap fir filter

8 tap FIR Filter with	Area	Delay	Power	Memory (in KB)
Dadda multiplier	Used LUTs: 130 Total: 1920 Utilized: 6%	12.71 ns	32.65 mW	4537928
Wallace tree multiplier	Used LUTs: 150 Total: 1920 Utilized: 7%	17.47 ns	33.59 mW	4549976
Baugh-Wooley multiplier	Used LUTs: 150 Total: 1920 Utilized: 7%	15.673 ns	33.59 mW	4539852

Table 6 shows a comparative analysis of FIR filters. SPARTAN 3E FPGA board is used. Delay, area, power consumption, and memory utilization are reduced in the Dadda multiplier with the exact compressor. Area, delay, power. Furthermore, memory utilization has been reduced in the FIR filter with the Dadda multiplier. High speed of the multiplier and adder results in the fastest speed of the FIR filter circuit.

5 Conclusion

The high-performance design of the FIR filter has been implemented successfully. Low latency and low power consumption are achieved by using an FIR filter with a Dadda multiplier. In comparison to the FIR filter with the Dadda multiplier, the FIR filter with Wallace tree multiplier and the Baugh-Wooley multiplier has a large delay and high-power consumption. Dadda multiplier with exact compressor provides reduced 27.27% delay as compared to Wallace tree multiplier and 18.9% compared to Baugh Wooley multiplier.

LUTs are 14.28% minimized as compared to other multipliers. Xilinx ISE 14.7 is used for synthesis and simulation. In the future, an approximate multiplier could be used to design an FIR filter.

References

1. Patel, S., Khare, K., Yadav, J.S., Yadav, P.: High-performance robust FIR filter design using Radix-8 based improved booth multiplier for signal processing application. In: 2021 8th International Conference on Signal Processing and Integrated Networks (SPIN) (August 2021). https://doi.org/10.1109/SPIN52536.2021.9566058
2. Cho, S.M., Meher, P.K., Trung, L.T.N., Cho, H.J., Park, S.Y.: Design of very high-speed pipeline FIR filter through precise critical path analysis. IEEE Access **9**, 34722–34735 (2021). https://doi.org/10.1109/ACCESS.2021.3061759
3. Madhavi, L., Kavya, N., Sindhu, M.: Implementation of programmable fir filter using Dadda multiplier and parallel prefix adder. IEEE Xplore (2018). https://doi.org/10.1109/ICIRCA.2018.8597249
4. Ye, W.B., Yu, Y.J.: Bit-level multiplier less FIR filter optimization incorporating sparse filter technique. IEEE Trans. Circuits Syst.—I **61**, 3206–3215 (2014). https://doi.org/10.1109/TCSI.2014.2327287
5. Priya, S.S., Maheswari, M.: Low-power area efficient reconfigurable multiplier architecture for FIR filter. In: Proceedings of the 2nd International Conference on Communication and Electronics Systems (ICCES 2017) IEEE Xplore Compliant - Part Number: CFP17AWO-ART (2017). ISBN: 978-1-5090-5013-0
6. Mohanty, B.K., Meher, P.K.: A high-performance FIR filter architecture. IEEE Trans. Very Large Scale Integr. (VLSI) Syst. **24**(2), 444–452 (2016)
7. Dhivya, V.M., Sridevi, A., Ahilan, A.: A high-speed area efficient FIR filter using floating-point Dadda algorithm. In: International Conference on Communication and Signal Processing (3–5 April 2014). https://doi.org/10.1109/ICCSP.2014.6950126
8. Akbari, O., Kamal, M., Afzali-Kusha, A., Pedram, M.: Dual-quality 4:2 compressors for utilizing in dynamic accuracy configurable multipliers. IEEE Trans. Very Large Scale Integr. (VLSI) Syst. **25**(4), 1352–1361 (2017)
9. Edavoor, P.J., Raveendran, S., Rahulkar, A.D.: Approximate multiplier design using novel dual-stage 4:2 compressors. IEEE Access, Very Large Scale Integr. (VLSI) Syst. **8**, 48337–48351 (2020). https://doi.org/10.1109/ACCESS.2020.2978773
10. Narayanamoorthy, S., Moghaddam, H.A., Liu, Z., Park, T., Kim, N.S.: Energy-efficient approximate multiplication for digital signal processing and classification applications. IEEE Trans. Very Large Scale Integr. (VLSI) Syst. **23**(6), 1180–1184 (2015)
11. Manikantta Reddy, K., Vasantha, M.H., Kumar, Y.B.N., Dwivedi, D.: Design and analysis of multiplier using approximate 4-2 compressor. AEU-Int. J. Electron. Commun. **107**, 8997 (2019)
12. Gorantla, A., Deepa, P.: Design of approximate compressors for multiplication. ACM J. Emerg. Technol. Computer Syst. **13**(3), 1–17 (2017)
13. Ha, M., Lee, S.: Multipliers with approximate 4-2 compressors and error recovery modules. IEEE Embed. Syst. Lett. **10**(1), 6–9 (2018)
14. Janaki, K., Koteswararao, G.: Design of parallel prefix adders using reversible logic gates. IJSETR **04**(54), 11505–11509 (2015). ISSN 2319-8885
15. Marimuthu, R., Elsie Rezinold, Y., Mallick, P.S.: Design and analysis of multiplier using approximate compressor. IEEE Access **5**, 1027–1036 (2016). https://doi.org/10.1109/ACCESS.2016.2636128

MPPT Using P&O Algorithm for Solar-Battery Powered Electric Vehicle

Viswateja Anjuru and W. Razia Sultana[(⊠)]

VIT University, Vellore 632014, TN, India
Viswateja.anjuru2020@vitstudent.ac.in, wraziasultana@vit.ac.in

Abstract. Despite ongoing variations in temperature and irradiation conditions, maximum power point trackers (MPPTs) are essential to get the maximum power output from photo voltaic (PV). MPPTs, therefore, command the highest level of efficiency in the entire PV system. The DC voltage produced by the solar system is increased via a DC-DC boost converter. These trackers are operated using a variety of MPPT algorithms, with the P&O (perturb & observe) approach receiving special attention due to how easy it is to implement it in electronic programmable circuits. This study uses a model that integrates numerous environmental elements to examine how a PV panel's output, which is managed by MPPT trackers, behaves and a battery-connected electric vehicle. The suggested integrated system's components as well as their functions are followed by a simulation of a prototype system in the MATLAB/Simulink programme to confirm its benefits.

Keywords: Battery electric vehicles · P&O algorithm · Permanent magnet synchronous motor · Maximum power point tracking

1 Introduction

The global need for electricity is rising quickly. Due to its near-freedom as well as cleanliness, renewable energy has recently been taken into consideration. Energy from the sun is one of the most promising energy sources for the production of electric power among renewable energy sources like wind, thermal, ocean, etc. Sunlight may be used to produce electricity either through the photovoltaic (PV) effect [1] or by heating a fluid to produce power. Both of these technologies are frequently employed to provide electricity to independent loads or rather a power systems. Though, it is apparent that the solar PV cells' converting effectiveness, which ranges from 9 to 17%, is quite poor, especially in situations with low sun irradiation. Additionally, different weather conditions always cause the electricity produced by solar PV panels to alter. It is clear that the solar PV cell's V-I as well as V-P properties are non-linear and fluctuate with temperature and irradiance [2]. But the maximum power point, which is a singular point on the V-I or V-P curve, is always present (MPP). This point's attributes are unknown, however, MPPT algorithms can identify it and classify it broadly as follows: The methods Perturbation and Observation (P&O) [3–5], Incremental Conductance (InC) [6, 7], Constant Current (CC) or Voltage (CV) [8, 9], as well as Fuzzy based Logical Algorithms (FLA) [10,

© The Author(s), under exclusive license to Springer Nature Switzerland AG 2022
V. Arunachalam and K. Sivasankaran (Eds.): ICMDCS 2022, CCIS 1743, pp. 198–210, 2022.
https://doi.org/10.1007/978-3-031-23973-1_14

11], Artificial and Neural Network (ANN) [12], and a technique of Particle Swarm Optimization (PSO) [13, 14] are examples. These current methods offer a number of benefits and drawbacks related to simplicity and rapid convergence, additional hardware as well as cost. An alterable P&O method for MPPT of a Battery connected solar electric vehicle is suggested in this study. In comparison to the outcomes utilizing the P&O method, the produced simulation results demonstrate the usefulness and value of the suggested approach. The remaining part of the paper is organized as the mathematical formulation of solar photovoltaic boards is described in Sect. 2. Section 3 presents a solar PV system that is battery-connected. In Sect. 4, a flexible P&O algorithm intended for the MPPT approach is suggested. After that, the simulation outcomes are shown to support the applicability of the suggested approach in Sect. 5. Finally, the future scope to the relevant ANN technique with P&O (perturbation and observe) algorithm, the benefits of the new idea are summed up.

2 PV Panel

Mathematically a photovoltaic solar cell is as follows:

$$I = I_{sc} - I_o\left(e^{qv/kT}\right) - 1 \tag{1}$$

$$V_{oc} = {kT}/{q}\ln\left({I_{sc}}/{I_O}\right) + 1 \tag{2}$$

where
 I_{cell} = PV cell current in Ampere (A)
 I_{sc} = PV cell current under short circuit (A)
 V_{cell} = photovoltaic cell voltage (v)
 V_{oc} = PV cell voltage under open circuit (v)
 P_{cell} = PV cell power (W)
 T = PV panel temperature (K)
 I_o = PV panel reverse current of saturation in Ampere (A)
 q = 1.609 * 10^{-19} (C) charge of an electron
 k = 1.381 * 10^{-23} (J/K) which is Boltzmann's constant

Because of the shadowing, solar photovoltaic panels are particularly sensitive. As a result, a more precise same circuit for a solar PV cell is described that takes shading into consideration as well as losses caused by contacts, internal series resistance of the module, and connections between cells and modules [15]. The solar PV cell's V-I characteristic is therefore expressed as follows:

$$I_{cell} = \left\{I_{sc} - I_o\left(e^{q\left(V + IR_s/kT\right)} - 1\right) - (V + IR_s/R_p)\right\} \tag{3}$$

where Rs, Rp resistances of shading as well as losses.

Although the producers make an effort to lessen the impact of both resistances to enhance their goods, the perfect situation is not feasible. It is important to emphasise the importance of the open circuit voltage (Voc) as well as the short-circuit current (Isc) which are the two key components of the V-I characteristic [16–18]. At both locations, there is 0% electricity created. The output current I, of the cell is measured to calculate the Voc, whereas the output voltage Voc, of the cell is measured to get the Isc. The solar PV cell produces its most power at a characteristic point where the product of (V&I) is at its highest value. This point is distinct and is referred to as the MPP.

Irradiation and temperature are undoubtedly the two most crucial parameters that must be considered in order for a solar PV panel to produce power [19]. The features of solar PV panels are significantly influenced by these elements. As a consequence, the MPP changes during the daylight. Significant power losses happen if the operating Point is a long way from the MPP. Therefore, it is crucial to monitor the MPP in all circumstances to guarantee that the solar panel is generating the most electricity possible. The MPPT algorithms are tasked with solving this issue by looking for and identifying MPPs under diverse circumstances. For searching MPPs, this study suggests the adaptive P&O method, it is further explained in the section below.

3 Battery Associated PV System

Grid-connected solar PV systems, which are utilized in high power applications, and independent solar PV systems, which necessitate a battery to store the energy, may be divided into two groups. Figure 1 shows that the solar Photovoltaic array, DC/DC converters, DC/AC inverters, filters, transformer as well as energy storage are the essential components of the battery-connected photovoltaic System [2].

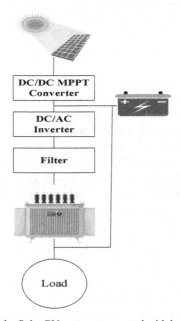

Fig. 1. Solar PV system connected with battery.

DC/DC converters are often used to maintain a steady output voltage from a variable power source, allowing several voltage levels to be generated from a single input voltage. Many DC/DC converters employ the buck (step down), boost (step up), include buck-boost topologies [20]. In addition, the primary function of DC/AC inverters is to convert a constant DC voltage into 3 phase voltages with variable frequency and amplitude, which are produced by controlling the semiconductor switches using pulse width modulation (PWM) methodology [21]. The phase locked loops (PLL) will provide the rotational frequency, direct as well as quadrature voltage elements at the point of common connection by resolving the grid voltage constituents a, b, and c.

4 MPPT P&O Algorithm Connected BEV (Battery Electric Vehicle)

P&O technique is the MPPT algorithm that is most often utilized. This method employs a straightforward feedback system with few parameters that can be monitored. This method involves regularly perturbing the module voltage and comparing the resulting output power to that from the prior perturbing cycle [16]. This algorithm introduces a little disruption to the system. The power of the solar module varies as a result of this disturbance [22]. The perturbation will persist in the same manner if the power of the disturbance increases. The power just at MPP is zero once it is reached and after instant power drops, as seen in Figures, therefore the disturbance reverses whenever the power level is reached.

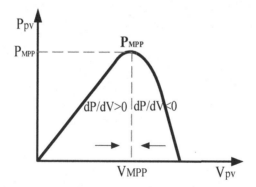

Fig. 2. Conventional P&O algorithm

It is clear that the P&O method often has a fixed step size, which prevents it from successfully tracking the MPP under rapidly changing atmospheric circumstances. Utilizing a variable step size under varying atmospheric circumstances helps get around this problem. In this traditional P&O technique, it is assumed that the perturbation variable serves as the reference value for the terminal voltage of the solar PV panel. Therefore, it is known that the operating point is on the left side of the MPP if the output voltage of the solar PV panels is disturbed and dP/dV > 0. In order to get the operating point closer to the MPP, the P&O algorithm would raise the reference voltage for solar PV panels

[23]. Alternately, it is known that the operating point is on the right side of the MPP if the solar PV panels' output voltage is disturbed and dP/dV < 0. To move the operating point closer to the MPP, the P&O algorithm would lower the reference voltage for solar PV panels [2]. Figure 2 and Table 1 both more succinctly illustrate this description. Up till the MPP is attained, the procedure is often repeated. However, it is clear that the traditional P&O method can falter in situations when atmospheric conditions vary quickly. When the pv System voltage V changes, the operating point shifts if the environmental conditions are nearly constant, and the voltage change is reversed whenever the power declines. In this, the power rises but the disturbance stays the same [24, 25]. As a result, if the sun's irradiation rises consistently, the operating point will continue to deviate from the MPP [15]. To make sure that the MPPs are followed during sudden changes in solar irradiation, an adaptive P&O approach with a variable perturbation scale factor that relies on power fluctuations is recommended. This shows that the perturbations step size adjusts and varies continuously in response to shifting atmospheric conditions. The key shortcomings of the adaptive P&O algorithm, which would include convergence speed as well as tracking efficacy, are one of the adjustments to the conventional P&O algorithm that can reduce expenses. The list of variable perturbation step sizes that alter with power changes is shown below (Fig. 3).

$$\Delta V_i = \Delta V_o \cdot dP_i/dV_i \tag{4}$$

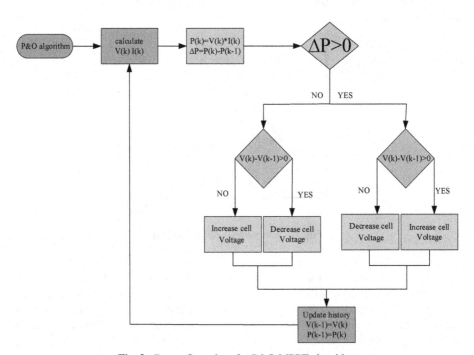

Fig. 3. Power flow chart for P&O MPPT algorithm

Table 1. Conditions of power perturbation

Power	Perturbation	Next perturbation
Positive	+ve	+ve
Negative	+ve	−ve
Positive	−ve	−ve
Negative	−ve	−ve

The goal of the MPPT technique is to automatically determine the current (IMPP) in turn voltage (VMPP) at which a photo voltaic PV array should operate in order to produce the maximum output power (MPP) at a certain temperature as well as irradiance. The majority of MPPT techniques adapt to changes in both irradiance and temperature, while others work better in conditions when temperature is roughly constant [26]. Despite the fact that certain MPPT approaches are open-loop and need for recurring fine tuning, the majority would automatically adapt to changes in the array due to ageing. In our situation, the module will normally be coupled with a power converter that can regulate the amount of current flowing from the PV array to the load [27] (Fig. 4).

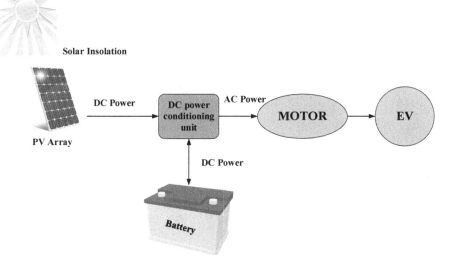

Fig. 4. Block diagram of solar powered battery electric vehicle.

5 Matlab/Simulink Environment

In order to simulate the MPPT of the solar PV system that is linked to the battery-powered electric vehicle, simulation results are produced using the MATLAB/SIMULINK program. The Simulink library browser's subsystem block was used to represent the PV panel as a constant DC source in Fig. 5, which incorporated all of the panel's functionalities. The model receives three inputs from the system as feedback: irradiance, temperature, and voltage. The parameters of solar panel ASEC-305G6M are listed in Table 2.

Apollo solar energy ASEC-305G6M with 6 parallel strings and 2 series modules are used to get the power rating of 3660 W. The Voltage-current as well as Voltage-Power characteristics depicted in Fig. 5 of the solar PV system, for solar irradiation G = 1 kW/m² at a temperature of T = 25 °C. Figure 5 demonstrates that the current of a photovoltaic System grows together with the sun irradiation.

Table 2. ASEC solar panel parameters.

Apollo solar energy ASEC-305G6M parameters		
Sl. no	Parameter	Value
1	Parallel strings	6
2	Series cell modules	2
3	Max. power	305.0063
4	Cells per module	72
5	Open circuit voltage	44.08
6	Short circuit current	8.95
7	Voltage at max. point	35.59

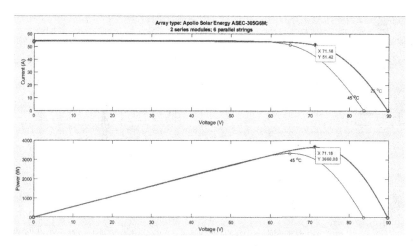

Fig. 5. V-P and V-I characteristics of solar panel.

For the simulation, a lithium-ion battery (Li-ion) with a nominal voltage of 12 V and four cells is used. The battery's rated capacity is 48 Ah, and its internal state of charge (SOC) is 80% with 0.0001 resistance (Fig. 6).

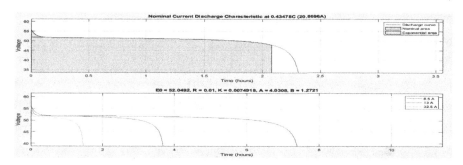

Fig. 6. Nominal discharge characteristics of Li-ion battery.

The suggested P&O algorithm is used to link the battery to the solar panel as illustrated in Fig. 7, transformer-free DC-DC converter links the solar panel and battery. The output parameters of the panel are measured at various temperatures and irradiations, and any inaccuracies are corrected by a DC converter before being delivered to the battery, which is utilized in electric vehicles to give power to the drivetrain.

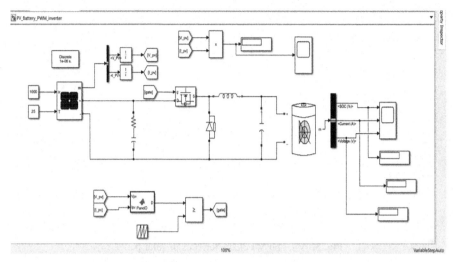

Fig. 7. Battery connected to solar PV array

Figure 8 depicts the whole simulation diagram of a solar-powered battery-connected electric vehicle, and Table 3 lists the specifications of a permanent magnet synchronous (PMS) motor.

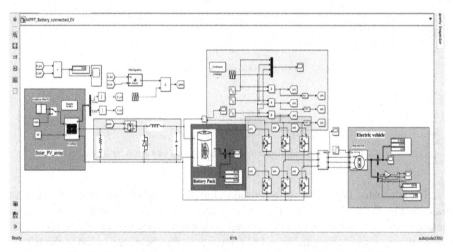

Fig. 8. Proposed simulation of solar powered battery electric vehicle.

The suggested P&O algorithm always attempts to pull the maximum power from the solar panel, providing supply to both the motor and battery for charging. The motor receives power from both the solar panel and the battery.

The parameter study of an algorithm for different temperatures and irradiation is tabulated below:

Table 3. Parameters at different temperatures and irradiations

Sl.no	Temperature (T) °C	Irradiation (G) W/m²	Voltage (V) V	Current (I) A	Power (P) W
1	20	500	70.65	26.37	1863
2	30	1000	67.11	52.51	3524
3	40	1500	64.40	76.35	4917
4	50	2000	64.22	89.30	5735

The results for maximum power point at irradiation of 1 kW/m² is as shown below (Figs. 9, 10, 11 and 12):

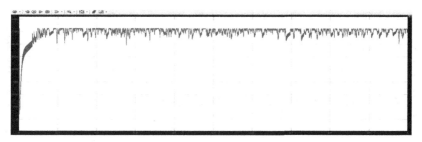

Fig. 9. Maximum power drawn from solar panel

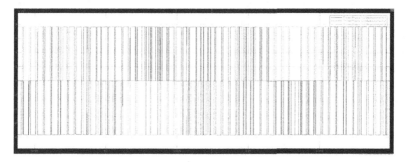

Fig. 10. Three phase output voltages of PWM inverter.

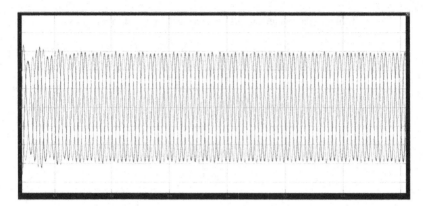

Fig. 11. Three phase stator currents of PMS motor.

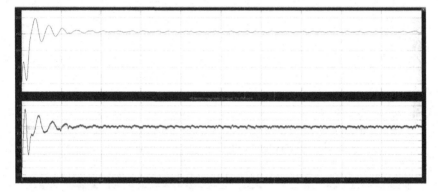

Fig. 12. Torque-speed characteristics of PMS motor.

6 Conclusion

A battery-powered electric vehicle with a PMS motor was driven in this study using an MPPT control system that effectively employed the P&O algorithm to get the most power from solar panels. The simulation results show how effective P&O algorithm-based MPPT is for a battery-powered solar vehicle.

7 Future Work

The algorithm will be modified utilizing the ANN-MPC approach for MPPT to properly draw the maximum power for expanding solar panel applications.

References

1. Yadav, P., Bhargava, A., Sharma, M.: MPPT using soft computing technique with MLI in photovoltaic system. In: 2016 International Conference on Micro-Electronics and Telecommunication Engineering (ICMETE), pp. 466–470. IEEE (September 2016)
2. Faranda, R., Leva, S.: Energy comparison of MPPT techniques for PV Systems. WSEAS Trans. Power Syst. **3**(6), 446–455 (2008)
3. Sridhar, R., Selvan, N.T., Jeevananthan, S., Chowdary, P.S.: Performance improvement of a photo voltaic array using MPPT (P&O) technique. In: 2010 International Conference on Communication Control and Computing Technologies, pp. 191–195. IEEE (October 2010)
4. Huynh, D.C., Nguyen, T.A., Dunnigan, M.W., Mueller, M.A.: Maximum power point tracking of solar photovoltaic panels using advanced perturbation and observation algorithm. In: 2013 IEEE 8th Conference on Industrial Electronics and Applications (ICIEA), pp. 864–869. IEEE (June 2013)
5. Razali, N.M., Rahim, N.A.: DSP-based maximum peak power tracker using P&O algorithm. In: 2011 IEEE Conference on Clean Energy and Technology (CET), pp. 34–39. IEEE (June 2011)
6. Ping, W., Hui, D., Changyu, D., Shengbiao, Q.: An improved MPPT algorithm based on traditional incremental conductance method. In: 2011 4th International Conference on Power Electronics Systems and Applications, pp. 1–4. IEEE (June 2011)
7. Liu, B., Duan, S., Liu, F., Xu, P.: Analysis and improvement of maximum power point tracking algorithm based on incremental conductance method for photovoltaic array. In: 2007 7th International Conference on Power Electronics and Drive Systems, pp. 637–641. IEEE (November 2007)
8. Huynh, D.C.: An improved incremental conductance maximum power point tracking algorithm for solar photovoltaic panels. Int. J. Sci. Res. **3**(10), 342–347 (2014)
9. Ye, Z., Wu, X.: Compensation loop design of a photovoltaic system based on constant voltage MPPT. In: 2009 Asia-Pacific Power and Energy Engineering Conference, pp. 1–4. IEEE (March 2009)
10. Aganah, K.A., Leedy, A.W.: A constant voltage maximum power point tracking method for solar powered systems. In: 2011 IEEE 43rd Southeastern Symposium on System Theory, pp. 125–130. IEEE (March 2011)
11. Kang, S.J., et al.: A novel MPPT control of photovoltaic system using FLC algorithm. In: 2011 11th International Conference on Control, Automation and Systems, pp. 434–439. IEEE (October 2011)
12. Padmanabhan, V., Beena, V., Jayaraju, M.: Fuzzy logic based maximum power point tracker for a photovoltaic system. In: 2012 International Conference on Power, Signals, Controls and Computation, pp. 1–6. IEEE (January 2012)
13. Ramaprabha, R., Gothandaraman, V., Kanimozhi, K., Divya, R., Mathur, B.L.: Maximum power point tracking using GA-optimized artificial neural network for solar PV system. In: 2011 1st International Conference on Electrical Energy Systems, pp. 264–268. IEEE (January 2011)
14. Azam, M.A., Abdullah-Al-Nahid, S., Alam, M.M., Plabon, B.A.: Microcontroller based high precision PSO algorithm for maximum solar power tracking. In: 2012 International Conference on Informatics, Electronics & Vision (ICIEV), pp. 292–297. IEEE (May 2012)
15. Ishaque, K., Salam, Z., Amjad, M., Mekhilef, S.: An improved particle swarm optimization (PSO)–based MPPT for PV with reduced steady-state oscillation. IEEE Trans. Power Electron. **27**(8), 3627–3638 (2012)
16. Esram, T., Chapman, P.L.: Comparison of photovoltaic array maximum power point tracking techniques. IEEE Trans. Energy Convers. **22**(2), 439–449 (2007)

17. Atallah, A.M., Abdelaziz, A.Y., Jumaah, R.S.: Implementation of perturb and observe MPPT of PV system with direct control method using buck and buck-boost converters. Emerg. Trends Electr. Electron. Instrum. Eng.: Int. J. (EEIEJ), **1**(1), 31–44 (2014)
18. Nguyen, T.P.: Solar panel maximum power point tracker. Department of Computer Science & Electrical Engineering: University of Queensland, vol. 64 (2001)
19. Chaudhari, V.A.: Automatic peak power tracker for solar pv modules using dspacer software. Maulana Azad National Institute of Technology. Master Thesis of Technology in Energy. Bhopal: Deemed University (2005)
20. Zainudin, H.N., Mekhilef, S.: Comparison study of maximum power point tracker techniques for PV systems (2010)
21. Ahmed, M.E., Mekhilef, S.: Design and implementation of a multi level three-phase inverter with less switches and low output voltage distortion. J. Power Electron. **9**(4), 593–603 (2009)
22. Mekhilef, S., Ahmed, M.E., Younis, M.A.A.: Performance of grid connected photovoltaic inverter with maximum power point tracker and power factor control. In: 2008 Canadian Conference on Electrical and Computer Engineering, pp. 001129–001134. IEEE (May 2008)
23. Chang, Y.H., Chang, C.Y.: A maximum power point tracking of PV system by scaling fuzzy control. In: International Multi Conference of Engineers and Computer Scientists, Hong Kong, pp. 271–350 (March 2010)
24. Kalpana, C., Babu, C.S., Kumari, J.S.: Design and implementation of different MPPT Algorithms for PV System. Int. J. Sci. Eng. Technol. Res. (IJSETR) **2**(10), 1926–1933 (2013)
25. Scheurer, A., Ago, E., Hidalgo, J.S., Kobosko, S., Shaffer, A.: Photovoltaic MPPT charge controller. Mentor Alan Shaffer Lakeland Electric, Sponsored by Workforce Central Florida, Spring (2012)
26. Azab, M.: A new maximum power point tracking for photovoltaic systems. Waset. Org **34**, 571–574 (2008)
27. Lee, C.S.: A Residential DC Distribution System with Photovoltaic Array Integration (2008)

Author Index

Printed in the United States
by Baker & Taylor Publisher Services